REBUILDING

COMMUNITIES

REBUILDING COMMUNITIES

Experiences and Experiments in Europe

EDITED BY VITHAL RAJAN

A RESURGENCE BOOK

Published in association with WWF

A Resurgence Book
First published in 1993 by
Green Books Ltd
Foxhole, Dartington,
Totnes, Devon TQ9 6EB, UK

in association with the World Wide Fund For Nature (WWF)
Gland, Switzerland

Designed by David Baker

Composed in Bembo 11/13pt
by Chris Fayers, Soldon, Devon, EX22 7PF

Printed by Hartnolls Ltd
Bodmin, Cornwall

British Library Cataloguing-in-Publication Data:
Rebuilding Communities: Experiences and
Experiments in Europe
I. Rajan, Vithal
361.6

ISBN 1 870098 50 1

Contents

Acknowledgments

I SHOULD LIKE TO THANK all the contributors, who have given so generously of their time and patience to make this book possible. It has been both a privilege and a great personal pleasure to work on this book, for most of the writers are friends of mine of long standing, and what can afford greater happiness than working with one's own community of affection on a book on re-kindling the community spirit? My thanks are also due to the friends whose photographs liven the pages. A special word of appreciation must be said for the generosity of the famous Croatian painter, Josip Generaliç, who has permitted me to use his beautiful painting, so suited for the theme of this book, as its cover.

I want to thank WWF-International, particularly my colleagues in the Communications Division, Robert SanGeorge and Zandra McGillivray, without whose generous support this book would not have been possible. A special word of thanks is due to Ms. Patricia Handley, my secretary, who gave unstintingly of her time, over weekends and late into the night, to get the manuscript ready in time.

Vithal Rajan
Gland, 1992

The publishers wish to thank the following for providing illustrations for this book: *Photographs:* p58 WWF/Jan Habrovsky; p90 Peter Earthy; p100 Peter Jackson; p110 Michel Bührer; p118 Hillka Pietilä; pp184, 190, 198, 205 WWF/ Marco Pagliani; p210 WWF/Georgia Vallaoras; p222 Greenpeace/M. Scharnberg; p226 Douglas Firth; p238 Hasse Zimmerman *Diagrams:* p92 Martin Rieser; pp95, 96 Amy Elvey.

Foreword

SATISH KUMAR

"It is better to light a candle than curse the darkness."

THIS BOOK CAN BE SUMMED UP neatly and precisely by the above maxim. No change of any substance and value can come about from the top; such as from the government or big business. Even when a change is imposed from the top, it is generally draconian and as such, disliked by the people. Then how do changes of consciouness and changes in social values come about?

It is not merely by criticising what is wrong with society, or with government, or with multinational corporations, but by initiating positive and constructive projects and taking actions at a grassroots level that a real transformation can take place.

At present in our social discourse and in the media, there is too much negativity. Many of us are busy analysing what is wrong with education, with the economy, with rural life and so on, but such analysis is mostly ineffective. There is always an explanation from the establishment as to why the status quo should remain. Much energy is lost in argument and counter-argument.

But there are many dedicated individuals and groups, quietly working away to bring about human values, ecological aspirations and social cohesion through small but significant projects, throughout the world. They are the guardians of the future, they are the salt of the Earth, and they are servants of the people. Our planet will be saved not by politicians or by ambitious industrialists, but by people of the spirit. This book brings together experiences and examples of pioneers who have put as their first priority the interest of the Earth and all life upon it. They provide inspiration to others without making media headlines.

I myself have been involved with a number of people engaged in such actions. First of all, Vinoba Bhave and his colleagues in India. Vinoba said that as Mahatma Gandhi brought about independence for India through non-violent means, we should do the same to bring about land reform by changing the hearts and minds of landlords, rather than imposing a system by the force of law. Thousands of Indians joined him, and we went from village to village, often on foot, saying to landlords: 'If you have five children, consider Vinoba your sixth child, representing the poor and the landless, and give one sixth of your land to ensure that no one in India lives without the means of earning a livelihood.' The force of compassion and persuasion worked. We collected four million acres of land which was distributed among over one million families. More land was distributed by such efforts than by government legislation.

On a smaller scale, I have been engaged in the establishment of the Small School in Hartland, in Devon. In order to attend the nearest comprehensive school for their secondary education, children of this village have to travel fifteen miles every morning and fifteen miles every evening. The school bus picking up children from village to village takes nearly an hour each way, resulting in a commuter's way of life from the age of eleven. I went to complain to the Chief Education Officer of our area, who flatly refused to contemplate the idea of providing school facilities in the village, on the grounds of economics. 'What is more important—economics or children?' was my reply. So a few of us gathered in my living room and nine parents came forward with the idea that we should start our own school. And so we did. For the last ten years the school has grown from strength to strength—from nine children to thirty-six, and the school is able to offer not only a successful academic curriculum, but also to bring in ecological and spiritual values as the basis of education. Teachers teach children—not subjects—and learning is a co-operative effort between children, teachers and parents.

At this moment, the Small School may appear to be a small, experimental project, but when the big system collapses—and the writing is already on the wall, as is shown by high rates of truancy, bullying, juvenile crime and dissatisfaction among parents—an example like the Small School will prove to be invaluable.

The third example I would like to mention in this context is the work of Schumacher College, where people come together to form a temporary community of like-minded individuals to learn new ideas, rethink the direction of their lives and recharge their batteries through intellectual and spiritual nourishment. It is clear that the world is at a turning point. As significant and important as the agricultural revolution and the industrial revolution, a new paradigm is emerging, and therefore a new kind of education is needed to respond to this situation. Existing universities and colleges underpin the research and development of the scientific and technological paradigm, which is the foundation of our industrial society.

We need to study and develop, in an interdisciplinary and holistic manner, concepts and lifestyles which can exist in harmony with nature, rather than dominating her. Five principles in particular have formed the curriculum of the college:

- *Gaia*—the whole Earth is one living organism, interconnected, interdependent and self-regulatory. This represents a move away from the notion of fragmented, disconnected and compartmentalised ways of looking at the world.

- *Deep Ecology*—not only is the whole Earth one living organism, but everything upon it has intrinsic value. Humans are no more important than the rainforests, worms are no less valuable than elephants and the trees, rivers and mountains are good in themselves. Their significance cannot be judged from the point of view of human use.

- *Permaculture*—every living thing is good in itself, but we humans have to relate with each other and with the multitudinous species of the Earth. This relationship should be based on the principle of permanence, of sustainability, of durability. Like the American Indians who believed that all present actions must be judged on the basis of how they will affect not only our children but up to the seventh generation, modern civilisation needs to relate with the natural world in the same spirit.

- *Bio-regions*—even though the whole Earth is our home and we humans are part of nature, we need to develop a sense of place and learn to live within the carrying capacity of a particular, biologically-given area. Enormous amounts of transportation, mobility, and exports and imports cannot be environmentally sustainable. Huge nation-states and free world trade bring injustice to the weak and the poor. So we need to develop systems of decentralised, small-scale, social, political and economic administration, based on democratic and ecological principles.

- *Spirituality*—all the principles stated above require a subtle perspective based on a sense that all life is sacred. We need to practice a profound reverence for all life. Human activities bring damage to the Earth and therefore, through spiritual and practical means, we need to act to replenish the Earth and the spirit.

These five principles correspond closely to the spirit of the projects and programmes described in the pages that follow. It is my hope that readers will study the rich variety of ideas and experiences, not only to be informed but to be inspired, so that they themselves can participate in many more new grassroots projects in times to come.

Introduction

THE RETURN
TO THE COMMUNITY

VITHAL RAJAN

WE LIVE IN A dramatically unstable world, with the loss of the certainties built up since the Age of Enlightenment. Unshakeable monolithic centres of power, whether in the Kremlin or in Pretoria, seem to have crumbled to dust. This destruction of empires has taken place without battling armies and the horrific slaughter of war. It will be years before humanity can begin to unravel the web of human struggles that have brought about these profound political changes.

The end of the Cold War, perhaps, signifies the end of World War III, which gave the laurels of victory to the economically most powerful nation, and left to the loser the shreds of a war-exhausted and indebted economy. The member nations that once formed the Soviet Union traded much more intensively with each other even than members of the European Community. Russia, which has the great bulk of the industrial plant and output, and of the natural resources of the Soviet Union, exported a fourth of its output to the others, while even the export-led economy of Germany exports no more than a sixth of its output to the EC. This life-giving interaction between the economies of the CIS has been ended in just a few years. Even more dramatic has been the shrinking of the Russian economy from a GDP of around US$800 billion in 1988 to around $500 billion last year, and the economy continues to decline perhaps by a further 10 per cent this year.[1] Such massive disruption and destruction of a giant economy happens only to the losers of great wars of attrition.

Since the American Civil War, victory has gone in long-drawn struggles not to the big battalions, but to the power of strong economies, built up by modern science, strengthened by political centralisation, and often sustained by jingoistic nationalism. It is significant that despite the United States unleashing its war machine on North Korea and Vietnam, no territorial or political gains could be made by the superpower. In fact the Vietnam war, far from defeating its peasant rivals, isolated the American ruling élite as never before or since, from public opinion both at home and abroad, and in fact brought the world's largest economy into a recession that has crippled it since. Within a decade of its defeat in Vietnam, the US had launched an attack against the weak Sandinista government of Nicaragua. If it won a stand-off here, it was due to the supremacy of its economic power and influence.[2]

If economic forces have become a struggle for supremacy by other means, and a real war is as outmoded as the cavalry, then this illuminates the remarkable prescience of Meiji Japan, and may prove that the Sandinistas, who let go of power in the face of overwhelming odds, judiciously foxed both enemies and friends. These possibilities open up new chances for the poor countries in their bid to retain shreds of independence, while classifying the Gulf War along with Omdurman as the mother of all futile battles.

The USSR's military might coupled with a bureaucratised economic structure imploded it into ruin. Its feeble attempts at establishing a countervailing cult of internationalism merely highlighted the great currents of ethnic and nationalistic struggles within its boundaries, which have now dismembered it into potentially warring neighbours. If these new states can avoid the fate of Yugoslavia, it will be commendable, and a sign that perhaps humanity can create communities even out of large agglomerations. But the credit will go more to an inherited wisdom based on shared culture than to newer politico-economic formations.

If the Russians skied down the tracks of the American economy, to use Sakharov's metaphor, their bureaucratised economy could never hope to catch up with their free-market imperial competitors, who understood better than most the machinery of power. If the Soviets waited for time and the disaffection of the masses in the West to manifest itself, unfortunately their own authoritarian rule eroded any hopes their people may have had for equitable social relations.

However, the undoubted success of the West's rampant 'military-industrial complex', the pride of the scientific age, has not brought its leaders, its politicians, its scientists, its generals, and its barons of industry, the plaudits of their peoples. Its workers have certainly engineered its victory over what was clearly perceived as centralised authoritarian power, but even before triumph was proclaimed, myriad dissidents have spoken out, many local movements have developed, ethnic voices have been raised, all demanding local autonomy, real freedom, and a living culture where people matter, not systems of power.

Most awesome of all, this disaffection has shown itself as simple unbelief in the new church of science and economics created by intellectual leaders, and an honest distaste for the new culture: homogenised, impersonal, distanced and coolly frightening. A culture that underlines in every social act the infallibility of its unapproachable scientific leaders, and the implacable necessity of its economic laws.

And yet, asks the man on top of the omnibus from Zagreb to Calcutta, is this for real? What he sees is failure, failure writ large across the face of the earth. Broken promises, moral confusion, an almost autistic inability of scientists and leaders to hear and understand what is important to people. Politicians as dream merchants and scientists at the hustings of their new culture promise that tomorrow 'development' will be achieved in the Third World; and individual fulfilment will become a pleasant reality here at home—if only people will stop being ignorant, unprincipled, resisting the brave new world.

People have listened to this hectoring and tried to move along the pathways created by the new powerful economic-scientific complex. Disillusionment has come only after social 'falsification' of the economic theories of 'development' and the scientific hopes of social fulfilment. Moral confusion throughout the world signifies the systematic devaluation of traditional cultures, the death of collective memories of the lives of past generations. The descendants of the Enlightenment have tried to clean the cultural slates and write with a logical pen the social products of fact and thought. The acknowledgement of the brutalities and the absurdities of 'modern times', and the failure even to counterfeit human happiness, is not ultimately a condemnation of humanity but rather an acknowledgement of the failure of linear thinking, of giving primacy to a culturally determined 'rationality' evoked by an imperial and deeply exploitative system.

Reagan's 'evil empire' has vanished in a bubble of soap. Where shall we now find evil? Is it not time for modern Western civilisation to confront its own Jungian shadow? Is not the very nature of its great power over people the cancer that kills its joy? Can there be a new, simple resurgence of social vitality by turning away from pathways of power towards creative involvement in one's own community? Is this being dull, being immersed in what the great Victorian Marx contemptuously called 'rural idiocy' — or is it a direct way, available to all of us, of achieving a meaningful sense of identity, a sense of belonging and continuity? At this moment of great moral and social crisis, is the return to the community the opportunity we are looking for?

To return is not easy. First we have to turn our backs on the most powerful myth built by Man. Then, we have to remember. We have escaped 1984; can we escape the Brave New World? Can we welsh on the deal struck with Mephistopheles? But it is Dr. Faust who made the deal, and it is still his key problem.

The intellectual élite of the world (and those in the Third World are an inextricable and decisive part of it) know that the world is their oyster and the sword they prick it open with is the scientific-industrial complex of the new world culture. The single-minded pursuit of power as decisive control over events needed the Enlightenment's separation of moral value from cognition of fact. A system of thinking and behaviour that based its truth on the manifestation of power could only be positivist and logocentric. Born out of war and conquest, this process strengthened all instruments and institutions of social control, including the Churches, while erasing the Spirit within them and at the centre of every human community.

Enemies within what seemed the 'astonishingly consensual'[3] circle of intellectual agreement have sprung up from the least expected quarters. Three decades ago the black movement in North America dismissed accepted history as white illiteracy. Amerindians combined their political work with a vigorous attack on the bastions of intellectual power. The most sustained and deep-felt discreditation of a knowledge system based on white patriarchal images of the world has come from the worldwide women's movement, which has combined excellent scholarship with an active pursuit of alternative modes of living and working, to change society in comprehensible and real ways.

Women have asked for a distinct 'feminist standpoint'[4] for understanding knowledge. Liz Whitelegg says: 'The kind of science we have been teaching is the kind that boys find most appropriate, divorced from an environmental, social or human context. But it isn't the most useful if we want life on earth to continue.'[5] There is an easy, arrogant belief among some vociferous scientistic interpreters of the theory of knowledge that such 'cognitive relativism' can be refuted without considering the genealogy of knowledge construction. In this context the scientists would do well to remember that the powerful intellectuals who imprisoned Galileo were supported by the 'astonishingly consensual' nature of the knowledge shared by them—systems of perception and cognition shared by concentric cliques of the intellectually powerful. Their very identity is based on the pursuit of power to control events, and hence people. The acquisition of such awesome power was made possible by asking power-related questions of Nature. The development of science, industry, and nationalism over the last few centuries can be seen as a response, in the words of Standing Bear, to the white man's 'primitive fears'.[6] But Nature's 'scientific' answers have only deepened and multiplied our sources of fear. Humanity has yet to ask Nature questions on how to nurture, how to be inclusive, how to live as part of Nature, and not as despoilers. Perhaps the new deep ecology movement will found a more relevant science,[7] which finds the links between energy and consciousness of more significance than those between matter and energy. Skolimowski asks: 'How does it happen that energy is transformed into life? Two grammes of energy into one gramme of life? What is this energy that becomes life? And then becomes consciousness?'[8] As many modern scientists such as Fritjof Capra are finding out, these are ancient questions; and many ancient texts, such as the Vedas and the Upanishads, have intuited answers that are bridging human philosophical and scientific enquiries. Perhaps we may yet find that the points of perfect symmetry sought in the physical world are points of cosmic consciousness.

The hunger for power is not a phenomenon of modern times alone. Perhaps its usefulness was realised in the early stages of pastoralism, when young bloods indulged in cattle raids. There seems to be growing evidence that a dramatic shift in human social values took place when, several millennia ago, Indo-European patriarchal tribes pushed out of south Russia in waves to colonise peaceful, gynocentred, matrifocal agricultural societies in ancient Europe, Sumer, and the Indus valley. What is significant since the Age of Enlightenment is the progressive orchestration of more and more realms of human activity to serve the concentration of greater amounts of power in the hands of the few. A crucial role in this social process has been played by modern scientists, whose ideology severs decisively the links between moral value, social fact, and political action.

Despite the undoubted material benefits that have been showered on those who can afford them, even the beneficiaries of the Western world display untutored dislike of, and distrust in, both scientists and barons of industry. Such consistent mass opinion cannot be put down simply to ignorance or lack of puritanical virtues. What people are spontaneously reacting to is the loss of personal autonomy, of creative identity, and of social cohesion; and the clear experience of moral confusion and social manipulation. The more the élite, intellectual, economic, or political, say the issues cannot be understood by the ordinary person, the stronger the conviction grows of being used. Pointing to undoubted benefits, or the 'astonishingly consensual' nature of élite agreement, did not save theocratic empires or feudal dynasties. It is not enough to save the modern élite, particularly in the context of massive social failure to alleviate poverty in the Third World, or to enable people in the West to lead creative, fulfilling lives. Centralised power has emptied social life of meaning.

Postmodern philosophers are beginning to describe the nature of emotional alienation of the intellectual élite. Some Third World scholars are deconstructing the myths of Orientalism and Oriental images foisted on their societies, very much as the Enlightenment foisted the image of the Noble Savage on indigenous peoples.[9] These are myths of social disarmament, of clothing other peoples in unreal and unliveable attitudes and beliefs, more a projection, even on the kindliest of terms, of how alienated Europeans would like 'the other' to be. Such projections have done as much to destroy the independence of other societies as have the cruder conquistadors and colonisers, and are instruments of dependency creation, just as much as are 'idealisations' of women.

The critics of modernism, then,[10] including élite philosophers, disadvantaged ethic groups, women, and Third World thinkers, join hands with arguments that are both cohesive and socially relevant to their experiences. The challenged élite find that to vacate the stage of power is to deprive themselves of their very identity of white men (and their brown, black and yellow intellectual gun-bearers) carrying the White Man's Burden. People are beginning to resist representational practices that would, in the words of two postmodernists, Ashley and Walker, 'traverse them, claim their time, control their space and their bodies, impose limitations on what can be said and done, and decide their being.'[11]

A world in change implies people who make things happen. Who are they? Who makes history, and whose history? The fabrication of history is moving from the production of learned texts, in order to illuminate 'reality, identity and truth'; these are now considered as unachievable as the Enlightenment goals of truth, virtue, and beauty, in a period of moral confusion. The focus now is on narrative, evoking personal testimony at the micro level, on what Foucault calls 'local, discontinuous, disqualified, illegitimate knowledges.'[12] Some time ago Brecht asked: 'Young Alexander conquered India—he alone?' Shakespeare the Hobbesian, for whom the separation of power from virtue or knowledge inevitably led to tragedy, commemorates the victory of Agincourt as being won by 'we few, we happy few, we band of brothers'. But long before him, the peasants who won that battle were demanding to know who was the gentleman when Adam delved and Eve span. Newton said that if he saw farther than most it was because he stood on the shoulders of giants. But who were these giants? Scientists such as himself? Or were they artisans, smiths and tool-makers, with names unknown to us?

The emphasis on the narrative, the personal, the local, is not only to set the record straight for a history that has become a 'Western myth',[13] but also to serve a clear social, community purpose among Third World activists—to seek a way out of the newly defined 'underdevelopment' trap created by imperialist powers after World War II to extend their areas of influence. In the terms of Clausewitz, Development is seen as Colonisation through other means. UN statistics show that in the Third World around 14 million children under five die every year because of starvation, malnutrition, or diseases produced by extreme poverty. These deaths are 'the equivalent of all the victims of all the armed conflicts that have taken place on the planet since 1945.'[14]

The process undertaken by voluntary activists working at the grassroots to help local communities to recover from the savage effects of development policies is that of community building, the empowering of the poor themselves to take control of their lives. The strengthening of local community knowledge in ecology, nutrition and medicine, as an organic part of social community life, is radically different from the researcher's quest for titbits of traditional wisdom that could be winkled out and plugged into the scientific-industrial system. There are, as everyone knows, innumerable examples of how pharmaceutical giants have profited from studying the practices of indigenous peoples. Now scientists are discovering that indigenous people have respectfully learned from animals.[15] The Navajo Indian learned the anti-parasitic properties of the *Ligusticum* plant from bears. Kenyan women know about labour-inducing plants from elephants. Tanzanian chimpanzees show people how to chew *Aspilia* leaves to kill parasitic worms. Will all this knowledge end up only as pills, or will modern society also learn something from the relationship that has existed between indigenous societies and nature?

Since development policies are being presented consistently as a moral crusade which taxes the generosity of the West, it is necessary to point to innumerable objective studies which have demonstrated how every aid dollar brings home two, how the debt trap wins the political compliance of the poor nations and enriches the rich, and how the primary beneficiaries of the development process are the imperialist powers themselves.[16] It is important to echo once again that Africa did not know a massive famine till our times. This year around 40 million people are starving in Africa. Zimbabwe, the renowned bread basket of southern Africa, is now starved by the worst drought of the century. The broad reaches of the Limpopo are now cracked earth, and the great river can be crossed on foot with dry shoes. The people have lost a greater proportion of their food crops than even the Sahelian countries. This is not merely a natural crisis, but as elsewhere a result of political struggles closely linked to agricultural policies promoted by the World Bank and the IMF, which put a premium on lucrative cash crops, plantation crops, and even flowers over food needed by the population.[17] Non-sustainability is a modern creation.

Traditional societies needed for their very survival to take long-term sustainable approaches. Even the forgotten Incas stored sufficient grain for their poor. Cieza de Leon, the chronicler of the conquistadors, wrote of the ample supplies which if there were no war would be 'divided among the poor and widows, the old, the lame, the blind and the crippled.'[18] One of the main causes of destitution and the perennial threat of drought the Indian peasants suffer was the British colonial system itself. One of the greatest of nineteenth century British engineers, Sir Arthur Cotton, of whom a statue still stands in Hyderabad, bemoaned: 'The natives think of us as civilised savages; civilised in the arts of war, but savage in letting fall into disrepair the waterworks created by their forefathers.' The need to remember that underdevelopment was the economic effect of political conquest is not only to voice once again one's moral indignation, and to correct the impression left behind by even benevolent Westerners, such as Marx, who believed along with Lord Macaulay that British imperialism was a boon for Indians; but also it is to de-construct the myths of underdevelopment which shroud the real levers of international political policy. The fact that these myths are accepted as a rational scientific understanding of reality shows that this is no mere palace conspiracy but a universalised, biased ideology accepted by the élites, of the West and the Third World alike, as received knowledge. If real alternatives are to be found, which can convert crises into new opportunities for rebuilding communities, then we must take the time at least to describe some of the process by which people's minds have been enslaved into imagining there are no other real alternative styles of thought and action.

Let us look at the case of India's struggle to proceed with development initiatives within the parameters of Western liberal thinking accepted by its élite. Indians are not alone in suffering such intellectual enslavement, but they do present a well-argued example of how the colonised can internalise the conqueror's mission.

The Depression of the 1930s, followed by World War II, led that generation of Westerners to think of the war and its aftermath as a 'crusade', to use Eisenhower's words, but a crusade that must lead to times of plenty, through social engineering, scientific development, and the interplay of 'free market' forces. Here was a grand synthesis of scientific determinism and gothic romanticism with a vengeance. A grand vision of continuous economic growth into prosperity for all presented itself as an achievable reality. Colonialism had been ended, with Britain divesting herself of the greatest Empire the world had known. International functional instrumentalities were available through the United Nations' structures and its organisations, or could be called into being. Economic Science had removed all mysteries from the problems of growth or change faced by societies. This was a compelling vision shared by all the élite, whether of the West or of the newly independent countries of Asia and Africa. Pandit Jawaharlal Nehru was as much a believer in this vision as any in the West.

This was the dominant vision of economic and political reality, but there were also very many other visions of reality, of the colonial experiences, and of what was to come. For one, the Marxist interpretation which held the imagination and political loyalties of many of the activists among the poor in India, and the most 'progressive' of the political opposition, saw exploitative economic relations between the West and India, between the haves and the have-nots, as the enduring mark of the times. Independence for them was a mere formal transaction which did little to mitigate oppression of the poor, and while many internal struggles and convolutions were gone through, the Left in India was not sanguine about any simple road to development, as long as class struggle to oust those in power was left out of the equation. There was also the Gandhian vision, which while being equally critical of Western pretensions of knowing how to develop India, parted company with the Marxist Left, who rigidly adhered to the industrialising, high technology path of development.[19] In a sense, the élite in power under Nehru, and their Marxist opponents in Parliament and at the grassroots, were one in believing that development could be achieved, and poverty removed from the midst of the masses, only by learning and following the paths of Western science, technology, and industrialisation.

The differences between Mahatma Gandhi and Pandit Nehru were of long standing. While love and comradeship bound them together, their visions of what could be achieved, and what was desirable to achieve, were very widely different. Pandit Nehru was impatient to enter the modern world. Mahatma Gandhi viewed the modern world with profound regret, and wanted development, if his views could be encapsulated in a sentence, to centre around the idea of 'Gram Swaraj', or freedom at the village level. He envisioned a world of self-sufficient, self-provisioning village communities at the core of Indian life. He considered no other form of development was possible, or moral. To the accusation that his policies would perpetuate poverty, he replied his path would make the masses of the poor far better off than they had ever been before. Nor was he a strict socialist in the Marxist sense. He developed the concept of 'trusteeship' for the rich, and hoped a change of heart would render them servants of the poor. All this made little sense to the mainstream of Indian political and economic thought, led by Pandit Nehru. Gandhi was considered, reverentially, as a visionary and a romantic—strangely almost as Mao Ze-Dong was considered in China in the late 1950s—and he quietly refused to battle for his own cause.

The slowdown of growth under the five-year plans by the mid-1960s is too well known to need further comment. Gunnar Myrdal, in his seminal work on South Asian economies,[20] highlighted the differences in 'initial conditions' between India's and Western countries' industrialisation in the nineteenth century, and spoke of the 'soft state', where political and social factors held the key to development. This was an important discovery—that there was no scientific method, or package of technology and planning, which could drag a society into industrialised development if there were not the political will and conducive social processes.

Actually there was a tragic similarity between the start of the process of industrialisation in England and in India, which has led many development planners and economists already in the fast track to believe all will turn out well. In England, as in India, the accumulation of wealth was heralded by the destruction of its peasantry. But the process was centuries in the making. Long, long before Goldsmith, Shakespeare would make John of Gaunt bemoan that England was leased out like a pelting farm, and that England that was wont to conquer others had made a shameful conquest of itself. There was, luckily for England, no foreign imperial power to suppress its many political and tenurial adjustments. But by the early nineteenth century England, followed by other European nations, had found an empire which could absorb the tensions of its internal conflicts. England could appease its impoverished by offering them the spoils and spaces of its empire, and transfer to the colonies the burden of poverty. Japan, the one Asian power to escape colonisation, found its first rungs on the ladder of industrialisation by stamping on Korea and China as early as the 1890s. The equal impoverishment suffered by all the ex-colonies does not leave any of them, even huge countries like India—however much they may wish it—the option of unthreatened overlordship of their region. As the United States showed in the Gulf War, this will not be allowed to happen, except in controlled ways which actually weaken all the countries of the region.

Caught in a massive dependency trap, the pundits of countries like India can only hope, like Mr. Micawber, that something will turn up— breakthroughs in bio-technology or fusion power, which can be managed by the few, to buy on the one hand time from the many, and on the other the right to exist from the superpowerful. Perhaps, this is one psycho-sociological reason why the intellectual élites of Third World countries like India cling to outworn nineteenth century concepts, when even Western intellectuals are beginning to explore alternatives. However, one minor breakthrough did occur, which saved the Indian government from the American threat of using food aid as a political weapon.

The alarming spectre of political breakdown, endemic starvation, and dependence on import of grains, was staved off by the dramatic cereal production increases under the Green Revolution. Under that programme India gained a much-needed breathing spell, and freedom from being crushed by dependence on grain imports, and by systemic breakdown at home as a result of a perennial scarcity of grain. By the late 1970s comfortable buffer stocks of grain had been built up, and industrial growth exceeded the so-called 'Hindu rate of growth', even during years of monsoon failure.

And yet the planners, economists and high-level government circles were left deeply worried. The Green Revolution has rightly been called a cereal revolution, or even a wheat revolution. Its effects have not spread outside the richly endowed areas. The heartland of this development, once touted as an alternative to Red Revolution, is convulsed with communal violence, and some writers, such as Vandana Shiva,[21] trace the seeds of violence to the Green Revolution strategies which have further widened the gap between the haves and the have-nots. In a caste-ridden society, where rules of marriage are strictly defined and people usually marry only within their own sub-castes, the Punjab till recently was remarkably free of this practice, and Hindus and Sikhs inter-married freely. In fact it is hard to come across a household that does not have such links. The demands of modernistic development and commercial competition produced ethnic division and unprecedented violence: a clear demonstration of how unsuitable development strategies are for societies which require a community focus even for their very survival.

Over the four decades from the early 1950s to the late 1980s, agriculture has failed in over a dozen years, and recurring droughts, with increasing environmental stress, make this a pattern to be expected in the future. As Amartya Sen and others point out,[22] even the per capita availability of food grains in drought-stricken areas of India has been lower than that of the Sahel, and if India has scraped by without a famine, it is due to the excellent food-for-work programmes and public relief works that the government manages efficiently. Acknowledgement must also be made of the frugality of the poor, and their own community-based devices which, ranging from local credit management to seasonal migrations, have prevented extreme hardship from turning into political catastrophe. While this social fact gives governments some margin for manoeuvre, it can give them no sense of comfort.

David Seckler, researching the question for USAID a few years ago, pointed out that while India may have escaped the first Malthusian trap, it has not escaped the second—that is, labour availability outstrips labour demand. Chronic and soaring unemployment and underemployment is the result. He has also pointed to the fact that if a mechanism could be found by which the sector of the population below the poverty line could find access to the grain surpluses stored in government warehouses (around 20 million tons in most years), then by the simple fact of consuming the food they are deprived of, they would be lifted above the poverty line, since any increase in income would go directly to buy food for the malnourished and the perpetually hungry![23]

The Indian government has called for increased people's participation, decentralisation of decision-making, and more power to the Panchayats or village councils. From the early 1950s, 'Block Development' programmes were designed with the expectation of decentralising to the local level, and a few years later the traditional 'Panchayati Raj', or system of village councils, was revived. But the essential hierarchial system of government could not be transformed, and all these innovations merely added more layers of intermediaries, power brokers, élite interests and political influence to an already formidable top-down command structure the British had inherited from the Moguls and refined to suit imperial interests.

Within the last decade the government has started to take a close interest in the voluntary sector, trying to invite it to participate in development, and at the same time trying to curb it to conform to centralising interests. The voluntary sector itself has changed directions many times over the last three decades. In the early years of Independence, it saw itself as complementing government efforts at the local level. The famines of the 1960s, the growth of the communist opposition, the splitting of the Indian Communist parties, the staging of post-colonial struggles around the world, the adoption of liberation theology by many Christian grassroots movements; all these influenced the Indian voluntary sector to take on a confrontationist role and join hands with local political action groups to defy power structures, official and unofficial. In India, as in some other countries, there was a general running out of steam of all such protest movements, following the economic recessions of the 1970s. Voluntary agencies settled into a role of advocacy, neither rejecting government overtures, nor trying to lead grassroots opposition. While rejecting a 'professional' approach to grassroots development, in order to distance themselves from conventional social workers, they are content to be seen as a voice of the people, but at the same time not as political activists; rather as concerned community workers, who have alternatives to offer the people and their decision makers.

But what are these alternatives? After many consultations, seminars and sharing of experiences, still no clear consensus has emerged. When voluntary agencies speak they are very clear and forceful in rejecting the paths they do not want to follow, but are less sure what are the concrete step-by-step options that are available to reach the broadly defined goals of social justice, sustainable development, and environmental conservation. To confuse matters, these goals are also those of the government. The dispute arises over measures.

It is in such a context that 'survival strategies', community-based action, have come to be seen as a solution, especially in resource-poor, poverty-stricken areas. Bertrand Schneider has called this 'the barefoot revolution', in which the poor hope to alleviate their poverty through the regeneration of their depleted environment, because they have no other resources left.[24] The government, while wedded to its high-tech top-down strategies, is not unsympathetic to interventions that can give life to its 'Lab-to-Land' programmes (attempts to extend technology to farmers), which have so far produced few results. The vocal and active members of the patriotic opposition are also wedded to a high-tech approach to modernisation and industrialisation. Besides the ruling circles, those on the Left are extremely critical about traditional strategies, for they fear it is another term for romanticising the past, for letting the poor remain poor, for giving prominence to 'feudal forces', obscurantism, and, in short, mumbo jumbo. People who have opposed nuclear energy, for example, have been roundly abused by the Left, much more than by government circles, and denounced as CIA agents bent on weakening the country!

In such a charged and suspicious environment, all movements to establish a third approach to development, that neither espouses the modern high-tech option nor the necessity for a Marxist revolution as a pre-condition for development, must tread carefully. The voluntary movement, with its origins in the 'constructive work' programmes initiated by Mahatma Gandhi during the 'freedom struggle' days, is beginning to feel its way towards exploring this third option. This is a time of both opportunity and confusion.

The modern bourgeoisie of a post-colonial country such as India are trapped by the Western 'Enlightenment' education they have received, and the new homogenised culture of modern times. They seem destined to repeat the errors of the West, but from a position of dependence and inferiority, caught in a nightmare of trying to catch up, though they know they will never be able to do so. Mahatma Gandhi, though a product of Western liberalism, had found an escape by mixing a powerful political amalgam of a struggle for independence with traditional values. He chose the traditional individual quest for spiritual growth as a path for public service; and confronted Western imperialism from a popular basis of reaffirming the sanctity of community life. Indian philosophical thought has generally accepted without argument that 'man does not live by bread alone', though the shortage of food is not only of modern making. The search for realism is also seen as leading to its very opposite, to delusion, if pursued with mere rationality. For example, mainstream Hindu philosophical tradition has accepted that 'true' or relevant knowledge, including the scientific, is to be found only through the pathways of spiritual enquiry. At the same time, the validation of the spiritual or religious mode is to be found in its ethical applicability to everyday situations. Such statements are not seen as circular, or mystical arguments, but as clarifications of human experience.[25] It was the traditional acceptance of such perception that enabled Mahatma Gandhi to launch a massive political freedom struggle, in which the boundaries of the personal and the public, the political and the spiritual, were blurred, and the movement was seen as emancipatory but still traditional in social content, as modern but still native in origin and spirit.

The spontaneous support Mahatma Gandhi received from the untutored masses was in essence dissimilar to the mass hysteria created by fundamentalists today. His support came from a profound understand among people of the value of their community spirit, the richness of their cultures which had attempted to integrate the spiritual with the material, the community with nature. Such integration was widely achieved in all cultural traditions. The Buddha, in a famous discourse to the people of Kesaputta, told them not to seek knowledge from reports, tradition, hearsay, texts, inference, appearances, speculation, deduction, or from 'the teacher.' How then can a person arrive at truth? Only by following a path of spiritual enquiry. If this sounds impossibly ancient, it is interesting to hear a post-modernist say: 'The problems are the traditional problems of any philosophy which leads knowing to a knowledge of ultimate unknowability, and thereupon summons knowing to unknow itself—as by an active forgetting.'[26] There is no mystery here for any student of philosophy even today, from Tabriz to Kyoto.

Why was the traditionalist comfortable with such a deliberately accepted sense of philosophical insecurity, which could possibly permit moral and cognitive confusion, and make nonsense of social order or ethical principle? It was precisely because this living on the philosophical knife-edge[27] secured ethical behaviour while permitting the evolution of human society according to the turnings of the wheel of Dharma. The source of this regenerative power lay for the Buddhist in the *sangha* or egoless, free association of the community, one of the Three Refuges of Buddhism, after the Buddha himself and Dharma, or cosmic law. It was perhaps the very neglect of the third principle, of community, that has led to Buddhist social stagnation in many countries.[28] In the second Beatitude Jesus says: 'Blessed are the poor in spirit, for theirs is the Kingdom of Heaven.' A theological explication, which is closest to my heart, says that the poor and the humble form a natural community, a human fellowship, who come together in His Name and with whom He dwells also.[29]

Is not the community an inclusive extension of the Gaia principle to humanity? The community encompasses commitment, compassion and consensus, by which we can live again as a people. In search for genuine alternatives anywhere, we turn instinctively to the living community in order to recover an untortured sense of self, and an identity that is rounded because it is an inextricable part of a wholeness, of humanity as a part of nature. The search for power over others, and the desire to exalt oneself, shatters the wholeness of the community. It is in attempts to destroy this wholeness that we can locate 'evil.'[30] And it is to this knowledge of the uses of power that we owe the separation of humanity from nature.

It is important to remember that humanity has never forgotten this simple message. Even the great minds of the Enlightenment were clear that humanity was searching for a new integration: of people in living communities, and of communities with nature. For Schiller, the higher restoration of humanity's unity with nature can only occur by our overcoming the fragmentation of our faculties and restructuring the original unity of being. But this can only be done by returning to Nature's simplicity and preserving our spirituality. For Schelling, this moment will be signified by the unity of the world of thought and the world of reality. For Kant, the moral destiny of the human race is that of 'fulfilled art' once again becoming Nature. Mozart's Magic Flute is to be heard as a parable of the power of music to redeem humanity and reunite it in harmony with Nature.[31] The desire for the unity of truth, virtue, and beauty has never left us, whatever the philosophical style of the period. In our times, Schumacher writes: 'Wisdom demands a new orientation of science and technology towards the organic, the gentle, the non-violent, the elegant and beautiful.'[32]

A return to the community in Europe is a return to the very ancient roots of her gentle matrifocal culture several thousand years ago when her unwarlike agriculturists lived under the sign of the Goddess of the Community and Nature.[33] Women in these ancient times did not dominate—there were no Amazons. They held places of veneration in a nurturing culture that affirmed life not power, the joys of being together, not holding mastery over others. This new understanding of the very origins of civilisation in Europe is beginning to be shared by hundreds of archaeologists involved in field research over the last several decades. Professor Marija Gimbutas shows that in conventional understanding 'civilisation' has meant a hierarchical structure, warfare, class stratification and a complex division of labour. Research led by her shows that the civilisation of Old Europe was woman-centred, peaceful, and artistic. It was a civilisation of very large towns, with high temples, a sacred script, spacious houses, and 'professional ceramicists, weavers, copper and gold metallurgists,' involved in a flourishing network of trade.

Gimbutas emphasises that 'it is a gross misunderstanding to imagine warfare as endemic to the human condition.' For several thousand years, at the dawn of civilisation in Europe, people lived peaceful lives. Nor was this because of rule by women. The emphasis of the people was on a culture and technology that nourished people's lives. This civilisation worshipped the Goddess who is Nature herself. She was the primeval Virgin. 'The abundance which flows from her body represented a harvest to the gatherers of the Palaeolithic. Before she was mother to domesticated grains, she was mother to the wild plants... Knowing the sacred earth as Mother, pregnant in spring, ripening into the birth of harvest, her fruited vines cut like umbilical cords and celebrated in autumn are beliefs that are thousands of years old. The belief that earth's forces are concentrated in mounds, hills, rocks, and trees; a gratitude and profound respect towards the earth for providing continuing nourishment for all of life; and the necessity for ritually participating in the holy round of nature continued with great intensity from prehistoric times into the historical era.' (It is refreshing to come across a unity of erudite scholarship and sympathetic understanding of people, but not too surprising when it comes from a woman scientist.) The Goddess of Nature and Community, who has come down to us through folklore in many forms, exemplifies, says Gimbutas, the infinite powers and patterns of nature in plant, animal and human life. The continuous tradition of the Goddess has her associated with a circle of priestesses, and implies in Old Europe that communities were governed by collectives of women, not autocracies.

This benevolent order was lost through the dominance of migrating Indo-Europeans whose powerful armies of horsemen, unmatched at that time, devastated other cultures. Humanity lost the peace of Eden not through the acquisition of spiritual knowledge, but through its subordination to material knowledge of how to acquire and wield power. As the Enlightenment itself knew, a return can only come through a recovery of the true knowledge of the community of people living in harmony with nature. But, as Goethe warned: 'Nature scorns the inadequate student. Mere empirical intelligence cannot reach her.' To be adequate, we must relearn the art of community building by actually living the community in reality. Perhaps, having conquered the world, and having reduced other peoples to dependency, Europeans, for their own survival, will return to a gentler memory.

PART ONE

GLOBAL
ISSUES

'Wisdom demands a new orientation of science and technology towards the organic, the gentle, the non-violent, the elegant and beautiful.'

E.F. Schumacher, from *Small is Beautiful*.

GLOBAL ISSUES

Introduction

THIS IS A BOOK about rebuilding the community. Many of us who have worked on the book hope that it will also be an action book: that the ideas, the stories, the struggles of people to find meanings in community action, and new hope in re-kindling the community spirit, will lead others to turn towards their own communities for sustenance, both material and spiritual.

People have always lived in communities. Their histories, their cultures, and their identities spring from this togetherness. However, the features of modern life, the pressures of earning a living as a member of complex socio-economic organisations, and the myths created by modern times and its machines seem to have made us, in ways sometimes subtle and sometimes brutal, suddenly lonely in the midst of vast crowds. Sages, poets, and humorists have all seen the signs of the times and warned and laughed at humanity. But the problems remain; they grow, and continue to grow.

This is also a time of multiple crises—of our global environment that is being depleted by human shortsightedness and greed; of the horrendous link-up between the arms and the drugs trades; of famines and deepening poverty in the Third World; of loneliness and the lack of security and meaning even among those who are better off here in Europe; of the spreading of AIDS; of ethnic violence and civil war engulfing parts of Europe.

As at other times of great moral confusion and threat, there is a growing disenchantment among ordinary people with their institutions and the promises of the high and mighty. There is a natural turning away from looking for something to be done towards trying to do something ourselves. We rediscover our neighbours, and ourselves in the process. We all know the simple slogan: Think Globally, Act Locally. It is by working in our own communities that we find our voices, our identities, and our strengths. A new birth of the community spirit can be seen all over the world, especially in the poverty-stricken parts of the Third World. There are beginnings here in Europe as well.

But somewhere at the back of our troubled consciousness there is still the lingering hope that 'the system' may after all have the answers; that it can spare us the need to re-invent, to re-make, to re-live. Recently, in the Rio conference, we had an enormous and extravagant exercise by which the great and the good came together, as they said modestly, to save the world. In his contribution to this book, **Professor Johan Galtung**, one of the foremost peace researchers of our times, with humour and with erudition, strips UNCED of all mystification. There is little left unsaid when he shows us that we cannot leave it to the bureaucracies, the intellectuals, and the corporations to save the environment, much less the world. There never really was that option for humanity. The so-called economic necessities of mega-organisation may not be so necessary after all for the rest of the world. As Galtung points out, echoing Mahatma Gandhi: 'Reasonable co-existence with the rest of nature, neither above it nor below, just as a part of nature, is entirely feasible at high levels of material comfort. And this applies to the whole world. We have a local vs global and élite vs people problem, not a "North-South" problem.'

At Rio, Fidel Castro said: 'The solution cannot be to prevent the development of those who need it most. Because today, everything that contributes to underdevelopment and poverty is a flagrant rape of the environment. As a result, tens of millions of men, women, and children die every year in the Third World.... Unequal trade, protectionism and foreign debt assault the ecological balance and promote the destruction of the environment.'

'The system', focused on initiatives by the various global élites, not only seems incapable of producing a way forward which will lead us out of our many-sided global crisis, but may actually be orchestrating and amplifying the scale of the multiple catastrophes. There is now clear evidence which shows links between the drugs trade and arms dealers; between superpower political manipulation, the rise of local warlords, and endemic famines; the accumulation of extraordinary wealth in the North and the channels of international debt, trade and aid, the transfer of technology and the imposition of development policies in the South; and even the university system and the genocide of indigenous peoples. Can more research solve all this? Will appeasing the growing aspirations of the rich turn the tide? Will a better reading of the texts teach us anything?

Paul Evans, of the organisation Plantlife, has this to say: 'Post-Rio we have to ask, "What do we want out of life?" The ecological crisis will not disappear: the environment and the challenges of nature conservation are the challenges of our very existence. The key to tackling this does not lie exclusively with science and specialised groups but in the world as we all live it every day: a popular movement for the community of life.'[1]

For several years now, Robert Chambers has pointed out society's need to focus on people's livelihoods, rather than on environment or development issues. Such an emphasis could lead to effective people's participation in solving local problems, with which they are dynamically involved anyway.[2] **Fulai Sheng** is exploring a framework for appropriate development strategies linked to the continuity of cultural and local knowledge traditions, as well as the conservation of nature. Far from seeing a contradiction between these interests, he sees them as different sides of the same coin. The focus on revitalising traditional economic activities, such as weaving, cattle-rearing, boat-building and cheesemaking, which feature in several of the CADISPA (Conservation and Development in Sparsely Populated Areas) projects described in Part Two of this book, is identified by him as a key component of an integrated approach. He suggests the incorporation of industries to reclaim deserted industrial sites, as is happening in the CADISPA Portugal project, and also judicious eco-tourism, as in the CADISPA Italy project in the Aspromonte region. But above all, he sees the question of social equity as having an important bearing on the viability of an integrated approach—in this he echoes the forceful sentiments of Jorge Revez, president of the lead NGO in Mertola, who sees his own work primarily as a fight against social injustice. However, Fulai Sheng warns that the answers to complex development-conservation issues may not lie in a simple dependence on NGOs, who concentrate more on conscientisation than on incomes, and who lack coordination abilities or institutional capacity to learn from their own experience.

We know that in Europe many traditionally grown crops no longer exist. The severity of genetic erosion throughout Europe, as **Michel Pimbert** points out, has shocked many grassroots groups into action. Arche Noah in German-speaking countries, the Fraternité Ouvrière in Belgium, and the Henry Doubleday Research Association in the UK, and the Swiss Pro Specie Rara, all aim to conserve plant and animal genetic diversity and encourage sustainable development by building on local knowledge.

This is a book of many voices: academic voices that elaborate on how we can restructure our communities, livelihoods, and political and economic patterns of interaction; intellectual voices that talk about the meaning of diversity in nature and how this is related to society; cultured voices that tell us how people managed in the past and why; simple and true voices of the poor that speak of life as they live it; young and strong enthusiastic voices that are battling for change. Though the theme of this book is that of a holistic integration of community life and nature, and of rebuilding our lives at the local level, the book by its very nature is not such an organic production. It cannot be. We have yet to see the growth of early promises into a strong, acceptable alternative to what exists today. This book is about these early promises and remnants of the past which—

if we all agree that is what we want—may be woven back again into vibrant life. This book is a demonstration of the hope that you will join the few in a peaceful, organic, struggle to bring back meaning.

Waiting for UNCED:
Waiting for Godot

JOHAN GALTUNG

THE BIGGEST CONFERENCE in the history of the world (The United Nations Conference on Environment and Development) was held in Rio de Janeiro in June 1992. It lasted two weeks and was supposed to find answers to the pressing problems of environment and development and their interfaces. This author expects very little to come out of the conference; the following are the reasons why, focussing on the environment issue.

1. A mini-theory of conferences

Conferences are important as markets for people and ideas, as articulation fora, particularly if adequate media can supply a multiplier effect, and as fora for the negotiation of ratifiable treaties. The first two functions are important and easily met. The third will also be met. The problem is whether the treaties are up to the problem.

There are three conditions for a conference to succeed:

[1] *Domain*—all relevant parties are around the table;
[2] *Scope*—all relevant issues are on the table;
[3] there is sufficient *Time*.

There should be no *a priori* ranking of parties and/or issues. Partner-coalitions, issue-bundling and trading are permitted.

UNCED satisfies [2], as considered a very impressive catalogue of issues, but not [1] and [3]. Of course, ample time was provided for Agenda 21; UNCED is but the visible part of the iceberg. But that is the part that counts in the minds of participants and observers. Compared with a highly successful conference, such as CSCE 1972-75 in Helsinki, this is a major deficit. Much better would have been a format fitted for three years of (almost) permanent session, and then a signing ceremony, not an open negotiation session of two weeks' duration. The current Israel-Arab states' negotiation is another badly choreographed process: ample time, but too narrow in domain and scope. But the real problem is the participants. They are of all kinds, but the core is governmental in general and ministers of environment and development (E&D) in particular; this is in addition to the world summit aspect. The argument here is that this abstracts, and deflects from the real issue. The real issue is between depleters/polluters on the one hand—usually companies although they may be backed up by states and by producer and consumer interests—and actual and potential victims, divided into present humans, future humans and nature (which may also be divided into present and future).

States will produce more or less ratifiable treaties which in turn will be more or less adhered to. Imagine now that the parties meeting would be Companies, Present Victims, Future Victims and Victimized Nature; in other words, more like a conference between slave-owners and slaves, drug dealers and drug victims, rather than of the governments of slaving and drugging states, and others. What outcome could they produce?

Before that there has to be an answer to the obvious objection: OK, thalidomide victims can meet thalidomide producers like Japanese victims of minamata and itai-itai diseases can meet the corresponding producers. But how does one get Future Victims and Victimized Nature into the conference room? As participants in the regular sense, perhaps not. But there are some very good second bests. Thus, the younger a person is, the more Future does the person possess, gradually trading Future for Past as s/he grows older. So the argument would be to have youth and children represent Future Victims rather than some abstraction like 'sustainability'. And as to Nature: badly damaged Nature, through depletion or pollution or both, live or dead, should simply be in the conference room as (mainly) silent witnesses and testimonies.

One possible outcome would be that, confronted with the implications of their depletion/pollution, the evil-doers would change their evil ways. Another outcome would be a possible redress of the grievances of the victims. And the States can be there as a Third Party, partly to see to it that the other two parties turn up at the conference, not only the victims, and partly to cast agreements in the shape of ratifiable and binding treaties.

But the role of the States would be very different from the role at an armament/disarmament, war/peace conference, the model which they (unwittingly) imitate. In those cases, the States are the parties since they usually have monopolies on ultimate arms, on foreign policy in general and the politics of war and peace in particular. Even in this case it may be argued, however, that it would have been very useful in such contexts to confront arms manufacturers/dealers with their victims, the dead and the bereaved, the wastelands made out of nature, in short the consequences of genocide and ecocide.

Why do such things not happen? One answer would be that it runs against the entire Western tradition in handling crimes; the crime is seen as being against the State (or the 'people'), the victim is forgotten, and the crime is converted to a relation between the State (Judiciary) and the criminal.

In the UNCED case the process of alienation from the concrete wrong-doing is actually taken one step further: only the third parties, the States, meet in the core conference; the Victims are easily forgotten except as statistics and abstraction; and the Companies get off the hook, one theory being that they were unwitting parties to less fortunate activities. They are all written off by means of an overused phrase for people in general: non-governmental organisations (like defining women as non-men, children as non-adults and environment as non-human).

However, the point would be to convert confrontations between wrong-doer and victims in the field of the environment into a court case, with States sending the judiciaries rather than the ministers and experts in the E&D fields. Rather, the point would be for the two to examine together other courses of action, less wrought with danger, even catastrophe. They are the ones directly involved; they know best the nature of the issues. In other words, the buddhist approach of 'We have been on a bad karma together, let us try and change it' rather than the Christian 'You were wrong, you have to confess, repent and be punished.' A good opening question for all parties concerned would simply be: 'How could it have been avoided? What could all three of us have done?' And then a thorough exploration among relevant, concerned parties. Let past horrors inspire a better future through dialogue rather than adjudication.

But would not this have been very emotional? Precisely, yes, and that is good. The issues are there for everybody to see. In no way does this exclude the third party and the expert unravelling chains and cycles of cause and effect in addition to the cycles and chains of crime and atonement, common problems and dialogue. But it lends realism and concreteness to the conference, rather than relegating it to 'NGO' fora.

As it is the States try to present themselves as third parties loaded with expertise, getting the emotions out of the way. Precisely by not having been directly involved, it may look as if they are above the issues. Of course they are not.

Take as an example the 450 nuclear reactors in the world today, ultimately producing plutonium as 'waste', with a lifetime of 40,000 years. Nobody knows how to get rid of it, only that drilling holes somewhere to encase it may be producing a ticking time bomb. There is one possible use: as 850,000 bombs of the magnitude of the one that caused the Hiroshima genocide. This presupposes that no new reactors are built and that the present ones are ultimately phased out.

Or, to take another example: are we really to believe in the CFC theory that refrigerators and spray-bottles are the only cause of the ozone hole, and not the rockets and space ferries?

The States are the culprits here, at least as much as the Companies, together with the intellectuals who produced the underlying theories without due consideration for the 'side-effects'. Actually, the very concept of 'side-effect', meaning effects outside the paradigm used, is indicative of the blinkers that come with the cult of intellectual poverty known as excessive specialisation. They are all effects, all intra-paradigmatic if only the paradigm is broad enough. A plea for holism!

And a rather basic question: if the eco-catastrophes we are in are also caused by a particularly mechanistic and old-fashioned Western paradigm referred to as 'scientific', are we really to accept that the remedies for the problem are located within the same paradigm? In its most simplistic form we are talking about the (X,Y) paradigm, X for cause and Y for effect; like $X=CO_2$ for Y=greenhouse effect, X=CFC+others for Y=ozone hole, or X=HIV for Y=AIDS. If we do not like Y the remedy is to decrease X. But how about the context and a host of other variables, not all of them within natural science paradigms, like the paradigms themselves? How about synergies and reverse effects? How about the factors generating the pressure for economic growth, probably restoring any X at some other place in the total *gaia*? How about the factors just discussed, which shunt power away from Perpetrators and Victims and their possible dialogue into the hands of the States and the Experts, thus removing the obstacles for unimpeded operation of the (X,Y) paradigm?

At least keep the dialogue open to all kinds of views!

2. A mini-theory of problem normalisation

It is interesting to compare the Stockholm Conference 1972, that gave rise to UNEP (The United Nations Environment Programme), and the Rio Conference 1992 that gives rise to—what? Probably close to nothing if the thesis of this paragraph is correct: UNCED is not a problem-solving enterprise, but a signpost announcing that the normalisation of the environment problematic has been achieved.

For this a model of standard 'modern' society is needed. The basic structure is tripartite. There are two pillars, State and Capital (allocating factors and products through Plan and Market), run by bureaucracies (S) and Corporations (C). Between them, around them or under them, but in general not above them (except as rhetoric), is the Civil Society (CS): people and their associations, family, friendship and neighbourhood groups, voluntary associations, etc. In a capitalist society S is in principle serving C, in a socialist society C is in principle serving S, both of them having, in principle, CS as their *raison d'être*. In democratic societies CS is supposed to control S or C, in capitalist or socialist democracies respectively.

An important question is where intellectuals are located, since they produce understanding and forms of understanding, and control the discourses for the dialogues. The answer has to be split into two: intelligentsia and (true) intellectuals. The former produce answers to questions put by others (usually S and C); the latter produce questions themselves. The former are often for sale, the latter more independent. The former run modern society in the form of BCI complexes (bureaucracies, corporations, and intelligentsia); the latter are their critics.

The case of biogas may serve as an introduction to the more general case of normalising the whole environment problematic. The enthusiasm for the biomass converter in the 1970s and early 1980s may be hard to understand today. Even primitive biomass converters worked if the temperature was not too low, processing organic material into methane for cooking and heating, and a residue for organic fertilisation. People could even do this themselves at the village level (China) or the household level (India). No need for the BCI complex.

How does BCI appropriate something like this? Through overt or tacit cooperation, of course. One approach would be to find the conditions for converters to function optimally: a task the intelligentsia assumes willingly. Once that has been solved an implicit formula exists for standardised production of converters; a typical task for the corporation. The link between abstraction/generalisation in science and standardised mass production in the economy is obvious. The state can now enter, taxing the corporation in order to provide more money for research on converters, thus closing the cycle, or intervene directly, for instance outlawing converters as hazardous.

In either case normalisation has taken place. The intelligentsia have proved themselves to be above ordinary people in their professionalism, the corporations to be above artisanal villagers in productive capacity, and the state to be above them all in power, providing funds (l'état provident) and prohibiting and protecting (l'état gendarme). Of course, the converters then become too expensive for the villagers so the gas has to be transported to the cities. To the BCI complex.

At the time of Stockholm '72 the environment problematic was not yet normalised. There was direct confrontation; there was raw anger, with civil society and the first environmental organisations pitted against the corporations. The corporations were totally unprepared for this, as mainstream economists had not warned them. Some of them must have been in a state of shock. Naturally the more intelligent understood that there was money to be made with recycling technology and cleaning-up technology, knowing that both depletion and recycling, both pollution and cleaning up would be counted as bona fide economic activities and enter the GNP and their own book-keeping on the credit side. There is still no public environmental accounting, checking whether the environmental damage resulting from producing, distributing and using the remedies is less than the evil to be remedied. But above all the state was suffering, having been marginalised by these direct confrontations. This did not last long. The obvious answers, Ministries of the Environment that could establish norms for pollution/depletion; Departments, even Faculties of the Environment at universities and technical high schools, granting PhDs in environmental science to those who could unravel chains and cycles; and an environmental industry for recycling and cleaning up could combine the classical roles of the State as provider and watchdog. Of course, the problems of exhausting nature beyond its carrying capacity were not exactly new. But the consequences were reaching the suburbs and the middle classes, not only the inner cities, the lower classes, and the ghettos.

Yet something was needed, a real ideology. And that is what the Brundtland Report provided, with the only two words that will remain in people's memory from that report, 'sustainable development'. As if anyone has ever argued for non-sustainable development; as if anything changes when the general problem of reproduction, *reproducibility*, is expressed by another word. However, what is meant is clearly not sustainable development, but sustainable growth, and in the report there is no effort to make any distinction between general economic activity and the type of economic activity that is registered positively in the economists' GNP: that of value added through higher levels of processing of nature into goods in the secondary sector and services in the tertiary sector of economic activity; and marketing, buying and selling.

A general rule-of-thumb is as follows: the higher the degree of processing, the greater the eco-degradation because of non-degradable pollutants, and the greater the use of non-renewable matter. *And* the more global the trade, the less local and transparent the chains and cycles of cause and effect; and the more difficult to act, even to think. In short, the worse the problem.

But this is obscured by the Brundtland Report. That report has a quite different function, whether intended or not:

- to reassure Capital: growth is still possible—take a little more care, but in general terms, go ahead;
- to reassure Civil Society: whatever happens will have to be sustainable, and in solidarity with future generations;
- to reassure the State(s): whatever happens will be under our leadership; our power will increase rather than decrease.

In other words, a perfect report—a hoax, but perfect.

With this report normalisation could set in, nationally and supernationally. The new eco-eco mixes sprouted everywhere: economists with ecological concerns, and ecologists with mainstream economic thinking. What they both try to do is obvious: to conceive of depletion/ pollution as costs unaccounted for in the production/consumption process, which can now be internalised by presenting the recycling/ cleaning up bill. The state will then be an honest broker, assuming some of the costs, and splitting the rest between producers and consumers. This presupposes State-Capital dialogue, the assumption behind social democratic theory and practice, and dialogue between both and Civil Society. Rather than dialogues with the 'environmental activists' that got it all going, the process is to be integrated into the normal political process, through parliamentary and presidential democratic procedures.

Having people push monetised costs around in this tripartite construction of modern society is, indeed, no answer to such problems as the greenhouse effect, the ozone holes, deforestation, desertification, decreasing biodiversity and toxic pollution contributing to cardiovascular diseases, malignant tumours and mental disorders. A conference on slavery organised along UNCED lines in 1792 would have come up with fines for the slave-owners, limits to flogging, obligatory bandaging of the wounds, funds for the schooling of children of slaves, possibly even for the development of badly affected societies deprived of their population. Slavery in general would have been deeply lamented. But: no end to slavery.

Some slavery is inevitable, a necessity for growth, the BCI complex would have informed the world. But it has to be more equitably shared by the countries of the world, not monopolised by some few slaving countries who greedily have monopolised the slavery cake instead of dividing it more fairly. There would be statistics all over demonstrating what a small proportion of humanity accounts for the overwhelming part of the slavery; using the slaves for economic growth, and now trying to deprive others of that ability. The foresighted might even think in terms of slavery certificates, giving each country of the world the right to possess a certain number of slaves, for example in proportion to their own populations. Trading with certificates would be possible, for a natural equilibrium, defined by the market, could be obtained. Serious talk about over-slaving and under-slaving countries would emerge.

The slaving nations would have had a trump card up their sleeve: the United States will never accept any serious limitation. All we have to do is to wait for the US to vote against, maybe deplore it, and travel home. Not only in 1792, but much later. The argument would have been: US interests first, abolition later—much later. For review conferences between 1801 and 1809 they could have relied on President Jefferson, himself a slaver (about 150 slaves on his thousands of acres). Secretly the slaving countries would have been reassured: the US can be relied upon to block anything. 'If the US did not exist we would have to invent it', would have been the whispering in the corridor.

Or take a more recent example: armaments and the Cold War. Disarmament conferences by and for states were not only irrelevant but counter-productive, even legitimising existing armaments, and being cloaks for the transition to new weapons systems. In the early 1980s people on both sides lost faith in their governments, and communicating in their own way, making people-to-people contact and exchanging information, millions in the street simply demanded an end not only to the nuclear threat but also to rotten regimes. The Berlin wall fell. The Cold War was over. The managers of the states all exclaimed: 'Nobody could have predicted this.' Why? They thought the problem had been normalised. But people did not believe in that system and took the matter in their own hands, mindful, among other things, of the states' interest in the arms trade and in piles of weapons as symbols of prestige and power.

What would conferences to control the production, distribution and consumption of drugs look like, given the considerable interest of some states in the economics of production and distribution while deploring the consumption? They might reduce or eliminate some excesses, not much more. In no way would they compare with a televised confrontation of drug victims with pushers, dealers of all kinds and growers. Much naivety is needed to assume that the committed can be shunted aside and the non-committed will carry the same message into ratified and binding treaties. They may even stand in the way of progress by giving people illusions. Some consciousness-formation may emerge, but some may also be blunted; that the net balance is positive is far from clear.

3. A mini-theory of alternatives
If there is anything we can learn from the history of major, deep-rooted problems of exploitation and repression, then it is this: a change of system is needed, as otherwise the same phenomena of slavery, arms manufacture and armed conflict, drug consumption to the point of enfeebling whole populations and depletion/pollution to the point of biocide, killing whole regions, will be reproduced. *The problems will be sustainable, not the development.* Thus the slavery economy yielded to a capitalist economy where labour, not labourers, were traded; and slavery was, *grosso modo*, not reproduced. For the other three problems, no alternative social formation has been introduced and the problems proliferate, as post-Cold War history informs us.

Of course, the best alternative social formation from the point of view of the countless eco-problems would be a world economy based on countless local economies with highly transparent eco-cycles so that people become the victims of their own anti-ecological action; *and* there would be either a lower level of processing or processing using renewable matter and energy only. This is what humanity would do today were we guided by rationality. Reasonable co-existence with the rest of nature, neither above it nor below, just as a part of nature, is entirely feasible at high levels of material comfort. And this applies to the whole world. We have a *local vs global* and *élite vs people* problem, not a 'North-South' problem. Not only the effects, but also the causes have to be handled. And they are in the eco-eco cycles themselves, not only in some points of emission and impact, e.g. in the growth-aid-debt triangle.

Malthus was an optimist: he talked about the arithmetic growth of food production and the geometric growth of population (today we would say linear and exponential). In the coming hundred years or so the population increase may well be from 5.5 billion to 11 or 12 billion, very many of whom will be trained in the irrational behaviour of today and shown no real alternative by their political leaders. At the same time, the inevitable under the present system will happen: food production will not remain constant, but decrease, possibly dramatically. Decreasing biodiversity, increasing toxicity, deforestation, desertification and the ozone holes all impact negatively on food production; their synergies, basically unknown due to the ubiquity of the (X,Y) model, may possibly be fatal. Recently the socialist countries have been particularly badly hit (it is said that the life expectancy of the population in the Moscow area decreased by ten years in the two decades of the 1970s and the 1980s). Maybe they polluted more than before. What is sure is that socialist ideology of self-sufficiency placed the impact of their eco-irresponsibility on themselves, to the point of committing some kind of eco-suicide. The capitalist countries, through their world-encompassing cycles, distribute the impact globally—mainly on Third World countries, but also on themselves. Seventy per cent of the deaths in the US are probably now caused by the biggest form of pollution, neither air, nor water—but through food and diet.

One day, when the disaster is obvious to everybody, people will again be on the streets, in their millions. They will demand their planet back—with a sustainable system.

Should the people (meaning all of us) really act locally and think globally? Of course we should think and act both locally and globally—that frequently quoted saying excludes two rather important categories. The BCI complex is acting globally all the time. The clones in the Third World countries are more a part of that system than a part of the local populations who see the basis for their livelihood ruined more and more, every day. To speak of the Third World élites as representing the victims when what they go in for is their part of the expanding depletion/pollution cake may be correct in a formalistic sense, but in the end only the people can think, speak and act for themselves.

Some causes are locally expressed, in manufacturing processes. But with the globalisation of the post-modern economy, and under the standard ideology of comparative advantage, this usually means that capital, technology and management are located in the First World and labour and nature in the Third; Union Carbide is a good example. Was the cause of the Bhopal tragedy in Bhopal? Was the cause of Chernobyl not rather with some planning agency in Moscow? And is it really true that the effects are global? Some effects are carried by air and water and transportation, but the diseases of modernisation tend to hit very locally, inside single human beings. So, act and think everywhere! Only Civil Society can manage that. In the end, when problems are close to being solved, the States may celebrate with a treaty which then has become meaningful. Let us only hope UNCED has not had too much demobilizing impact, but at least has stirred some sluggish consciences.

Postscript

The final outcome of the UNCED conference was, of course, very disappointing. The US refused to sign the crucial biodiversity treaty (more interested in patents and their own gene technology industry that could come in as a substitute and benefit from decreasing diversity). The US also eliminated concreteness from the climate convention. And the Rio declaration and Agenda 21 also suffer from a lack of concreteness (Tagesanzeiger, 15 June 1992, or other reviews).

Integrating Economic Development with Conservation

FULAI SHENG

SOME PEOPLE BELIEVE that economic development and conservation are mutually exclusive. They argue that a given habitat can either be destroyed for economic development or preserved in its natural state for the survival of species: there is no compromise.[1] In their view, if you cut trees in a forest, then it is impossible to preserve the biological diversity at the same time; or if you protect the forest, it is impossible to carry out any economic activity there.

There are two factions within this group.[2] One complains that conservation castrates economic development. In the Pacific Northwest of the United States, for example, the protection of 1.2 million hectares of federal forest land (the habitat for the spotted owl) is said to have cost 150,000 jobs in the logging industry.[3] The attitude towards conservation is that economic development should not be sacrificed for the protection of the spotted owl. The bumper sticker 'Save a Logger. Kill an Owl', which is very popular in that area, says it all. Similar sentiment is shared on this side of the Atlantic Ocean: as the Spanish Prime Minister Felipe Gonzalez announced recently: 'When the survival of a peasant or a duck is at stake, it can be guaranteed that it's the duck that goes.'[4]

The other faction, however, condemns economic development for destroying the environment. The logging of tropical rainforest, for example, is estimated to cause the extinction of 50,000 invertebrate species per year—about 140 each day.[5] This attitude towards conservation is that the environment must be protected from economic development. It is this perception of the relationship between economic activities and conservation that has led to the preservationist approach to environmental protection.

But the relationship between economic development and conservation must be a complementary one. Conservation provides a material basis for sustained economic development, whereas economic development provides incentives and financial resources for carrying out conservation activities. The conservation of forests is again a good example. On the one hand, conservation ensures a sustained supply of wood for housing construction, furniture manufacturing, and other uses. On the other hand, the use of forests not only creates material incentives for conserving forests as a long-term money-making asset, but also generates funds necessary for conserving the forests.

Many community-based economic activities, in particular, can directly contribute to conservation. In the peasant/duck example, if the peasant sets up a duck farm, both conservation and development objectives can be achieved: there will be reduced pressure on land and forests, greater attention to the pollution level of rivers and lakes, the duck will not become extinct, and at the same time there will be a stable duck-meat supply and increased income from the sale of ducks which will further encourage and enable the farmer to maintain the farm. In fact, many Chinese farmers have become millionaires through setting up duck farm businesses in the last ten years.

There is great potential for integrating such community-based activities with conservation. These activities are on a small scale, are highly labour intensive, and require a low input of natural resources. Activities such as basketry, knitting, weaving, bee-keeping, flower growing, the farming of local food specialities (Peking duck, for example) and aquatic farms all have minimal impact on the environment while producing substantive economic benefits for the local people.

This chapter discusses such a complementary relationship between economic development and conservation with a view to promoting the integration of the two. The focus is on rural community-based activities, because the most serious environment degradation and resource depletion are taking place in rural areas, and because those rural activities can be most readily incorporated into conservation.

The remainder of this chapter is broken down into four sections. The first introduces the preservationist approach towards environmental protection and points out its unsustainability. This is necessary because the preservationist mentality represents the most serious threat to an integrated way of conservation; to see clearly the complementarity between economic development and conservation, we must first demonstrate the unsustainability and unrealistic nature of the preservationist approach.

The second section describes the transition from the preservationist approach to an integrated approach and analyses the need for such integration. This section intends to demonstrate that an integrated approach has become the mainstream of conservation and that such integration is not only driven by the failure of the preservationist approach, but also by the positive linkages between economic development and conservation.

The third section outlines the major components of this integrated approach, which include various community-based economic activities, some of which have already been touched upon above, the supporting mechanism for the integration, and the governing principle of sustainable resource use (SRU). The emphasis in this section is placed on community-based activities for the purpose of promoting these activities in rural communities that are confronted with the development-conservation debate.

The final section summarizes the major points of this chapter.

A. THE PRESERVATIONIST APPROACH

Preservationists reject economic development. Their approach to environmental protection is typified by protected-area projects, which consist of:

1) declaring a certain area as a protected area;
2) demarcating the area;
3) removing the inhabitants from the area;
4) building fences and check points around the area;
5) training and arming guards to police the area; and
6) punishing people for violating the rules of protection.

The basis of this approach is the belief that economic development and environmental protection are mutually exclusive. The export of tropical timber, for example, is viewed as a threat to the protection of rainforests; preservationists believe that the only way to save rainforests is to make them protected areas, reserves, or national parks, thereby denying people access to forest resources and excluding any economic activity in those areas.

This approach might have come about as an understandable reaction to the alarming environmental crisis at a global level: a minimum of 140 plant and animal species are becoming extinct each day; forests are disappearing at an annual rate of 17 million hectares, about half the size of Finland; heat-trapping carbon dioxide in the atmosphere has increased by 26 per cent over the pre-industrial level; and the temperature on the earth's surface has reached a record high: of the seven warmest years in recorded history, six have occurred since 1980.[6] These environmental trends are, of course, inseparable from the pressure of economic activities. In the past 100 years, for example, industrial production has increased by over 100 times.[7] Faced with an environmental crisis of such proportions, the immediate response of preservationists has been to oppose all economic activities in sensitive areas.

But such a preservationist approach cannot be sustained in the long run. First, the measures prescribed under protected-area projects, particularly the fences, checkpoints, and armed guards, virtually treat local people as enemies of nature; this necessarily invites people's resentment towards environmental protection. Second, the establishment of protected areas sometimes disregards traditional land tenure practices, giving rise to land-use conflicts which are counter-productive for environmental protection. Third, the preservationist approach does not deal with the roots of environmental problems; displaced people without alternative livelihoods will either bounce back to where they were before, or exert pressure on the environment elsewhere.

Empirical evidence has shown that protected-area practices have largely been a failure. In the twenty years between 1950 and 1990, for example, although the number and extent of protected areas increased more than fivefold, the average rate of species extinction continued to increase substantially over the same period of time.[8]

B. TOWARDS AN INTEGRATED APPROACH

The fundamental flaws of the preservationist approach have prompted growing international recognition of the need to integrate economic development with environmental protection. As early as 1980, the World Conservation Strategy stressed the importance of integrating economic activities of local communities with protected area management.[9] The message is that 'conservation is not the opposite of development'.[10] In 1991, the second world conservation strategy 'Caring for the Earth' further underscored that: 'We should stop talking about conservation and development as if they were in opposition and recognise that they are essential parts of one indispensable process.'[11] More recently, in June 1992, 'Agenda 21' of the Rio Summit specifically calls for 'integrating environment and development at the policy, planning and management levels'. [12]

Such a shift from a preservationist approach towards an integrated approach represents a fundamental change of perception with regard to the objectives of conservation. It is reflected, for example, in the growing replacement of the term 'preservation' by 'conservation', which, by definition, 'includes both protection and the rational use of natural resources'.[13] A notable change came when WWF, the largest conservation NGO (non-governmental organization) in the world, changed its name in 1989 from 'World Wildlife Fund' into 'World Wide Fund For Nature'[14] with a newly defined goal to 'stop, and eventually reverse, the accelerating degradation of our planet's natural environment, and to help build a future in which humans live in harmony with nature'.[15]

The need to integrate economic development with conservation can be analysed from five angles:

1) economic activities that damage the environment result from the pressure for development and such pressure will not disappear

through excluding economic activities from conservation;

2) economic under-development and uneven development are often the roots of many environmental problems and need to be addressed directly in conservation activities if we want to go beyond the treatment of the symptoms;

3) economic activities provide material incentives for local communities to implement conservation activities;

4) economic activities can directly contribute to the attainment of conservation objectives; and

5) the financial sustainability of conservation ultimately depends on economic activities.

First, economic activities can be environmentally destructive. For example, in the Castilla-La Mancha region of Spain, the least populated region in the country, recent economic initiatives supported by the European Structural Funds encompass reservoirs, irrigation projects, river dredging, canal-building, road networks, and afforestation;[16] these development activities threaten to intensify soil erosion, uproot native vegetation, drown thousands of hectares of Mediterranean forest plains, destroy river systems, and adversely affect the wild flora and fauna.[17]

In Extremadura, another sparsely populated area in southwestern Spain, economic activities financed by the European Structural Funds also have serious environmental implications. For instance a commercial re-afforestation project in the area has led to the loss of over 30 tonnes of soil per hectare every year.[18]

Such economic activities reflect the pressure for development. The pressure can come from local people who legitimately aspire to a better material life, from national governments under political pressure to reduce unemployment, or from external agencies concerned with regional economic disparity. In the case of Spain, for example, the pressure mostly comes from the government and the European Community (EC), which have been trying to align the economic development of Spain with that of the richer members of the EC family.

The pressure for development always exists, as people's aspiration for a better life is rooted in human instinct. Rather than turning a blind eye to development pressure, therefore, it is best to acknowledge its existence and to reformulate economic development plans in an environmentally friendly manner. In this way, economic development can continue to be pursued without unduly exerting a negative impact on the environment. In the case of the Castilla-La Mancha region of Spain, WWF-Spain has initiated a good example of the integrated approach. In its critique of the development plan for the region, WWF-Spain suggests various viable alternative schemes that will, on the one hand, accommodate development pressures, or at least partly so, and on the other hand minimise the adverse impact of development on the environment.

Secondly, economic under-development and uneven development are often the forces behind the pressure for development. Both the Castilla-La Mancha region and Extremadura are among the poorest and most sparsely populated areas of Spain. The desire to modernize these areas generates the development pressure which has the adverse environmental impact described earlier.

Economic under-development and uneven development can also affect the environment through mass emigration to relatively wealthier areas, home and abroad. For example, the lack of economic opportunities in Mértola County in Southern Alentejo of Portugal has caused an emigration of the core of the local labour force.[19] Mértola's population dropped from 26,026 inhabitants in 1960 to 11,693 in 1980. Most emigrants were the young and strong members of the local labour force. They either moved to big cities in Portugal or abroad. The environmental impact of such economically induced emigration is three-fold:

1) increased emigration to urban areas aggravates human pressure on urban infrastructure and contributes to urban environmental problems;

2) the depopulation and ageing process in rural areas makes local communities unable to manage local resources sustainably; and

3) the disintegration of rural communities as a result of such emigration makes the local environment vulnerable to the invasion of external interests: in the case of Mértola, the planting of eucalyptus by paper-pulp companies has turned the county into one of the largest plantations of eucalyptus in the country, and the construction of a toxic waste dump has made the area, in effect, a national toxic garbage can.

Economic activities, which create employment opportunities and income for the poorer segments of society, must therefore be an integral part of conservation in those areas. Otherwise the pressure from the lack of economic opportunities in an area, or from uneven development among different areas, can lead to destructive environmental impact in both urban and rural areas. The same reasoning can be applied to economic underdevelopment in low income countries and to the uneven development between North and South.

Thirdly, environmental protection often incurs costs on the part of the people and communities affected. Even the enlightened version of environmental protection, i.e. conservation, which includes sustainable use of natural resources, involves costs in terms of reduced access to, and use of, local resources, at least in the short run.

True, there are benefits from conservation, but they usually accrue over a long period of time and are beneficial to a larger group than the ones who have to bear the costs. The positive impact of curbing greenhouse emission, for example, is not likely to be substantively felt by the current generation and will benefit all people rather than any individuals or groups of individuals. Such implicit or explicit cost/benefit comparisons may discourage people from carrying out any conservation activity.

To induce people to get involved voluntarily in conservation activities, the cost/benefit picture in their mind must show a clear margin of benefits over costs. Economic activities generate employment and income and may be combined with conservation activities to win the support of local people for conservation.

Fourthly, economic activities can directly contribute to the achievement of conservation objectives. Many environmental problems are economic problems as well. The deterioration of capital infrastructure such as waste treatment plants and sewage facilities are basic economic problems, but have important environmental implications. The solution to these problems will at the same time tackle the associated environmental problems.

Sometimes economic development and environmental protection can be viewed as the same thing. For example, in Ireland and Greece, 35 per cent of household waste and 20 per cent of municipal waste are disposed of by unmonitored tipping on to the land. In Ireland, Italy, Belgium, and Greece, only 20, 26, 24, and 19 per cent of the population respectively have access to the sewage system.[20] Pollution problems are tremendous. In these cases, to provide waste-disposal and sewage facilities can be seen as both an economic activity and a conservation activity.

Fifthly, the long-term sustainability of conservation requires the financial resources generated by economic development. Conservation activities cannot be implemented without money. In the Ruhr District of Germany, for example, the total costs of reclaiming derelict industrial sites amount to 15 billion Dm (6.8 billion ECU). Where will the money come from? If a conservation activity is to be self-sustaining, economic development must be part of the scheme and must be promoted to yield financial resources to fund the implementation and maintenance of conservation on a sustainable basis. It is true that funds for conservation may come from governments or other external assistance, but ultimately these funds must come from economic activities somewhere.

C. COMPONENTS OF THE INTEGRATED APPROACH

The need for an integrated approach is evident; but what exactly does it consist of? This question can be answered on three parallel levels. On the first level, an integrated approach consists of economic incentives and activities. On the second, it consists of political, social, cultural, and institutional factors that together form a supporting mechanism for successful implementation of the integrated approach. On the final, but most important level, the approach must be governed by the SRU principle—the balancing instrument to reconcile the short-term conflicts between economic development and environment.

ECONOMIC INCENTIVES AND ACTIVITIES

Economic incentives refer to financial instruments used to alleviate the pressure of economic activities on the environment. In a rural context, they can include compensation payments and substitution programmes.[21] Compensation payments are direct monetary transfers to the affected population whose access to local natural resources is denied by conservation schemes, whereas substitution programmes are those that provide alternative natural resources to the ones that are being protected.

These instruments are often found in developing countries where conservation activities are characterized by protected reserves that block local people's access to their traditional sources of livelihood. In the Oban area of Nigeria, for example, as the establishment of a national park has reduced local people's incomes from hunting and gathering, and any economic benefit from the protected area is either insufficient to compensate for the loss of income or can be realised only over a long period of time, compensation payments are made to local communities on a quarterly basis for a period of seven years, but will be suspended if people are found to be violating park policies.[22] With regard to substitution, if a protected area was a source of livelihood based on hunting and fuelwood gathering, then animal husbandry and woodlots outside the protected area may be proposed as substitutes.

These incentive instruments are justified on two grounds.[23] Firstly, local natural resources are the basis for local people's survival, and the protection of those resources without any compensation or substitution or both will condemn people to poverty, which in turn will aggravate pressure on the environment. Secondly, compensation and substitution can be provided in the form of cash payments, goods and services, in return for local people's promises to waive their rights of access to the protected areas.

But these incentive instruments cannot have a sustained effect. They are no more than an extension of the preservationist approach; their overriding objective is protection, rather than integrated economic development and conservation. While there can be short-term relief of pressure on the protected area as a result of incentive instruments, the long-term impact is by no means clear. Compensation cannot last forever; in the case of the Oban National Park, for example, compensation payments will last no more than seven years. What happens afterwards? There is also the question of where the compensation funds come from. Whether the funds will come from the government or external sources including bilateral donors, multilateral institutions, and NGOs, there is always a problem of uncertainty about the availability of funds, which can be affected by global and domestic economic situations. Finally, local natural resources often provide a wide range of services to local people, and it is not possible to substitute the functions of all those resources.

Sally Jeanrenaud of WWF-UK has identified four major areas of complication related to compensation and substitution schemes:[24]

1) the difficulty in identifying the appropriate political forum for negotiations and regulations;
2) the difficulty in determining the form, total value, period of payment, and target (communities or individuals) of compensation or substitutions;
3) the impossibility of providing substitutes for all resources formerly used in a protected area: e.g. medicinal plants, building materials, and particularly wild foods;
4) the complexity of negotiating explicit agreements setting out the rights and obligations of both sides.

To promote a real integrated approach, therefore, we cannot rely on the use of these incentive instruments; rather, we should focus on substantive and viable economic development activities. In a rural context, these activities can include traditional economic activities, tourism, wildlife use, extraction of reserves, and environmental enterprises.[25]

1) Traditional economic activities

These activities are characterized by their indigenous nature, small scale, high labour input, and low resource input. For example, in Mértola County of Portugal, where WWF has recently promoted an integrated approach named CADISPA (Conservation and Development in Sparsely Populated Areas), the types of traditional activity that are being encouraged include:[26]

a) traditional weaving
b) bee-keeping (for honey-making)
c) traditional boat-building
d) basketry
e) cheese-making
f) sweet-making.

Such activities can be important components of an integrated approach. First, they generate economic benefits in terms of livelihood, income and employment for the poorer segments of local communities, rather than the privileged and external interests as is often the case when large development projects are undertaken.

Secondly, the impact of these activities on the environment is minimal because of their low resource input and high labour intensity. Basketry, for example, is based on crop residue without having any significant impact on the environment.

Thirdly (but no less important than the previous two), such activities unite people in communities, create a sense of local integrity and responsibility, and help prevent the disintegration of rural communities. For example, local women in many rural communities often get together to engage in traditional weaving while they share their sorrows and joys and offer help to each other. This is an effective way of communication among the local people themselves and it helps stabilise the rural communities.

One should not, however, confine rural economic activities to traditional activities. People in the North and in urban areas tend to romanticise simple ways of life in rural areas. Many Western tourists, for example, are often enchanted by the primitive features of the places they visit, rather than by the modern facilities. They hope that those traditional features will be retained, as they fulfil their nostalgic dreams. Such sentiment has nothing to do with conservation, and would condemn local people to a life at a subsistence level and even poverty. Local people have the same aspirations for a better material life as everyone else. They have the right to benefit from the economic wealth of the mainstream of society. To demand that they live on a subsistence basis is both morally wrong and unrealistic. It is up to local people (particularly the indigenous ones) to decide their own lifestyles.

2) Tourism

Tourism, if properly managed, can contribute both to the economic well-being of local people and to conservation. First of all, tourism generates employment opportunity and income. It accounts for 5 to 10 per cent of GDP in many countries.[27] In the European Community, tourism accounts for 5.5 per cent of GDP, 5 per cent of export revenues, and 6 per cent of total jobs, involving over 7 million full-time jobs.[28] The Mediterranean basin, in particular, represents 35 per cent of the entire international tourist trade and is the world's leading tourist spot.[29]

Secondly, the economic benefits from tourism, in terms of employment and income, should create incentives to preserve the environment as a money-making asset.

Thirdly, tourism in conservation areas can serve an educational function; tourists, whether from local areas, other parts of the country, or abroad, will gain a better understanding of the specific environment as well as the functions related to it, thus generating broad awareness of the importance of conservation.

Viable recreation management has been reported, for example, on the coast of North Holland, which consists largely of beaches and sand dunes.[30] At peak time, there are about 250,000 visitors on the beaches along the coast. Each year, 4 million people visit 17,000 hectares of sand dunes there. In spring and autumn, 70,000–80,000 visitors go to the dunes per day. The tourism in this area generates 'a stable and growing source of employment'. A total of 76,500 beds are provided for long-stay visitors, accounting for 50 per cent of all beds in the region, excluding Amsterdam.

Such pressure for recreational use, however, can also cause damage to the fragile coastal areas, particularly to the dunes where there is inadequate natural vegetation. When the vegetation is uprooted, the sand can blow away, not only threatening to cover farms and residential areas, but also render low-lying areas of the west Netherlands vulnerable to flooding.

Control measures are therefore necessary to reconcile the conflict between the demand for recreation and the protection of the environmental functions of coastal areas. In North Holland a recreation planning policy has been implemented: zoning regulations promote day-recreation facilities in areas where the recreation pressure is particularly heavy, and long-stay facilities in areas where the pressure is less heavy. The plan has also spread the load by creating recreation facilities in inland towns, extending the dune area, expanding and renovating facilities at existing sites. 'This example shows that recreation development can be achieved without adversely affecting the natural and landscape qualities of this area.'[31]

Great caution must be exerted in developing tourism, because of the potential negative impact of unregulated tourism on the environment. Together with the tourists come the waste, pressure on local infrastructure (water, electricity, transportation), and disturbance to the ecosystem. The threat is most evident in the Mediterranean region. For the EC members located in this region the increase in tourism is estimated to require the doubling of space occupation by the year 2000, and solid waste and waste water could more than triple by the year 2025.[32]

Since many of these problems are externalised by the tourism business, the promotion of tourism may not be based on the principle of sustainability. People in the tourism business now have a tendency to label their businesses as 'green' and promote them as eco-tourism or nature tourism in order to manipulate the environmentally conscious public. But if they do not have to internalise the costs such as increased waste, deterioration of infrastructure, and disturbance to the habitat, then the type of tourism that they are promoting cannot be ecologically sustainable.

In the EC's 'Towards Sustainability: The European Community's Programmes of Policy and Action in relation to the Environment and Sustainable Development, 1992', the major elements of developing sustainable tourism are outlined.[33] They include:

1) controls on land use;
2) strict rules on new construction;
3) controls on illegal housing;
4) management of private traffic flows to and within the tourist sites;
5) diversification of tourism;
6) strict implementation and enforcement of environmental standards on noise, drinking water, bathing water, waste water, and air emissions;
7) creation of buffer zones around sensitive areas such as wetland and dunes;
8) better dispersion of summer holidays;
9) awareness-building and education of local people and tourists;
10) education and professional training of people involved in the management of the areas involved.

On the economic side, there are two areas that must not be overlooked. One is the seasonal nature and unpredictability of the demand for tourism. For example, an average of 50 to 70 per cent of tourism in the Mediterranean takes place in summer.[34] The demand for tourism is affected by political, economic as well as climatic events, and may not necessarily be a reliable source of income.

The other area, which is probably more important, is that tourism may not actually benefit the local people and contribute to the growth of the local economy. In the Dutch example given above, it is not clear who in fact has benefited from the increased coastal tourism: whether it is local people, the government, or large businesses in the resorts.

This problem is more prominent, perhaps, in developing countries, where local people may actually become worse off from tourism development, because of the loss of their access to national parks reserved for tourists, and because of the type of development that is often dominated by outside commercial interests.

In Rwanda, for example, revenues from tourism has never gone to the local people.[35] In the CAMPFIRE project in Zimbabwe, tourism revenues have entered the pockets of local government officials.[36] The World Bank has estimated that as much as 55 per cent of gross revenues from tourism in developing countries flow back to developed countries.[37] Sally Jeanrenaud concludes that 'grassroots participation in ecotourism to date is extremely limited'.[38]

3) Wildlife exploitation

Wildlife can provide several important economic benefits to local people. It is an important source of protein, particularly for rural communities in developing countries. The meat and hides from wild animals can provide income. For example, hunting and trapping of wildlife contribute up to a quarter of villagers' income in the Korup National Park of Cameroon.[39]

But these economic benefits are sometimes achieved at the expense of the survival of the animals themselves. The fact that the animals are 'public goods' serves as a disincentive to manage wildlife on a sustainable basis. The high market prices for wildlife, which are themselves based on increasing scarcity, have further encouraged unsustainable exploitation.

The way to conserve wildlife, however, does not lie in the across-the-board prohibition of wildlife exploitation. The economic imperative to exploit wildlife is such that legal enforcement can be ineffective. Except in the case of genuinely endangered species where absolute protection may be justified, a more effective approach to conserving wildlife is to encourage its sustainable exploitation to the benefit of local people.

First, local people's livelihoods may partly or completely depend on wildlife; the protection of wildlife without providing viable alternative means of livelihoods will drive people into poverty, the pressure of which can render any protection scheme ineffective.

Secondly, the exploitation of wildlife can be made an incentive for people to conserve it. The question of course is how to do this. While no perfect solution has yet been found, some field experiences in Africa suggest that empowerment of local community and community participation in wildlife management may be the only way to bring benefits to local residents and at the same time secure wildlife populations.[40] A good example is a village-based wildlife management project in Zambia, which has been very effective in reducing poaching of wildlife, increasing wildlife populations, contributing to the material welfare of the local people, and is 10-50 times cheaper than law enforcement.[41]

Thirdly, wildlife whose population needs to be controlled for ecological reasons can be exploited without endangering its survival. The deer population in the UK, for example, has been a major factor in causing traffic accidents on motorways. Organised culling of the deer population not only generates benefits in terms of revenues from the sale of deer meat, skins, and horns, but also in terms of reduced traffic accidents.

4) Extractive reserves[42]

The concept of extractive reserves has recently been developed from the conservation practices of rainforests. These reserves are demarcated for the harvesting and marketing of non-timber (and to a less extent, timber) products, particularly fruits, nuts, plant oils, resins, medicinal herbs and rattan, which can yield higher net revenues than the timber. The forest itself is kept intact in order for it to continuously provide essential environmental services but the products of the forest are made available to local communities to support their livelihoods. A cost-benefit analysis for the Korup National Park, for example, has demonstrated that the economic benefits from this approach can amount to US$25 million per annum, whereas the benefits from unregulated exploitation would only produce $1 million p.a.

This concept can (and has) been applied to other resources as well. Examples include butterfly farming, rattan cultivation, the harvesting of giant snails, and the cultivation of ornamental and medicinal plants.

Several conditions need to be met in order to make this concept a viable one. First, there needs to be an international market for non-timber products, because if these products remain non-tradable, the pressure for the logging of the tradable timber will not diminish.

Secondly, political support for extractive reserves is necessary because logging concessions often reflect the government's interests.

Thirdly, land tenure or forest tenure systems must ensure communities' control over local resources; without a secured property rights system, there will be little incentive to manage the resources sustainably.

Finally, scientific research is urgently required to determine the sustainable harvesting rates of various forest products, as otherwise the chances of exceeding the underlying sustainable rate are great, particularly when viable markets for the resources have been established.

5) Environmental enterprises

Environmental enterprises are those that provide goods and services for the purpose of environmental protection. They include waste treatment plants, sewage facilities, recycling factories, reclamation services, and plants that produce pollution control and waste treatment equipment.

The development of these environmental enterprises both generates economic activities and contributes to conservation. On the one hand, these industries create employment opportunities and generate income. On the other hand, they reduce the waste and pollution levels through treatment and recycling and through making the treatment equipment available to other sectors of the economy.

In many old industrial towns in Europe, a major environmental industry is the reclamation of deserted industrial sites. In the Nord-Pas-de-Calais region of France, for example, there are about 10,000 hectares of derelict industrial land due to factory closures and the decline of mining activities and heavy industries including chemical, steel, metallurgy, energy production, cement and textiles.[43] Soil contamination is serious in these areas because of the type of products formerly produced and the processes employed. The needs for economic recovery and job creation have prompted the Regional Council to initiate a reclamation programme of about 73 million francs per year, which has maintained and created 340 jobs directly involved in the reclamation work in the region.

SUPPORTING MECHANISM

An integrated approach consists of not only economic activities and conservation, but also a whole range of supporting factors encompassing political, social, cultural, and institutional dimensions. For example, the extractive reserves approach requires governments' political will to cut logging concessions; and in addition secured land tenure, which is also the product of political will, must be in place to encourage local people to extract non-timber products in a sustainable way.

Each of these factors in turn has various elements that affect the integrated approach. Along the social dimension, for instance, education, the health of the population, social equity, land tenure systems, and population growth all have implications for the integrated approach. As another example, along the institutional dimension, government administrative capacity, local organisations, and the roles of NGOs all have an impact. To sharpen the focus of analysis, we focus on a few of them without trying to be exhaustive. This, however, should not imply that other elements are less important.

1) Empowerment and participation of local communities

The empowerment of local communities and a participatory approach are the political basis for conservation. Politics is a science of power. To delegate control over local natural resources to communities and allow local people to participate in the management of these resources involves a political process in which the transfer of power takes place. Such a transfer of power is necessary to enable conservation activities to be owned by local people. The second world conservation strategy, 'Caring for the Earth' states that:

> Most of the creative and productive activities of individuals or groups take place in communities. Communities and citizens' groups provide the most readily accessible means for people to take socially valuable action as well as express their concerns. Properly mandated, empowered and informed communities can contribute to decisions that affect them and play an indispensable part in creating a securely-based sustainable society.[44]

The World Bank's World Development Report 1992, 'Development and the Environment', also admitted that: 'Many environmental problems cannot be solved without the active participation of local people.'[45]

In 'People and Parks', empowerment of people is identified as consisting of five major elements:[46]

a) Information gathering: local people participate in collecting information and have access to information;

b) Consultation: people are consulted on the objectives, design, and management of conservation projects;

c) Decision-making: people have inputs into and control over conservation projects;

d) Initiating action: people identify and respond to conservation/development problems;

e) Evaluation: people participate in evaluating conservation activities and provide insights for future project design.

Participation must be carried out on an equitable basis. Various interest groups are involved in conservation activities. They can include local resource users, governmental officials, local and external NGOs, multilateral and bilateral organizations, and outside commercial interests. Insufficient representation of any one party could lead to coordination difficulties. But given the extraordinary importance of the local population's participation, sufficient representation of local people should be guaranteed.

Equitable participation is equally applicable to the communities themselves. One tends to talk about communities in general without distinguishing the levels of authority within them, whereas in fact many are hierarchical with privileged local leaders. The underprivileged groups can be under- and mis-represented. To ensure that an integrated approach benefits the entire local community rather than just a few privileged village heads, attention must be paid to the adequate involvement of the disadvantaged groups.

The participatory approach and the empowerment of local people need to be supported by the system within which they operate. Environmental education, for example, is necessary so that people can make informed decisions. When there is an irreconcilable conflict between conservation and economic development, participation and empowerment alone will not solve the problem; alternative sources of income must be found. There is also a need for strong local institutions to speak in one voice, in order to avoid disorder and loss of direction. Furthermore, the participation and empowerment need to be given legal form so that governments cannot easily deprive the people of their right to participation.

2) Social equity

The question of equal distribution of wealth has an important bearing on the integrated approach. Unequal distribution, which exists in more or less every society (see Table 1 below), affects the environment in two ways: the rich use resources wastefully because they can afford to do so, and the poor continue to exert pressure on the environment as they become marginalised both politically and economically. An integrated approach may generate economic benefits, but not necessarily for the poor segment of the society if they are not well-targeted, and if the unequal distribution pattern remains unchallenged.

Table 1: Unequal distribution of income

Selected developing economies	% share of household income by top 20% of population	Selected developed economies	% share of household income by top 20% of population
India	41.1 (83)★	Spain	40.0 (80-81)
Pakistan	45.6 (84-85)	Singapore	48.9 (82-83)
Ghana	43.7 (88-89)	Hong Kong	47.0 (80)
Sri Lanka	56.1 (85-86)	New Zealand	44.7 (81-82)
Indonesia	41.3 (87)	Italy	41.0 (86)
Philippines	48.0 (85)	Australia	42.2 (85)
Cote d'Ivoire	52.7 (86-87)	France	40.8 (79)
Guatemala	55.0 (79-81)	Canada	40.2 (87)
Peru	51.9 (85-86)	United States	41.9 (85)
Columbia	53.0 (88)	Switzerland	44.6 (81)
Jamaica	49.2 (88)		
Costa Rica	54.5 (86)	★the years for which data are	
Botswana	59.0 (85-86)	available are shown in brackets.	
Malaysia	51.2 (87)		
Venezuela	50.6 (87)		
Brazil	62.6 (83)		

Source: World Development Report 1992, World Bank.

In rural areas, unequal distribution of land is a major form of social inequity. In many countries, around 20 per cent of the rural population have no land, 50 per cent of the farmers together occupy 3-4 per cent of the total agricultural areas, and 10 per cent of the farmers together occupy 50-75 per cent of the total agricultural areas.[47]

In Brazil, for example, land ownership is among the most concentrated in the world and remains an important cause of poverty, which in turn exerts pressure on the environment in the cities and in the Amazon region. In non-Amazon Brazil, 4.5 per cent of the landowners control 81 per cent of the land.[48] In the 1980s, 1.8 per cent of the farm units in Brazil occupied 60 per cent of the total agricultural land in the country.[49] Many farmers have been driven from the land and have migrated to cities or to the Amazon. In less than 30 years, 20-30 million people have moved into cities, and the rural population in the Amazon has increased from 1.6 million to 3.8 million.[50] By the early 1980s, 75 per cent of the rural population were living in poverty, and half of them were destitute. The numbers of urban poor and destitute had increased rapidly. Poverty in the Amazon region was higher than the average for the country.[51]

The equity issue should also be applied to North–South relations. The existing unequal distribution of wealth, as reflected in the terms of trade and resource consumption, for example, affects conservation efforts on a global level. The deteriorating terms of trade, being unfavourable to commodity exporters, have forced developing countries to extract more resources in exchange for a given unit of foreign currency, in order to develop their economy or to service foreign debt. In terms of resource consumption, the Brundtland Report pointed out that industrial countries, with only 26 per cent of the world population, consumed 80 per cent of world energy, steel and other metals, and paper, and about 40 per cent of food.[52] This situation condemns developing countries to a subsistence standard of living, and can hardly lead to sustainable development at a global level. Profound changes in international relations are therefore needed.

3) Land tenure and property rights

Related to the question of social equity, land tenure systems and property rights are important factors in influencing people's behaviour towards conservation. First, contradictions in the definitions of land tenure will lead to land-use conflict, which can render conservation ineffective. Sally Jeanrenaud gives an example of a forest reserve in the Mont Etinde area of southwest Cameroon, which is on state land, but which also includes communal land where usufruct rights and the system 'he who clears the land owns the land' are recognised by the legislation; this has led to conflict between conservation projects and local communities.[53]

Secondly, local control over resources through specified land tenure systems is essential for an integrated approach. Local control creates a sense of responsibility and authority for the management of local resources. People thus have a vested interest in managing resources sustainably.

Thirdly, as discussed previously, unequal distribution of land is a cause of poverty, which compels people to encroach upon reserves and marginal lands, and to cultivate steep slopes in order to survive. Land reform is needed to take pressure off the environment; otherwise, conservation threatens to aggravate the inequalities by denying the poor their access to resources, which will have the opposite results to those intended.

Fourthly, insecurity of land ownership, which gives a short-term perspective, encourages the unsustainable use of resources and makes it difficult to mobilize credit facilities which are needed for economic development.

In giving control over resources to local communities, it is important to establish a strong and cohesive community structure which provides control, incentives, regulations, and sanctions that help enforce sustainable management through access and usufruct rights. In the absence of strong community leadership, local resources tend to break down into open access, whose environmental damage has been extensively recorded.[54]

4) Indigenous culture and knowledge

Indigenous culture and knowledge have significant influences on the effectiveness of conservation. First of all, indigenous knowledge, which has developed over generations, often proves to be the most effective way to protect the environment. Compared to modern farming systems, for instance, indigenous communities contribute to the maintenance of genetic diversity by using a wide range of crops and natural products. The Pokot pastoralists in Kenya use more than 60 plant species for food and more than 100 for medicine.[55] For animal fodder, they can identify species that can serve as dry- or wet-season fodder, increase milk or meat production, or provide appropriate nourishments for different types of livestock. In Nepal, farmers use between 70 and 130 species of fodder trees.[56]

Secondly, cultural values, which may not be readily quantifiable, carry great weight in people's decision as to whether to participate in conservation. These values, whether based on economic benefits or spiritual importance, determine attitudes towards conservation. If these value systems are not well understood and incorporated into the integrated approach, conservation programmes can be ineffective due to lack of support from the people.

5) Local institution-building

The strengthening of local institutions can have a significant impact on the integrated approach. Relevant institutions include government offices, people's organizations, and NGOs. The weakening of government departments in some less-favoured areas of Europe, for example, has aggravated environmental degradation, as governments at local level have become incapable of delivering necessary social services and infrastructure such as sewage disposal and waste treatment. There is a need to strengthen these offices and to provide basic government functions.

In recent years, the role of NGOs has gained important recognition as a force in carrying out conservation activities. Over the last decade, their financial resources (mostly donations from individuals or public organisations) have more than doubled.[57] Sally Jeanrenaud has outlined some of the important reasons for this:[58]

a) NGOs cut across conventional boundaries between disciplines and between sectors, and between stages in the traditional 'research-dissemination-implementation' continuum. This is considered particularly important in countries characterised by rigid bureaucracies and conservative departments.

b) They are considered better at responding to small needs and designing and disseminating appropriate technologies, often disregarded by public sector programmes.

c) They are better at supporting farmer innovations and designing innovative approaches themselves.

d) They are better at encouraging participatory approaches to rural development. One of the reasons for donor interest in NGOs lies in their perceived contribution to the wider process of democratisation.

e) They often have a stronger presence in remote areas with weak infrastructure where the majority of poor live.

f) They are better at articulating small farmers' requirements and getting them on to the public sector research agenda.

g) They have the administrative flexibility to respond to farmers' needs, and to modify interventions in the light of experience.

Despite these advantages, Sally Jeanrenaud also points out the limitations of NGOs, which include excessive reliance on the initiatives of individuals; weak institutional capacity to document and learn from their own experience and from the experience of other organisations; excessive concentration on community organisations and conscientisation to the neglect of income generation; inter-NGO rivalries; and the lack of coordination amongst NGOs' efforts, and between NGO and GO initiatives.

SUSTAINABLE USE OF RESOURCES

An integrated approach includes not only economic activities and various political, social, cultural, and institutional factors, but also the balancing factor of sustainable resource use (SRU). Integration does not mean that conflict between conservation and development does not exist: economic development requires use of resources, whereas conservation requires the protection of resources. Although conservation may generate long-term social benefits, short-term individual costs can be great.

The conflict between the two, however, is not irreconcilable. SRU is the bridge between development and conservation. SRU acknowledges the need to use resources for economic development, but also to condition that use by the sustainability principle. SRU should, in broad terms, cover all resources. The basic principles are:

1) The use of renewable resources should not exceed the regenerative rates of the resources;
2) The use of non-renewable resources should be fully compensated for by the replenishment of renewable substitutes;
3) The waste discharge to the environment should not exceed the assimilative capacity of nature (including human health);
4) Where the ecological implications of a particular resource use is uncertain, precaution must be taken to avoid irreversible loss and damage.

In order to implement these SRU principles it is essential to find out the scientific thresholds for the use of various resources, including the assimilative capacities of both the environment and human beings. Important work has been initiated in the Netherlands, where various environmental problems are identified and classified, ecologically sustainable standards established, and measures proposed to bring many unsustainable existing activities to the level of a sustainable threshold.

SRU has become the central theme of modern conservation. In the newly defined WWF mission, for example, SRU has become one of the most important elements in conservation policy, together with those of the preservation of biological diversity, and the reduction of pollution and wasteful consumption.

In fact, both biological diversity and reduction of pollution and wasteful consumption are closely related to the SRU principle. If people cannot benefit from biological diversity through the use of resources, for example, they will not have incentives to promote biological diversity; but in order to ensure that they continue to benefit from biological diversity, the use of resources must be sustainable, and not lead to the extinction of species. Applying this reasoning to wildlife management, if people cannot benefit from wildlife, they will have little incentive to protect it; but in order to enable them to continue to receive the benefits from wildlife, wildlife must be exploited on a sustainable basis.

In a similar vein, the reduction of pollution is also governed by the SRU principle. Pollution is often related to activities that produce economic benefits. For example, pollution in terms of waste can result from tourism, which at the same time can benefit both tourists and the people who work in the tourist business. But in order to let tourists continue to benefit from tourism, the pollution level must not be allowed to go beyond the assimilative capacity of nature. The mismanagement of the Adriatic Sea, for example, has resulted in a loss of 1.5 billion ECU from tourism income and fishing in 1990, indicating the cost of unsustainable pollution.[59]

The SRU principle can equally be applied to the reduction of wasteful consumption. Many important resources such as water are already being used unsustainably on a global level: the wasteful use of water has undoubtedly contributed to water shortages. Subjecting the use of water and resources in general to the SRU principle will therefore serve to curtail wasteful consumption.

D. SUMMARY

Conservation must incorporate economic activities in order to be effective. Such recognition has come about as the traditional preservationist approach which rejects economic development has proved itself to be a failure. Economic activities are not only the root causes of many environmental problems—and therefore must be directly addressed by conservation—but also are indispensable for achieving conservation objectives. Clearly the need to integrate economic activities with conservation is driven by both the positive and negative links between the two.

Such an integrated approach consists of three parallel levels. The first includes economic incentives and activities, of which rural community-based traditional activities are most readily incorporated into conservation. The second encompasses a whole spectrum of political, social, cultural, and institutional dimensions, which together form an indispensable supporting mechanism for the integrated approach. The third is the bridge between economic development and conservation, i.e. SRU, which reconciles the conflict between the need to use resources and the need to condition the use by the principle of sustainability.

SRU has become the major theme of modern conservation. Together with biological diversity and reduction of pollution and wasteful consumption, it constitutes a major element in WWF's Mission Statement for the 1990s. The SRU principle can and should be applied to both biological conservation and to the reduction of pollution and wasteful consumption. It is SRU that provides the fundamental philosophical basis for integrating economic activities with conservation.

The Making of Agricultural Biodiversity in Europe

MICHEL PIMBERT

THROUGHOUT THE WORLD human communities have found ways of securing their food and livelihoods from the wealth of nature's diversity. And, throughout history, people have played a central role in creating and conserving the diversity of nature.

Although they look untouched, many of the last refuges of wilderness that our societies wish to protect are inhabited and have been modified or managed throughout our human past. Recent scientific findings indicate that virtually every part of the globe, from boreal forests to the humid tropics, has been inhabited for millenia. The Kayapo of Central Brazil presently occupy a two million hectare forest reserve, but they used to practise their nomadic agriculture in an area approximately the size of France. The current composition and diversity of many tropical rainforests may well be the legacy of past civilisations, the heritage of managed forests and cultivated fields abandoned hundreds of years ago. In many cases, rural communities and their traditional land use practices have been partly responsible for the creation of nature's diversity and for its maintenance and protection.[1]

The creative genius of rural people is perhaps more immediately apparent when looking at the diversity of their traditional crops, animal breeds and associated farming systems (agricultural biodiversity). Since agriculture began, farming communities have helped create a broad range of genetic diversity that has been passed down from generation to generation. Women, men and children have selected, conserved and used a vast array of plant varieties and animal breeds adapted to different environments and needs. Plants and animals, both wild and cultivated, have been combined in complex and diverse agroecosystems. Cultural and biological diversity have evolved together, the one informing the other. For example, the gourd shows tremendous varietal diversity: it has been selected for a multitude of uses, including containers, pipes, floats, musical instruments, penis sheaths, ornaments and food.

Rare short-horned cattle from the central Rhodopes, Bulgaria.

Today much of the biological diversity of forests, wetlands and agricultural lands is threatened with extinction. Many strategies aimed at saving what remains of nature's diversity look towards governments, industry and experts for vision and appropriate remedial action. However solutions proposed by, and implemented from, remote central places often fail to address the root causes of the loss in biodiversity. Moreover, given the key role human communities have played in extending and conserving nature's diversity, it is ironic that ordinary people are seen as passive recipients of top-down conservation plans rather than active partners in their design and implementation.

After briefly highlighting the making and decline of agricultural biodiversity in Europe, this chapter looks towards a future that restores people's right to stewardship and broader social control over a collective patrimony: the diversity of plants and animals that feed and support us. Overcoming obstacles to informal innovation and people's participation in the management of agricultural biodiversity in Europe will be emphasised.

The making of agricultural biodiversity in Europe

Most of the world's biological diversity is found in vast managed forests, farmed lands and human settlements. However, nature's diversity is not evenly distributed around the globe. As a result of the Ice Age, the northern hemisphere was left biologically impoverished relative to the more southern latitudes. Tropical rainforests alone contain most of the world's plant and animal species thought to be alive today. Most of the crop and animal genetic diversity also originated in what is now known as the Third World, having been developed by generations of African, Latin American and Asian farmers. As centres of genetic diversity, developing countries today are Europe's major source of breeding materials to continuously adapt domesticated crops and animals to new pests and diseases, climate change or production systems.

But despite its relative genetic poverty, Europe shares part of an important centre of genetic diversity: the Mediterranean area. Southern Europe has been the home of crops such as wheat, rape, faba bean, olive, grape and barley. The caper bush, the cork oak, carob, and the stone pine (yielding pine nuts) also originated in the Mediterranean region along with a whole range of herbs and medicinal plants: sage, rosemary, thyme, laurel, parsley and lavender. Central Europe harbours a centre of diversity for other crops such as beet, lettuce, turnips, parsnips, horseradish and some forage grasses.

Historically, Europe has also played a leading role in amassing a large amount of exotic germplasm, particularly in the last 300 years. The wealth of Europe in the colonial era was to a large extent based on the exploitation of plant genetic resources developed by Third World people. The return of Columbus from the New World opened the way for the transfer of biological wealth from the Americas to Europe. Maize, potatoes, squash, tomatoes, peanuts, common beans, sunflowers and other crops crossed the Atlantic. Human diets and agricultural productivity vastly improved in Europe as skilful farmers further diversified and adapted these crops to their new environments, needs and fancies. Seeds were continuously selected and saved, and from generation to generation they were passed on as part of the family heritage. The art of informal breeding practised by rural people was such that crops and animals introduced from distant lands developed into a complex mosaic of uniquely adapted local varieties. Each village had its particular tomato or wheat. Each region had its particular breed of pig, chicken or cattle.

And, like rural people in Africa, Latin America and Asia, European communities also nurtured the knowledge needed to collect wild foods from common lands and forests. Until fairly recent times, more than two thousand wild plants were eaten by the rural populations of Europe. About sixty years ago, Greek farmers still had a similar diet to that of their ancestors at the time of Pericles. They cultivated cereals, olive trees and other fruit trees, but they did not have vegetable gardens. They ate the wild vegetable plants that surrounded them.[2]

All over Europe, small-scale farmers and gardeners nurtured difference and diversity in the countryside and in human settlements where large amounts of food were produced *intra muros*. Wild edible plants were either tolerated, actively protected, or even sown and harvested in forests, farms, gardens and orchards. Semi-domesticated and wild plants and animals were woven into complex, diverse farming systems. The long-lived manorial estates of medieval England relied on plentiful wild resources (including nuts, berries, fruits, herbs, grasses, deer, wild boar, and fish) to support and complement the production of arable, garden and orchard crops and livestock. Even today, balanced wood pasture systems can still be found in some Mediterranean countries. For example, the *dehesas* occupy over a million hectares in Spain. The *dehesas* are usually divided into four parts and several families manage them on a four-year rotation. This rotation helps protect fragile soils and create an immensely rich habitat for birds like imperial and short-toed eagles, red kites and black storks. Deer, lynx, wolf and rare breeds of goats are also found in the *dehesas*. Cork harvesting, timber, honey gathering, olive growing and hunting on a sustainable basis all provide additional income to the farmers.

For sure, the yields of traditional farming systems were and are generally not as high as the chemical-based monocultures and factory animal farming of today, but these systems provided security. In many cases farmers encouraged sustainability, stability and equity at the expense of productivity. Integrated farming and diversity promoted stability; diversity of the whole system together with varying livelihood strategies enhanced sustainability; and equity—when and where it was valued—was maintained by a high level of cooperation.

By experimenting, innovative and adaptive farmers also discovered how to use resources internal to these diverse agricultural systems to maintain soil fertility, feed farm animals and to control weeds, insect pests and diseases. For example, to control some weeds and slugs some farmers would march through their fields flocks of ducks and breeds of weeder geese. Rustic breeds of pigs and other farm animals were fed almost exclusively from the acorns, walnuts, chestnuts and beech seeds produced by nearby forests and woodlands. Several of the broccoli varieties developed in seventeenth century Italy were often grown in mixtures to reduce damage by insect pests like aphids. A common practice in traditional cereal production was that of mixing different species on the same plot. During the Renaissance in France, rye and winter wheat were often grown together. Farmers had noticed that wheat was protected from frost damage by the taller-growing rye. Modern science has since shown that diseases are also less prevalent in cereal mixtures than when rye and wheat are grown separately.

In these and many other ways, biological diversity was simultaneously used as a productive force and a source of security of livelihood by innovative rural people. But achieving food security and designing biological solutions to production problems like pests and declining soil fertility were not the only factors that contributed to the creation of agricultural biodiversity in Europe.

People's preferences for different foods were also a driving force behind the development of new crop varieties and animal breeds which, in turn, helped diversify farming systems. Desires for better taste, cooking, storage and cider-making qualities all contributed to the blossoming of literally thousands of apple varieties in different parts of Europe. After its introduction in the seventeenth century from Latin America, the potato was selected for boiling, frying, baking and for many more cooking and culinary uses. But diversity flourished in gardens, farms and orchards not only for utilitarian reasons. Cultural, religious and spiritual orientations were reflected in the colours, shapes, perfumes, textures and flavours of locally adapted crop varieties and animal breeds. Bloodthirsty societies that indulged in watching cock fights actively selected poultry breeds with more flamboyant and aggressive males. In the small village of Saint-Vérain, in the French Alps, it was customary for Catholics to grow yellow potatoes while the red ones were the domain of the Protestants.[3]

This rich tapestry of nature's possibilities and human culture embodies the knowledge and work of millions of anonymous people who, throughout Europe, have kept alive our heritage of crops, trees, animals and diverse agroecosystems.

The collapse of agricultural biodiversity in Europe

During the last few decades, this living diversity has been violently torn apart. As industrial methods of production and the market economy have penetrated almost every corner of Europe, diversity has been replaced with uniformity in agriculture, forestry, fisheries and animal husbandry.

We no longer eat as many locally produced foods as our grandparents did. Until this century, the Provençal diet in south-east France was rich in 250 different plant species, including vegetables, fruits and condiments. Today, about 60 are cultivated in the region, of which only 30 make up most of the local consumption.[4] In other parts of Europe some of the most nutritious wild edible vegetable plants like Good King Henry, nettle, coltsfoot, shepherds purse and great burdock are treated as undesirable weeds that must be exterminated. Powerful chemical herbicides are used to keep them out of our farms, gardens, forest plantations and towns.

Many of the traditionally grown crop varieties no longer exist. Instead of a huge patchwork of different varieties of a crop, most parts of Europe are now covered by a relatively small number of closely related high-yielding varieties that thrive on chemical fertilisers, pesticides and irrigation. There is a constant threat of new diseases or of chemical resistant insects evolving and this could wreak havoc in such large areas of single crops. Since the 1920s Greece has lost 95% of its traditional, locally adapted wheat varieties. A single potato variety (the Bintje) covers nearly 80% of the land sown to this crop in the Netherlands. The top four varieties cover 71% of Britain's winter wheat acreage. The many varieties of almonds on which Spain based its production have been almost totally replaced by a few high-yielding varieties from California. In several crops there is also clear evidence that the remaining high-yielding varieties have an extremely narrow genetic base. Plant breeders have been recycling uniformity by repeatedly using materials composed of breeders' lines and advanced cultivars from breeders' collections. Valuable genebank collections of wild species and traditional varieties have tended to be under-utilised. For example, researchers have shown that all of France's current wheat varieties are descendants of Noah, a variety developed in the Ukraine last century. By crossing a few well-known genitors, plant-breeding programmes have considerably reduced the genetic variability of French wheat cultivars grown today.[5]

As the number of crop species and varieties declines, local nitrogen-fixing bacteria, mycorhizae, predators, pollinators, seed dispersers and other species that make up the *bulk* of the biodiversity of traditional agricultural systems die out or become rarer. Deprived of the flora with which they co-evolved over centuries, these species become extinct or their genetic base becomes dramatically narrowed; they can no longer provide the environmental services that contribute to the sustainability and stability of traditional agroecosystems such as soil fertilisation, pest control, buffering against climate fluctuations, and crop pollination.

Hundreds of Europe's hardiest breeds of chicken, geese, ducks, pigs, cows and other farm animals have also disappeared forever or are on the verge of extinction. Half of all breeds that existed in Europe at the turn of the century have vanished and a third of the remaining 770 breeds are in danger of disappearing within the next 20 years. Whilst the livestock industry is heading for an emergency level of homogenisation in Europe, 115 breeds of cattle are severely threatened, and only 30 breeds seem to be holding their own. In the Rhodope mountains of Bulgaria, the Rhodope short-horned cattle breed has been reduced to 250-500 head. Locally adapted sheep like the Karakachan and the middle Rhodope are also being marginalised by less hardy breeds that require special extra care to achieve their potential for high yields in milk, meat and wool.

The concentration and intensification of our food system needs controllable uniformity, not the anarchy of diversity. A look at western Europe shows that, in the EC today, 60% of cereals come from 6% of the grain farms and 75% of milk is produced by a quarter of the diary farms; 90% of the EC's pork production comes from 10% of the intensive pig farms; and a full 98% of the fowl production comes from 10% of the poultry units.

The requirements of food industries for a uniform product—whether for processing or distribution—have further exacerbated the loss of biodiversity in the food sector. After the reunification of Germany in 1990, East German farmers were prohibited from growing varietal mixtures of barley, so that they would produce a more uniform product for the West German brewing industry.

One of the ironies of this model of agricultural development is that it destroys the resources it depends on to sustain itself. Plant and animal breeders no longer have the genetic resources needed to introduce resistance to diseases and pests, to improve food quality and taste. Possibilities of adapting crops and animals to new environments are reduced. Wild plants are treated as undesirable weeds instead of potential sources of food or animal fodder. As ponds, hedges, diverse woodlands and other wildlife corridors are cleared to make way for heavy machines, soil and water conservation functions are obliterated from the landscape. Options for the natural control of pests also disappear with the removal of the wild foods and homes of birds, insect predators and parasites. Local people's knowledge is marginalised by a more powerful tradition of knowledge that claims universal truth and validity. And, as the landscape is increasingly designed for dependence on outside agencies and industrial inputs for its continued functioning, rural communities lose their vitality and the source of their economic and political power.

Recent restructurings in the industrial sector are encouraging the push for uniformity still further. Since 1970, more than one thousand small seed companies around the world have been bought out by giant multinational corporations. In the Netherlands by the late 1980s three companies held 70% of the agricultural seed market and four companies controlled 90% of the market for horticultural seeds. In Britain, three firms controlled nearly 80% of the garden seed market. Today, the European seed market, which represents sales of US$5–$6 billion a year, is largely controlled by no more than ten to twenty firms. Corporate control over seeds, the first link in the food chain, has led to a reduction in the number of different varieties offered on the market. Similar developments are taking place in the livestock industry. The multinational companies involved also have parallel interests in agrochemicals, pharmaceuticals and food processing. They are all attracted to the enormous commercial opportunities presented by agricultural biotechnologies. For them, the seed is the vector of those biotechnological changes that could further integrate their activities. The present quest to genetically engineer herbicide resistant crops is an example of this trend along with attempts to develop 'artificial seeds': cloned plant embryos inside a jelly-like capsule that contains fungicide, fertiliser or other chemicals.

Along with their attempt to gain physical control over seeds and animal germplasm, the giant companies are trying to obtain full legal control over the exploitation of genetically modified organisms. Industrial patent regimes are now being extended to genetic resources. What was once the common heritage of European people and of humankind is becoming the private property of a few.

European grassroots conservation today

The logic which demands profits and corporate control over the food system is systematically excluding living diversity from agricultural production. It also devalues the knowledge, priorities and skills of farmers. In the EC, we are left with ten million farmers today, with nearly half a million closing down or going out of business each year. As Western technologies and aid programmes transform the face and orientation of agriculture in Eastern Europe many more farmers will go under, possibly increasing unemployment and violent conflicts.

Given these developments, one may well ask what possibilities are left for people to influence the future of agricultural biodiversity in Europe? What are individuals and grassroots organisations doing to conserve and sustainably use our dwindling heritage of biological resources? How do people's initiatives compare with government-run conservation programmes? How relevant are their ideas and practices for a more sustainable agricultural development in Europe? What changes are needed to allow more people to participate fully in the recovery and celebration of diversity in Europe?

Grassroots initiatives to save Europe's declining genetic diversity include the efforts of food growers' cooperatives, non-governmental organisations, amateur gardeners, networks of fruit tree growers, independent research groups, enthusiastic individuals and farmers' organisations. Their reasons for saving and cherishing diversity are many; they include aesthetic and intellectual appreciation of variety and difference, cultural identification with a genetic heritage and pragmatic concerns about survival. The knowledge that tomorrow's options will be reduced if genetic resources are not saved is also one of the reasons why local conservation efforts are gaining momentum in Europe. Such people seek to conserve and manage resources in a way that is informed by 'an ecology of the heart' rather than being concerned only about 'rational uses', 'cost efficiencies' and 'direct economic benefits'. Unlike the uncritical, 'objective' rationales offered time and again by the formal sector, grassroots organisations consciously advance their more subjective reasons for conserving nature's diversity, both cultivated and wild. They acknowledge that their ethical, emotional and spiritual ties to organisms, habitats, places, processes and traditions guide them as much as their scientific reasoning.[6] Many individuals involved in these grassroots initiatives have a different vision of agricultural development to the one that is taught in universities and encouraged by the companies that sell agricultural machinery and chemicals. For these ordinary folks, saving and creatively using diversity through production is a source of security and independence from harmful industry; a possible way towards more peaceful, caring relationships with the natural world and amongst themselves.

Since the 1950s and 60s the various organic or biodynamic farming movements have been actively involved in the conservation of farm-level genetic diversity. Old crop varieties and rare animal breeds were and are maintained because of their resistances, rusticity, nutritional qualities, fertility, or compatibility with farming systems that do not rely on massive chemical inputs for production.

Other groups have sprung up more recently, shocked and alarmed by the severity and extent of genetic erosion throughout Europe. Deep concern has moved ordinary citizens to take direct action as they have learnt how government policies encourage the loss of genetic diversity. On June 30th 1980, the EC established the Common Catalogue of varieties that could be sold on the market.[7] The lists were largely drawn up through consultations with private seed companies. This gave the private sector a wonderful opportunity to eliminate competition and 'rationalise' the market. Virtually overnight it became strictly forbidden to commercialise seed and plantules of unlisted varieties, transport them for the purpose of selling them, advertise them for sale through the press or sell them on market stalls and fairs! Anyone peddling unlisted seeds could be fined. This is how more than a thousand traditional varieties of vegetables were purposefully written out of existence in the EC.

From the 1970s onwards, motivated individuals developed their own organisations and informal practices to involve people more fully in the management of genetic resources. Without government support, grassroots organisations began systematic efforts to inventory, collect, test, select and multiply threatened crop varieties and animal breeds. Rare genetic materials were regenerated and exchanged with others throughout Europe. The interests of these groups go beyond food crops and animal breeds: they include wild plant and animal genetic resources as well as medicines, ornamentals, wild flowers and multi-purpose trees.

Passion and dynamism characterise grassroots conservation groups such as those listed in the Appendix [see pages 257-259]. For example, Arche Noah (Noah's Ark) is a network of seed savers in the German–speaking countries of Austria, Germany and Switzerland. Today, over 350 network members actively collect, maintain and exchange seeds. Further north, in Belgium, a broad-based worker solidarity movement promotes small-scale urban gardening and conservation techniques involving over 1,200 plant varieties. The overall aim of Fraternité Ouvrière is to improve family nutrition among low-income households. Not far away, in the Netherlands, the Court of Eden holds perhaps the biggest private seed collection of Europe. It has about 30,000 samples of different crop varieties—more than the better-funded official Dutch genebank holds in Wageningen, with its 25,000 samples of spinach, lettuce, cabbages and cereals. Every year, staff and friends of the Court of Eden grow out twelve to eighteen thousand seed samples in the outskirts of Utrecht. Individual seed samples are regenerated by growing the plants in tiny plots among the fields of small-scale farmers in the area. Seeds are then harvested and carefully packaged in sealed envelopes, and stored for a few years before being planted out again. Samples are clearly labelled and all the information concerning each sample is kept up to date on a computer.

Many seed-saving groups rely on computers to help them monitor which varieties are about to be dropped from national lists and which ones are at risk because they are only sold by one or two small seed companies. This information is crucial for grassroots conservation programmes and is circulated as widely as possible. In the UK, the Henry Doubleday Research Association has recently published a catalogue of seed catalogues, 'The vegetable finder'. This comprehensive publication lists all vegetable varieties legally available today in the UK. Out of the 1,973 non-hybrid vegetables listed, nearly 85% are only being maintained by a single supplier. The endangered varieties are marked with a special symbol and British gardeners are urged to save them by growing them in their backyards.

Grassroots organisations have also developed innovative schemes to maintain the genetic diversity of farm animals. The Swiss association Pro Specie Rara (PSR) was set up in the early 1980s, largely in response to government failure to inventory and conserve rare animal breeds. Cattle, sheep, goats, pigs, chicken and geese are the main focus of PSR's conservation activities on animal genetic resources. PSR works as a sort of trust fund for endangered animals that is financed by its own shareholders, by donations and grants. PSR uses its working capital to buy the last individuals of a breed and lets them out free of charge to interested farmers. The farmer can use the animals on his farm but PSR keeps the right to buy the offspring and enlarge the herd. PSR also directs mating strategies and, when the breed is out of danger, the association gives up its rights over the animals.

Moved by the fear that the economic restructuring of former communist regimes would worsen genetic erosion, PSR has extended its activities into eastern Europe. Along with other grassroots groups in Central Europe, PSR is setting up an umbrella organisation to link up and strengthen animal and plant conservation groups throughout the region.

The federation of local initiatives into regional conservation programmes is an important feature of people's collective and creative response to the loss of agricultural biodiversity. The regional genetic heritage program of the Provence-Alpes-Cotes d'Azur, in south-east France, involves a wide range of actors spread across six administrative *departments*—about 31,500 square kilometres of extremely diverse ecosystems.

As one travels from the sandy shores of St. Tropez to the Upper Alps, the plains, prairies, farms, orchards, small river valleys and lower mountain chains offer a rich panorama of genetic and cultural diversity. However, profound changes in the agriculture and the use of the region's resources are threatening the biological heritage of Provence and the strong cultural identities associated with it. The development of people's initiatives to keep their links with the past alive and diversify their future is truly inspiring. Having realised that actions to combat the threat of uniformity cannot be carried out in a fragmented way, all the concerned parties came together: organic farming associations, national parks, schools and non-governmental organisations. Over 30 different groups came together under an umbrella organisation set up in 1983: PAGE PACA. Their aim is not just to conserve plant and animal genetic diversity; they also want to encourage sustainable economic development in the region by building on local knowledge and resources.

PAGE PACA has for this purpose inventoried the traditional fruit in the region. Succulent and exceptionally pest-resistant varieties of figs, peaches, almonds, plums and cherries have been saved from near extinction as a result of the spread of high-yielding varieties imported from California and elsewhere. Ways and means of reintegrating the traditional fruit varieties into the economy are now being studied. The tasty local fruits often cannot be transported over long distances—they lack the hard skins that have been deliberately selected for in the high-yielding varieties. To overcome this problem enterprising people want to develop processed foods based on the local fruits: jams, juices, purées and syrups. This could mean working with local industrialists willing to try out novel ways of processing the fruits and able to market the products. Alternatively, it could mean encouraging smaller-scale processing units (e.g. autoclaves) run by producer cooperatives or by members of a town neighbourhood. Apart from encouraging local consumption, much of the added value associated with processing would benefit a wider circle of people and could help create new employment.

Creating viable economic channels is now an important focus of PAGE PACA's multi-faceted activities. In raising public awareness about the value and uses of local genetic resources, PAGE PACA has run successful campaigns with slogans like 'Resources of the future, Jobs for tomorrow'. Members of PAGE PACA pass on both ideas and germplasm to others through tours, farmer groups, open days and popular information brochures. To design and run some of its projects, this federation of grassroots initiatives draws on the skills and expertise of official research institutes, sympathetic agricultural extension services, as well as ethnobotanists and economists.[8]

Having realised the importance for the future of the region of PAGE PACA's work, local government has recently decided to support and encourage these initiatives. But we should remember that these and other creative steps to conserve and utilise diversity are the product of an ongoing, participatory, bottom-up process—not the result of a government-led programme.

There are, in fact, fundamental differences between government approaches to conservation and community-based initiatives. Whereas people conserve *through* utilisation, official programmes conserve *for* utilisation.

Government conservation relies on *ex situ* (offsite) and *in situ* (on site) measures for that purpose. *Ex situ* approaches rely essentially on genebanks in which seeds, animal sperm and eggs are maintained in cold storage inside cans or glass tubes. *Ex situ* also refers to the maintenance of living plants and animals away from the areas where they developed their distinctive properties, e.g. in botanical gardens. *In situ* generally refers to protected areas and nature parks set aside to preserve wilderness from the human hand. Reproducing organisms are maintained in the areas where they developed their distinctive features. As an example, wild pistachios, almonds and apricots are conserved in a protected area east of the Caspian sea, in the Kopet mountains.

Both *ex-* and *in-situ* systems are favoured by governments and mainstream conservation experts. In both approaches people tend to be excluded from conservation sites. Moreover, key decisions on what to inventory, collect, save and use—and for whom—are firmly under the control of experts.

Fortunately, grassroots conservation is beginning to turn this logic of exclusion on its head as it challenges the formal sector's assumptions about appropriate means and ends. Growing endangered species to better conserve them, and diversity as a principle of production, are common unifying themes running through grassroots conservation work.[9] In the dry mountains of the French Oriental Pyrennees, a group of farmers have diversified their production by including a rediscovered speciality plant: the pepper of Espelette, a tasty plant that had been uncultivated. The farmers and local administrators have made moves to obtain an official quality label for their produce. Elsewhere in France, inhabitants of the village of Roquebrun have designed mediterranean gardens to grow nearly extinct local fruit tree varieties of quince, apricot, pistachio, fig, and almond, and also herbs and aromatic plants. The gardens of perennial plants exert many beneficial influences on the environment: the enhancement of wild life, the control of soil erosion, and the improvement of the microclimate. In the Central and Western Rhodope mountains of Bulgaria, efforts are being made to save and reintroduce the Karakachan sheep into the rural economy, gastronomy and culture of the region. Throughout Europe, permaculture approaches to food production in rural or urban settings functionally integrate a great deal of both wild and cultivated diversity in their designs. Permaculture is a philosophy and practice of whole-system design that seeks to supply human needs (food, shelter, and energy) while retaining the self-sustaining features of unmodified ecological systems.[10] Neglected, despised or quasi-extinct plants and animals are saved by becoming the building blocks of new, gentler agricultures and patterns of human settlement that help regenerate local ecologies and economies. This promotes greater consumer choice and security of livelihood.

Other empowering initiatives are opening up more social spaces in which diversity can flourish. The co-operative housing movement and eco-villages described elsewhere in this book nurture cultivated ecologies that allow diversity to thrive in orchards, gardens, greenhouses and roadsides. Other examples can be found in the growing Community Supported Agriculture (CSA) movement in Europe. In these initiatives, a specific group of people from one local area agrees to share the risks and responsibilities of food production with the farmer. Farmers know that their income is guaranteed and that they are growing food for local people as opposed to the open market. They aim to provide what people want, instead of concentrating on the crops and animals that give the highest returns. This diversity of crops and animals encourages the development of integrated farming systems that are sustainable, productive and less vulnerable to pests and other agents of crop failure. The active involvement of shareholders in farm work is encouraged. This helps 'reconnect' people whose primary activities lie outside farming and brings urban and rural communities together. The comments below, by one of the pioneers of community-supported farming in the USA, apply equally well to the European scene:

'Some things are typical for all community-supported farms. In all of them there is a strong dedication to quality; most of them are organic or biodynamic farms, most of them show great diversification, most are integrated farm organisms having their own livestock and thus their own source of manure, or they are aiming in this direction. At all of them, far more people are working regularly per 100 acres than in conventionally-run farms; and generally there are just many more people around participating in all of the dimensions of agricultural life: working, relaxing, storing, shopping, celebrating. This human element is of enormous importance. It shows that these farms have something to offer beyond good food. They embody educational and cultural elements that draw the interest of many people. Besides clean, healthy, life-giving food, and a strong contribution to an improved environment, the educational and cultural elements constitute the third great gift that farms of tomorrow have to offer.'[11]

In effect, by saving biological diversity through the production and reproduction of daily life, ordinary people are giving their own meanings to development.

People and the future of diversity in Europe

The initiatives and struggles described above do not share a uniform vision of the future. However, there are recurring themes in many of these approaches to conservation and sustainable development at the local level. Mutual support, responsibility, trust and group action are key to sustaining and caring for biodiversity and the environment. Community empowerment means reclaiming the political process and re-rooting decisions on the management of agricultural biodiversity within the local community and enabling all people, including women and children, to secure their rights and needs.

These social and participatory processes cannot be legislated into existence by policy makers and development planners or other paternalistic outsiders. After all, many of these grassroots initiatives belong to a long tradition of active minorities who, throughout history, have resisted the imposed enclosure of the forests, fields, rangelands, fishing grounds, plants and animals that they rely upon to maintain their ways of life and ensure their wellbeing.

But in seeking solutions to the alarming loss of agricultural biodiversity in Europe, policy makers, development planners and scientists need to recognise the enormous contribution and potential of the conservation work carried out by this so-called informal sector. Grassroots conservation networks and isolated initiatives fill gaps in the formal system of gene banks, universities and research institutions by focussing on regionally important crops and animals, marginal areas and ecologically sound agricultural practices. Because of their decentralised nature, these organisations are often better suited than national institutions to saving and reintroducing local genetic diversity and making it available for local needs. In many cases more genetic diversity is conserved in decentralised networks than in high-tech gene banks—and at a lower financial cost. The best documented example comes from the United States: of the 1,799 varieties of beans held by a non-profit network of farmers and gardeners (the Seed Savers Exchange), only 147 are found in the US government-supported collections. It is truly amazing that, even today, many of these grassroots conservation efforts are still unheard of, unseen, and their relevance unimagined by experts tied to textbook recipes for conservation and development problems!

Despite their lack of funds and exclusion from much of the formal scientific research system, it is undeniable that grassroots conservation initiatives are critically important participants in innovation today. Indeed, there are many similarities between this contemporary European stream of agricultural innovation and the informal R&D carried out by rural people in pre-industrial Europe and in the Third World countries of today.

During the agricultural revolution in Britain in the seventeenth to nineteenth centuries, innovative technologies and techniques developed by farmers were extended to others through tours, farmer groups, fairs and open days, and popular publications.[12] The technologies were then adapted to local conditions by rigorous experimentation to maximise the use of on-farm resources. Many experiments were first conducted in kitchen gardens where they could be protected and closely monitored. If successful they were then spread to the rest of the farm and the neighbourhood. The success of small gardens as sites for experimentation was clear during the seventeenth century, as commercial gardening grew rapidly to supply new vegetable and fruit crops to cities. London became surrounded by market gardens increasing in number from 4,000 to 45,000 between 1660 and 1720.[13] Over a period of two centuries crop and livestock production increased three- to four-fold. And yet, in those days, farmers' innovation, extension practices and technology adaptation were not supported by a government ministry of agriculture, by research stations, nor by extension institutions.

Times have changed. But, although they are far less numerous than the farming populations of pre-industrial Europe, people involved in the initatives described above rely on similar research modes to break new ground in the conservation and creative use of agricultural biodiversity today.

This is not to say that all is well within grassroots conservation circles. The work of the informal sector is fragmented. Local associations often lack funds, and also information and methodologies for small-scale conservation activities, e.g. guidelines on pollination distances and on optimal backup storage techniques. The (re-)introduction of local varieties, neglected crops and animal breeds into the economy needs better communication between those involved in conservation programmes, the agricultural sector and local industry. Complementarities and synergies are required among these groups to help diversify local production systems and the market.

There is clearly much scope for potentially fertile interactions between grassroots conservation efforts and the formal sector dealing with the conservation and management of agricultural biodiversity. This is already happening here and there, but such cooperation could be more systematically encouraged if:

- outside professionals (such as scientists, development planners, and policy makers) did not dismiss non- scientific or 'people's' knowledge; nor should they adopt the naive, uncritical, view that grassroots organisations and farmers always know best. There is now considerable evidence that experimentation is the norm rather than the exception among rural communities, particularly—but not exclusively—in developing countries.[14-17] However, it is still heresy to many of today's agricultural scientists and economists to suggest that farmers and grassroots organisations have much to say in the process of technology generation, diffusion and adaptation. Nevertheless many of the conceptual initiatives, conservation practices and more equitable social relations of production advanced by organisations such as those described above have immense relevance for solving the deep social and ecological crises induced by industrial agriculture.

- grassroots conservationists met scientists on terms of equality. Outside professionals should be persuaded that ordinary people have something to teach them and can become involved in key decisions relating to R&D priorities for conservation and use (from plant and animal breeding to the overall design of diverse farming systems in urban or rural contexts).

- innovative participatory methodologies were used by outside professionals to encourage reversals in roles, locations and learning. A reversal of learning would have outside professionals learning with and from farmers, gardeners and their grassroots organisations. Analysis, choice, experimentation, evaluation and development planning would be conducted by and with farmers and other non-specialists, with outside professionals in a facilitating and support role.

Making this happen in real life implies radical changes in at least three mutually reinforcing areas:

- the public research agenda and the way scientific research is organised, planned, carried out and evaluated;

- the legal frameworks which dictate what seeds and animal germplasm can be sold on the market and those that determine who owns them;

- the agricultural policies and prices that currently promote standardisation, specialisation and intensification in farming.

This trinity largely determines the fate of agricultural development and biodiversity in Europe. It is therefore important to look at each area in turn and identify levers for significant change.

Democratising research

Back in the 1980s, member states of the United Nations Food and Agricultural Organisation (FAO) adopted the concept of farmers' rights. 'Farmers' rights' recognise that, as a group, both past and present farmers are remarkably ingenious plant breeders and managers of biological diversity.

The concept of farmers' rights offers a unique opportunity to officially re-establish farming communities and the grassroots groups previously described as the key players in the creation, conservation and sustainable use of genetic diversity (and, more generally, of agricultural biodiversity). The concept legitimates bottom-up approaches that take grassroots conservation groups and farmers' needs, their priorities, their knowledge, and their agricultural practices, as the platform for an alternative development that could lead to a more dignified existence.

The notion of farmers' rights calls for a radical restructuring of national agricultural research systems to include farmers and grassroots organisations as equal partners in innovation and to give them more control over research priorities. Top-down approaches to the transfer of technology need to be replaced by more participatory research modes that broaden the circle of social control over decisions on how biological resources are managed and used—and for whom.

Worldwide, there already exist examples of participatory research in which farmers and rural people play a greater role in shaping the directions taken by science and technology. The gene bank of Ethiopia involves farming communities in the conservation of genetic diversity. On-farm conservation of landraces (traditionally grown local crop varieties) focusses on major food crops like sorghum, chickpea, teff, field peas and corn. The complementary knowledge and skills of scientists and farmers ensure that germplasm is conserved in a more dynamic and safer way than is the case in most other gene banks of the world.[18]

In Zambia, Columbia and India, participatory plant breeding and germplasm evaluation efforts that involve farmers, non-governmental organisations and scientists have consistently better served the needs of farmers and rural people in complex, diverse and risk-prone environments than conventional top-down approaches.[19-22]

A rich repertoire of participatory methods is increasingly allowing outside professionals to learn with, by and from rural people and to create a working relationship in which people's priorities and values become more fully expressed in projects aimed at conserving and using biological diversity—be it in agriculture, forests or wetlands.[23, 24] Appropriate behaviour and attitudes allow outsiders to establish rapport, convene, catalyse, facilitate, adapt, watch, listen, learn and respect. Meanwhile, rural peoples' sense of empowerment grows as *they* map, model, diagram, interview, quantify, rank and score, inform and explain, show, discuss and analyse, plan, present and share their knowledge and experience with others.

These examples from the South prefigure, here and now, some of the working relationships needed between public sector research, non-governmental organisations and farmers dealing with the management of biological resources in Europe. However, whilst these approaches support diversity, decentralisation and democracy they do not, in and by themselves, guarantee public participation in science and the design of technologies. Democratising research obviously implies broader reforms within the scientific community itself and the social forces that largely determine today's public research agenda.[25]

In European countries, most public plant and animal breeding work is determined by the needs of the various industries on the input and output sides of food production proper. The social context of public plant and animal breeder's work is such that the directions and uses of publicly funded research are increasingly specified by those who hold power in the food system. Official conservation programmes (germplasm collections, gene banks, use of genetic materials, etc.) often reflect and reinforce these commercial imperatives. These trends have become more apparent recently as private companies have massively invested in biotechnology research and development. Life processes are being engineered for commercial purposes through the application of modern science and technologies. The biotechnology revolution planned by and for corporate capital is transforming and further subordinating much of public research to its own ends.[26] Universities and public research institutes doing work contracted by the private sector are increasingly finding that they have to keep their research results secret while the corporations apply for patents on products partly or entirely developed with taxpayers' money. This greatly restricts the free flow of scientific information, to the detriment of learning and innovation.

Equally disturbing is that direct corporate control over public research is being accompanied by a dramatic decline in the public sector's role in the management of agricultural biodiversity. In 1987, the Thatcher government sold off the prestigious Plant Breeding Institute in Cambridge to Unilever. The French government nearly did the same thing a few years later: the National Institute for Agronomic Research (INRA) backed out at the last moment from selling its main plant-breeding station to the chemical giant Rhône-Poulenc. Meanwhile, public sector gene banks are being starved of funds, with staff demoralised and hampered in their survey, collection, evaluation and storage work. Under such circumstances more germplasm will no doubt be irrevocably lost in gene banks as a result of human errors, technical failures, and neglect[27]—accentuating the already severe 'gene bank erosion' problem of *ex-situ* conservation programmes.

R&D priorities for agricultural machinery and food processing technologies are also biased in favour of controllable uniformity. For example, current harvesting technology cannot cope with multiple-cropping systems and situations where several different varieties of a crop are grown together on the same plot of land. Current food processing technology only works within narrow tolerances of variety in the raw materials.

In this disturbing context, democratising research means increasing public funding for research on the conservation and use of agricultural biodiversity and, at the same time, restructuring agricultural R&D to allow for people's participation at all levels. Budgetary allocations should clearly reflect and reinforce the goals of sustainable agricultural development. Appropriate changes in the training and reward systems of scientists and extension staff [28] are required to encourage more equitable, participatory research modes in collecting and conserving genetic and species diversity, and in designing agroecosystems that rely more on nature's diversity and resilience than on capital-intensive 'solutions'. Farm tools, machines and food processing technology should be redesigned to cope with, and encourage, increasing biodiversity in agriculture. Public participation is also essential in the various bodies responsible for key decisions on overall national research priorities and R&D funding.

Clearly, powerful alliances need to be built between people working within public research institutes and other groups in society in order to reclaim more democratic and equitable spaces within science and the design of technologies. Today, in Europe, we are very far indeed from a 'mass practice in which scientists must loose all élitism and paternalism so as to re-acquire the whole knowledge fossilised in objects and techniques whose apparent neutrality hides their political and ideological role'.[29] Nevertheless, there are radical and socially sensitive men and women within the scientific community who, with broader popular support, could help transform the theory and practice of agricultural R&D as we know it today in Europe.

Changing the legal frameworks

The legal frameworks that regulate the activities of the genetic supply industry are also contributing to the decline of agricultural biodiversity in Europe. In the case of seeds, two sets of rules need to be changed to encourage diversity and sustainable agricultural development.

The first concern the rules that dictate what seeds can be sold on the market. To be registered on a national list and certified for sale, a variety has to fulfill a set of specific criteria. In most countries, a variety must be Distinct (distinguishable from all others on the market), Uniform (all individuals of a variety must be the same) and Stable (salient traits must be passed on from one generation to the next) – the DUS test. The initiative to set up standards for selling seeds came from the plant breeding profession itself, especially the flower and fruit breeders keen to rationalise market supply. However, these varietal certification laws impose extremely rigid standards. If a variety does not live up to the DUS test it cannot figure on an official list and be legally sold. This effectively excludes from the market a huge range of genetically diverse varieties of cereals, fruit, vegetables and other crops. In the EC, the strict demand for uniformity has reduced genetic diversity to such a degree that none but the most advanced varieties are allowed to be sold on the market. In turn, legally induced uniformity at the genetic level reinforces the ecological simplicity and homogeneity of modern farming and the costly dependence on industrial inputs for pest control and soil fertilisation.

Moreover, to pass established certification procedures and get a variety registered on the lists costs time and money. In the UK, it costs the equivalent of US$10,000 to register a new variety and keep it on the list for ten years. In France, the fee is even higher— the equivalent of US$40,000! These certification schemes clearly discriminate against the spread of informal innovations.

One response of grassroots conservation groups to the absurdity of the law has been to ignore it or formalise acts of civil disobedience. In Germany, local groups began packaging and selling old, diverse varieties labelled 'For test purposes' to bypass the law. In France, family seed companies like Le Biau Germe received threats from the authorities because the varieties they offered on the market were not on the French national list of seeds that could be legally commercialised. Based in southwest France, Le Biau Germe is one of the most well-respected biological seed companies. Over and above the distinct, uniform and stable varietal features required by the law (DUS test), French organic farmers prefer the quality of Le Biau Germe's seeds and their potential for adaptation in complex, diverse and low-input farming systems. To this day, Le Biau Germe continues to produce and sell seeds out of sheer obstinacy and hopes that the law will be rewritten to recognise the value of our genetic heritage.

There *are* instances where the law has been changed to encourage wider circulation and use of genetically diverse plants in society. France created a special parallel registration system for old fruit tree varieties in the mid-1980s. It is the only European country to have done so, but a precedent now exists that could be extended to all crops throughout Europe. Political will is all that is required to lower certification standards and registration fees.

The second set of legal instruments that need to be reconsidered are intellectual property rights (IPR) – the rules and rights that determine who owns genetic materials.

From the 1920s onwards, professional breeders began to lobby for some legal protection of their work in Europe. They wanted specific rewards and remuneration for the products of their plant breeding efforts. A special form of intellectual property right was thus created: plant breeders rights (PBRs). The UPOV convention (an international convention for the protection of new varieties of plants) was signed in 1961 by European states. Although PBRs provide a form of monopoly control over new varieties, this only covers the commercial use of the variety. Varieties temporarily protected by PBRs could be freely used by breeders to develop new varieties, the so-called 'breeders' exemption'. Farmers had the right to use their harvest from protected crops as new seed, a secular right that has been misleadingly called 'the farmers' privilege'.

However, in March 1991 the UPOV convention was revised and PBRs strengthened to look more like a patent right. The farmers' privilege and breeders' exemption have been drastically limited. If farmers want to reuse protected seed now they will have to pay additional royalties on them.

The drive to slap industrial patents on to the living world will only further restrict the availability and exchange of plant and animal genetic resources. If patents are extended to plants and animals, the few corporations that already control much of the genetic supply industry will derive enormous benefits. Farmers will be forced to pay royalties on every generation of plants and livestock they buy and reproduce for production purposes. Breeders will no longer have free access to germplasm to develop new varieties of plants and animals. Licenses will have to be obtained from the top biotechnology firms and royalties paid for the right to incorporate patented genes and characteristics into new crops and animal breeds. Most independent breeders and informal innovators will simply go out of business or be pushed into more civil disobedience.

It is not too late for public pressure to halt these destructive trends. Legal frameworks governing the activities of the seed and livestock sectors can still be creatively transformed to encourage rather than restrict nature's diversity. The rights society decides to grant to the developers of technology can and should be balanced by a set of obligations. For example, measures to promote genetic diversity could include obligations for the industry to diversify breeding programmes and adhere to strict genetic uniformity ceilings in a given region.[30]

Reforming agricultural policies

Over the last thirty years farm price policies have promoted standardisation and intensification in agriculture in the European Community. Between 1963 and 1983, EC cereal prices were reduced by 45% and since then another 30%. During this period, agricultural production increased along with huge food surpluses and escalating damage to the environment and wildlife.[31] Whilst increased production became concentrated among fewer and fewer farms, the EC's farming community declined by 35% over the past 15 years. Each year in the EC, 250,000 farms are forced to close down.

The policy behind these changes is known as the European Community's Common Agricultural Policy (CAP). The CAP is essentially a system of guaranteed farm prices for specific commodities, well above the world market prices, combined with measures to block the entry of cheaper products from outside the Community. In 1991, the EC spent 60% of its entire budget on the CAP alone. But most of the money does not go to farmers. A full two-thirds of it is allocated to non-productive activities like stockpiling and destruction of surpluses or getting rid of them on the world market through export subsidies.

In May 1992, EC ministers agreed to a reform of the CAP—largely in response to negotiations on the General Agreements on Tariffs and Trade (GATT). They presented the new measures as an important contribution to saving Europe's environment. However, a closer look at the CAP reform suggests that Europe's agroecosystems will be further standardised and production concentrated in fewer areas, to the detriment of both people and nature.[32]

The major thrust of the CAP reform is a 30% cut in prices paid to cereal farmers over the next three years, a 15% reduction in beef prices, and a 5% lowering of butter prices, among others. Policy makers clearly recognise that the newly imposed price levels are below the production costs of three-quarters of Europe's farmers, who will have to retire or find another job, if nothing else is done. A system of compensatory payments has therefore been proposed to take care of this potentially explosive situation.

However, the new compensation system is linked to yield and area farmed: 80% of the compensation payments will thus end up in the hands of 20% of Europe's farmers. These are the farmers who run the large chemical- and energy-intensive farms that provide the bulk of Europe's agricultural output: the genetically uniform crop farms concentrated in northern France, parts of England and Denmark, as well as the polluting, intensive animal production units of the Netherlands, parts of Belgium, northern Italy and northern Germany.

Under the new CAP, these large farms can only receive compensation provided they have set aside 15% of their arable land. This measure is meant to reduce EC farm surpluses and is often presented as a way to reduce production. But in the new policy 'setting aside' land is not defined as leaving it alone to recover from intensive practices: chemical fertilisers, toxic pesticides, heavy machines, massive irrigation and draining. It simply means that farmers are not allowed to grow food *per se* on it. Other crops can be grown on the set aside land if they are used for non-food purposes such as making biofuels, bioethanol, starch and other raw materials for industry. Rather than reduce production, the set aside rule may well intensify the use of land to meet the requirements of the newly emerging biomass industry.

Moreover, by lowering prices and channelling most of the compensation payments to the already 'advantaged' regions and farms, the new CAP basically rules out any agricultural future for 75% of the Community's farmers. The latter are relatively small farmers eking out a living in Spain, Portugal, Greece and in the so-called 'unproductive' parts of other European countries. It is in these less intensively farmed holdings that one can still find some of Europe's remaining regionally adapted, genetically diverse crop varieties and animal breeds embedded in traditional or low-input agroecosystems. The reformed CAP will simply drive this diversity of plants and animals to extinction, along with the agroecosystems and people's knowledge associated with them. The environment remains marginalised: the new CAP separates environmental protection from methods of agricultural production.

For sure, 'accompanying measures' are planned to promote some sustainable farming and nature conservation within the reformed CAP. Its 'Agri-Environmental Action Program' offers subsidies to farmers if they start growing organically, or stop draining wetlands, irrigation and ploughing up species-rich meadows. Farmers can even get money if they continue to rely on local crop varieties and rare breeds in danger of extinction.

The snag, of course, is that the budget is extremely small: 400 million ECU in the first year and up to 900 million ECU in the fifth year. This is merely 1-2 % of what Brussels currently spends on its agricultural policies! And these meagre financial provisions are aimed at 75% of EC farmers who otherwise have no future at all!

The new CAP will lead to a deep split between a 'productive' and 'competitive' minority that produces most of Europe's food and raw materials for industry on an increasingly narrow genetic basis and a written-off, 'non-productive' majority of farmers who will be asked to go out of business or to indulge in environmentally friendly activities for a while.[33]

However, broad alliances between all sections of society affected by these sweeping changes in agriculture are now emerging to build alternatives to the present CAP from the bottom up. Real change to the system cannot be achieved by individuals and groups acting on their own.

For example, in the UK a range of farming, organic, animal welfare, consumer, environmental and Third World development groups have created the Sustainable Agriculture, Food and Environment 'SAFE' alliance. Members of this alliance are collectively struggling for a radical restructuring of present systems of farm support. SAFE seeks to switch farm support away from price support towards payments for environmentally enhancing farm management practices based on the whole farm. The effect of providing 'tiered' support through whole farm management agreements would be 'to put smaller family farms (the mainstay of many rural economies) back on a level playing-field with larger farms, and to remove the present in-built bias towards increased farm size'.[34]

Such whole farm management payments could encourage farmers to modify their production methods to take full account of environmental factors and simultaneously reward those already practising environmentally sensitive farming, such as organic farmers and permaculturists. Reintroducing a wider range of crop varieties and animal breeds, varietal mixtures, multiple cropping and diverse agroforestry systems would thus be an integral part of such efforts to develop sustainable modes of production: all aiming towards high-quality food, regional rural development, maintenance of a more diversified environment, equity and a stable livelihood for farmers and farm workers.

Broad-based alliances, such as SAFE, also exist in France, Spain, Germany and Belgium. They all offer hope for changing agricultural policies and restructuring rural development in ways that support democracy, decentralisation and diversity (both cultural and biological) in Europe.

For details of grassroots conservation initiatives in Europe, see Appendix.

PART TWO

LIVING IN HARMONY

Your love of your country will extend to a feeling for the earth beneath your feet; like the ancients, you will come to regard the earth as a sentient being. You will feel your kinship with the earth and wish to protect its waters from abuse. You will not exploit them to their detriment by making them plunge through hydroelectric turbines, but wish to restore to them their natural courses with their bends, narrows, and broads. You will develop a sense of the oneness of all living things and realize your dependence upon them. Your growing respect for the earth will check the abuse of chemicals, both in the destruction of so-called weeds and in the unnatural forcing of your crops. You will learn the art of building up the humus and of leaving the earth a little better for your having lived on it.

You will become wise, not only book-learning, but by being able to read the book of nature.

Richard St. Barbe Baker, from *Land of Tane*

LIVING IN HARMONY:
SOME CONCEPTS

Introduction

ALTHOUGH THE WORLD only recently became aware of the scope of
the environmental tragedy we are creating—in the years following
publication of Rachel Carson's book *Silent Spring*—there is an older
history to conservation action to regain harmony with Nature. In the
eighteenth century, the Dutch translated into Latin the texts of the
Ezhava—a lowly, untouchable caste of Indians in Malabar—and published
them in twelve volumes as the *Hortus Malabaricus*. These books, the
knowledge of an ignored people, formed the basis of all subsequent
European classifications of South and Southeast Asian plants. As the
eminent environmentalist Richard Grove said: 'Although it may have been
novel in a Western context, the protection of natural resources has been
promoted since time immemorial.'[1]

It was in Mauritius that the French discovered how people can live in
harmony with Nature. Philibert Commerson, trained by Linnæus himself,
and the most experienced botanist of the eighteenth century, became state
botanist on Mauritius. He was inspired by his wife, Jeanne Baret, the first
woman to circumnavigate the world. The governor of Mauritius, Pierre
Poivre, a former Jesuit missionary, studied Indian and Chinese botanical
texts. This group was instrumental in promulgating comprehensive
environmental laws and regulations protecting forests, mountain slopes,
soil, water, and fish stocks. Thus the early damage done by colonists was
restricted to some extent. The Mauritian experience led half a century
later to forest protection systems in India, to mitigate the great damage
done by the heavy felling of trees to supply wood for the Royal Navy and
for the railways. The German geographer, Alexander von Humboldt,
influenced by Hindu philosophy, conceived of the ecological principle of
the interrelatedness of people and Nature.

Humboldt's concept, if we can call it such, was widely accepted, if not
commonplace, in ancient societies. Communities grew in harmony with
Nature, and their people were dependent on local resources they drew
from their environment. No part of the world seems to have been an
untouched wilderness, from deserts to boreal forests. Even the dense
Amazon basin was peopled for millennia, and consciously managed in

environmental terms. The Kayapo, for instance, believed in maintaining an energy balance between the natural and the spiritual worlds by regulating animal and plant use. Arturo Gomez-Pompa and Andrea Kaus say: 'Emerging from Western history and experience in temperate zones, a belief in an untouched and untouchable wilderness has permeated global policies... causing serious environmental problems.'[2] Humanity was never apart from Nature. To conceive of policies or production systems based on a belief in natural apartheid is not only to destroy the environment but to threaten human communities as well.

It is in this context that we should see the popular turning back to organic farming systems as more than a fad. It is popular recognition, far ahead of scientists and leaders, of the enduring reality that people are one with Nature. Ten years ago, Bill Mollison, an Australian ecologist, won the Right Livelihood Award for developing Permaculture, a designed system of organic and natural farming that enables all communities, even in urban centres, to relate to Nature, grow food for local use, and create human-scale habitations that are integrated with the environment around them. The ecological principle of sustaining biodiversity in Nature integrates with such farming methods.

Another pioneer in this field is **Robert Hart**, who has been working for many years in the field of forest gardening and agroforestry. In the next chapter, he shows each of us what we could do, in whatever small spaces are available to us, to turn these natural principles into a healthy way of life. Even small plots of land can help communities in most parts of Europe to be self-sufficient throughout the year. The basic principles of forest garden management, he says, should accord with the 'Laws of the Forest', such as ensuring maximum biodiversity; mutual protection and support; symbiotic interaction; multiplicity of functions; economy, and recycling ability; minimal disturbance of, and continuous maintenance of, soil cover; and the provision of niches for wildlife, including insects—all practical principles for establishing harmony between human society and nature.

Richard St. Barbe Baker, the Man of the Trees, regarded the forest as 'a society of living things, the greatest of which was the tree'. He called the forest the skin of the earth. To lose it is to lose the earth. Franklin Delano Roosevelt told him once that Gifford Pinchot, the creator of the first US Forestry Service, showed FDR two pictures: a 300-year-old Chinese painting of forest-covered hills overlooking a fertile valley with a gurgling river running past a populous town; and a recent photograph of the same place with barren hills, rock-strewn valley and derelict huts. FDR never forgot that lesson. Similar stories of destruction are all too common throughout the world.

But the reverse is also true. In their chapter, **Peter and Adrienne Jackson** show how the community-conscious and hardworking Swiss replanted their forest and recovered their environment from the brink of disaster. This can be done elsewhere by other people provided they have the will and the determination of the Swiss, and the community spirit to convert possibility into reality.

In his book *Immortality*, Milan Kundera describes the Alps as the heart of Europe. But the Alps, which have fired the European Romantic imagination, and still continue to do so for people such as **David Pitt**, are in danger of being vandalised by 'industrial skiing'. Sadruddin Aga Khan, the founder of Alp Action, says that the Alps are prey to every environmental problem encountered anywhere else: deforestation, air and water pollution, erosion, vanishing habitats, and the decline of agriculture. The world's busiest mountain network crisscrosses the Alps, bearing 20 per cent of all passenger and 15 per cent of all goods transported in Western Europe. Alp Action brings corporate partners into conservation work to maintain an ecosystem that is a 'source of sustenance—human and spiritual—for the entire European continent'.

A Forest Garden System for Self-Sufficiency

ROBERT A de J HART

BY MEANS OF a forest garden system, as practised in one form or another in many parts of the world, it would be possible for a community in most parts of Europe to achieve a high degree of self-sufficiency throughout the year from a small plot of land. A wide diversity of plant foods could be grown organically—foods best adapted to ensure positive health for every woman, man and child. Medicinal herbs and timber for building and fuel as well as plants to provide fibres, gums and other necessities could also be grown.

A forest garden is a small-scale reproduction of the natural forest and is thus the most intensive of all forms of land-use, because, like the natural forest, it comprises a number of different levels or 'storeys', so that vertical as well as horizontal dimensions are involved. Some might argue that factory farming is still more intensive, but it must be remembered that large areas of cereals are needed to feed the animals confined in factory farms.

The 'storeys' of which a forest garden consists are at least seven in number:

1. canopy, comprising high, light-demanding trees;
2. low-tree layer: shorter, shade-tolerant trees;
3. shrub layer: bush-fruits, such as currants and gooseberries;
4. herbaceous layer: herbs and vegetables, mainly perennial;
5. ground level: plants that spread horizontally, such as certain *Rubus* species;
6. rhizosphere: plants grown for their edible roots;
7. vertical dimension: vines and other climbers.

The system is self-perpetuating, because almost all the plants are perennial; self-fertilising, because deep-rooting trees, bushes and herbs draw up minerals from the subsoil and make them available to their neighbours; self-watering, because deep-rooting plants tap the spring-

Original area of author's forest garden: 30-year-old pear surrounded by herbs, red, white, and black currants, and raspberries.

veins in the subsoil and pump up water for the benefit of the whole system; self-mulching and self-weed suppressing, because rapidly spreading herbs, such as mints and balm create a 'living mulch'; self-pollinating, because the trees are carefully selected to be mutually compatible or self-fertile, and because the flowering and aromatic herbs attract beneficial insects; self-healing, because the aromatic herbs undoubtedly deter pests and disease-germs and exhale healthful radiations; and resistant to epidemics, because of the high diversity of plant species.

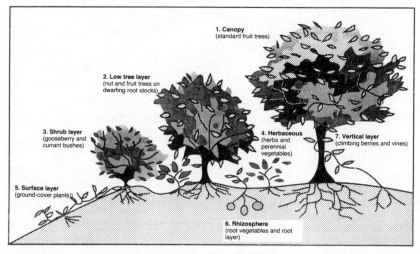

Fig 1: Cross-section of a temperate forest garden, showing seven 'storeys'.

The forest garden system has a very important role to play, not only in providing an answer to problems of hunger and malnutrition, but in the conservation of the environment. Trees counteract the greenhouse effect and atmospheric pollution, by absorbing carbon dioxide and other harmful gases, while exhaling the oxygen on which all life depends. They also transpire large quantities of water into the atmosphere, which fall as rain, while their roots exert a controlling influence on the groundwater system, inhibiting both floods and droughts. They create beneficial microclimates and moderate winds, providing shelter and pleasant living conditions for human beings, animals and other plants. Moreover, they prevent and can cure the erosion which has, in recent decades, transformed vast tracts of the earth into uninhabitable deserts. By programmes of re-afforestation, especially in the form of multi-purpose and multi-species systems, such as forest gardens, extensive arid areas in many countries could be rendered fit for human habitation. Quite high densities of population would become possible without endangering the environment, as human activities would everywhere be screened by trees. The environment, with its multitude of plant species, would provide useful and healthful occupations for most of the inhabitants, in food-processing, craftwork and the manufacture and maintenance of different forms of 'alternative technology' devices for the production of energy.

In order to build up and maintain a healthy and successful forest garden system, it is essential to ensure maximum biological diversity. This is done by planting the largest possible selection of species and varieties of useful trees, bushes, herbs, vegetables and fungi. This, in turn, will ensure that the forest garden fulfils its main purpose: that of providing a diversified and balanced diet for the community that operates it.

A forest garden can be established in any area where trees will grow. The initial preparation of the ground is the only time when hard work is needed. The soil must be thoroughly dug over, ploughed or rotovated and the roots of perennial weeds removed before the first plantings. Many forest gardens, especially in the tropics, have been established in old woodlands or orchards. Then the most valuable of the existing trees are retained to provide 'nurse conditions' for the new crop plants. In fact, the best way to conserve natural forests, including the rainforests, with their resources of enormous potential value for mankind, is not merely to 'protect' or 'preserve' them, but to develop them in wise and sustainable ways, enriching them with an abundance of new, economic plants, carefully selected for compatibility with existing conditions. The greater the diversity of plants, the greater the fertility, vitality—and beauty—of the landscape.

The established forest is a symbiotic organism, with an elaborate network of beneficial relationships between the plants themselves and between the plants and wild-life, from microscopic soil organisms to pollinating insects, small mammals and birds, which fertilise the soil and control pests. In a multi-species system epidemics seldom occur as they do under monocrop conditions. Plants, in general, attain a condition of positive health, which enables them to resist diseases, and even pests, without external aid. No chemical sprays should be necessary, though an occasional spray with a seaweed foliar feed or nettle-water can enhance the disease resistance of the leaves.

Little research has been done into the complicated question of plant relationships, both above and below ground, except in the case of leguminous plants and mycorrhizal associations. As is well known, leguminous plants—members of the pea and bean family—generally have the ability to extract nitrogen from the atmosphere, injecting it into the soil, where it benefits the plants' neighbours as well as themselves. In the case of mycorrhizal associations, certain fungi create protective sheaths for the roots of many plants, especially trees and orchids, which facilitate the flow of nutrients. If possible, therefore, forest garden systems should include leguminous plants and fungi, preferably of edible species, the spawn of which can be injected into the mulch covering the ground.

According to traditional lore, many other plants, especially aromatic herbs and members of the onion family, exert beneficial influences on their neighbours. As the biological function of plant scents and essential oils seems to be to attract beneficial insects and deter harmful ones, it is reasonable to suppose that this protective and stimulating role can be extended to neighbouring plants. A wide diversity of aromatic herbs creates a delicious and healthful atmosphere in the garden, while the plants' health-giving properties can also be enjoyed if they are made into teas or added to salads, stews or soups.

The many traditional plant associations, involving not only aromas but exchanges of root exudates, could easily be confirmed or disproved by science, as they have in the case of leguminous plants and mycorrhizal associations.

If a forest garden is to be established on a site where shelter does not already exist, such as an exposed hillside, the first essential is to create a series of windbreaks, as young trees are very susceptible to wind damage. These should take the form of strong wooden fencing with fast-growing trees, such as Leyland cypresses, behind. These, in time, will grow far higher than the fences, providing continuous shelter for the ever-growing trees of the forest garden. It is important to ensure that the belts are not too dense; they should filter the wind rather than checking it abruptly. Complete obstruction, forcing the wind upwards, causes turbulence and eddying round the plants which the belts are designed to protect. Eddying is also reduced by giving irregular profiles to the belts, which should curve into the predominant wind.

Another form of windbreak that has proved effective in windswept areas, such as an island off the coast of Wales, is the French Bouché-Thomas apple hedge. Vigorous young trees are planted obliquely so that they grow into each other, affording mutual support. Contrary to orthodox practice, the graft union is planted deep enough for the scion to take root as well as the rootstock, and thus a very strong framework is developed rapidly, capable of withstanding violent gales.

Once established, a forest garden requires minimal maintenance. The main work required during the growing season is cutting back plants that seek to encroach on each other. Throughout the year the ground is kept mulched with compost or straw. This suppresses weeds and provides the best possible conditions for the soil-organisms responsible for fertility: relatively warm and dry in the winter, relatively cool and moist in the summer. The herbs and perennial vegetables rapidly spread over the years, providing a 'living mulch', which weeds have little chance of invading.

Fig 2: Bouché-Thomas hedge.

An enormous variety of perennial fruit, nuts, herbs, vegetables and edible fungi are available for growing in the forest garden, the vast majority of which are never seen in shops and markets, and there can be little doubt that, for optimum health, the human system, in all its complexity, needs a wide diversity of proteins, carbohydrates, vitamins, minerals, trace elements, hormones, enzymes and other nutrients. Plant life, which is incredibly complex and contains many wonderful substances, can supply most, if not all, the nutrients essential for human wellbeing. For commercial reasons, the range of plant foods available to the average European housewife has been severely restricted and those that are available have generally been devitalised by the use of chemical fertilisers, sprays and processing. Anyone establishing a forest garden should therefore seek out specialist nurseries, seedsmen and possibly peasant growers, if they wish to accumulate a wide diversity of natural, nourishing plant foods—with their wonderful flavours.

While many food-plants are extraordinarily versatile and adaptable and can flourish in a number of different climatic conditions, the staple fruit that will constitute the backbone of forest garden systems will vary considerably between South and North. In the Mediterranean area the classic fruits must still predominate: figs, olives, grapes, peaches, citrus fruit and almonds. In the North, the apple must be preeminent, closely followed by pears, plums, damsons, gages, currants, raspberries, goose-berries and strawberries. In the Far North a surprisingly wide range of hardy berries is available. Probably the most northerly fruit tree in the world

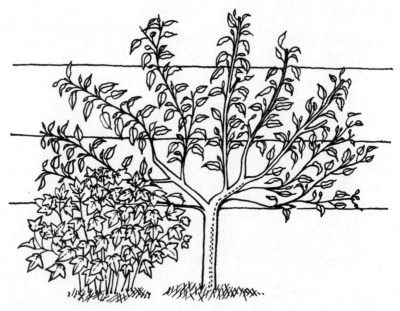

Fig 3: Fan-trained plum tree with blackcurrant bush.

is the rowan, the commercial potentialities of whose tart berries are now being explored by the Finns, together with blueberries and arctic raspberries.

In order to ensure regular harvests from the plants of one's choice over the longest possible period, it is essential to grow a number of different varieties. Many fruit trees and bushes are divided into early, mid-season and late categories, while apples are divided into six categories according to time of ripening. By careful planning it should be possible to enjoy one's own fruit almost throughout the year. Late apples, in particular, have a long keeping period after picking. Some crabapples are worth growing, not only for the beauty of their foliage and blossom and the sometimes surprising palatability of their fruit, but also because many of them, above all 'Golden Hornet', are excellent pollinators of ordinary apples. If space is very limited, 'family trees' may be planted: three or more varieties of fruit on a single rootstock.

If a community or family living off a limited plot of land is to enjoy a balanced and diversified diet of plant foods throughout the year, and also attain a degree of self-sufficiency in fuels, fertilisers, electricity generation and craft materials, the forest garden can be supplemented by a number of adjuncts.

One essential is an intensive vegetable garden. Other adjuncts can include:

• mounds for marrows, courgettes, squashes or asparagus;

- beds and logs for edible fungi or a small mushroom house;
- wetland area, comprising reedbed, bog-garden and watercress bed, if running water is available;
- strawberry bed;
- small grove of bamboos to supply edible shoots;
- bed of sun-loving herbs;
- greenhouse, plastic tunnel or cold-frames for tender plants and raising seeds;
- row of tubs on paved area for super-dwarf fruit trees, bushes and lime-hating plants in ericacious compost;
- willow coppice, to be cut periodically for stakes, fuel, shredding for compost or basketry;
- wild area, left uncultivated to provide compost material and niches for wild-life;
- windmill, watermill and/or biogas digester for electricity;
- sewage treatment area, comprising reedbeds with 'flowforms' for activating water.

As wind shelter is desirable in order to get the best results from most plants, all supplementary planted areas should, as far as possible, be sited in the lee of the forest garden, so that it can afford protection from the prevailing winds.

The aim of the intensive vegetable garden is to provide the greenfoods, roots and tubers which are part of the staple diets in all European countries, especially during the winter, when little or no produce is available from the forest garden.

Many systems and techniques can be employed in order to extract maximum nutriment from a restricted area, saving space, promoting the highest possible productivity and ensuring continuity throughout the year.

The first principle of space-saving is that of the forest garden itself: to provide vertical as well as horizontal dimensions of growth, where possible.

Many vegetables, in fact, have a natural proclivity to climb. These, which include many beans, peas, marrows, cucumbers, tomatoes, nasturtiums and hops, can be trained up fences, wooden or plastic trellises, wigwams or even trees. They can thus be accommodated, either in the forest garden itself, on any enclosures round or inside the garden, and up toolsheds or other buildings, when wire, plastic or wooden supports must be provided.

Other space-saving devices include intercropping and undercropping. Quick-maturing crops can be grown among slow-maturing plants; they will be cleared away before their slower friends are ready for picking. Low-growing plants can be grown beneath tall, non-spreading plants, such as sweetcorn and leeks, which will not shade them or impede their growth.

The first principle of productive vegetable growing is also shared with the forest garden. It is that of making use of Nature's laws and processes of symbiosis, of mutual aid. Many beneficial plant associations have been observed and practised by vegetable, herb and fruit growers down the ages, and a number have been confirmed by modern gardeners.

Among plants which the German garden writer Gertrud Franck stresses are 'good neighbours' to others are the leguminous plants—peas and beans— which inject nitrogen into the soil. Combinations comprising other vegetables which she claims are mutually beneficial include:

beetroots/brassicas	beetroot/lettuce
brassicas/cucumbers	brassicas/tomatoes
carrots/onions	celeriac/tomatoes
celery/all green vegetables	cucumbers/lettuce
onions/parsnips	onions/tomatoes

Combinations which she claims are harmful include: beetroots/ tomatoes, cabbages/onions and potatoes/onions.

Just as perennial, shade-tolerant, aromatic herbs undoubtedly play a role in stimulating the growth and enhancing the pest-and-disease resistance of plants in the forest garden, so annual, sun-loving herbs can play a similar role in the vegetable garden. These include anise, basil, borage, buckwheat, centaury, wild chamomile, coriander, dill, fenugreek, garlic mustard (Jack-by-the-hedge), heartsease (pansy), marigold (pot, Africa, French, Mexican) and summer savory ('the bean herb').

A useful economy technique is cut-and-come-again. Many leafy vegetables will re-sprout after cutting, just as many timber trees will send out fresh growth from 'stools' after coppicing. The seeds of lettuces, for example, can be broadcast, when they will create a miniature 'forest' of greenery, which thrives, even under drought conditions, far better than individual plants that have been transplanted. The seedlings can be pinched out again and again, leaving the bases of the stems to re-sprout. Mature brassicas will often re-sprout if a cross is cut across the stalk when the head is removed. Joy Larkcom, the salad expert, has made the interesting observation that cut brassicas will often survive lower winter temperatures than whole plants, re-sprouting in the spring.

As in the forest garden, it is desirable to keep the surface of the ground in the vegetable garden constantly mulched with compost, straw or vegetable residues ('leaf-fall'), so far as is feasible. This suppresses weeds, fertilises the plants, keeps the soil in good condition and enables the ground to be continuously used. After removal of one crop, the earth can be raked over and a new crop sown or planted.

An important reason for keeping soil constantly mulched is that it keeps the soil moist and therefore lessens the need for watering. Straw, in particular, remains moist for a surprisingly long time.

To avoid the soil being compacted by treading, it is best to grow annual vegetables in narrow beds, with still narrower paths between them. Then all cultivation can be carried out from the paths.

Raised beds and mounds are useful ways of economising on space, as vegetables and herbs can be grown on the sides as well as the tops. The easiest way to build them is to make a shallow trench, fill it with branches and twigs, lay turves grass-side-downwards on top, cover these with compost and cover the whole with soil.

The cultivation of a number of species of edible fungus is highly compatible with a forest garden system. This is an aspect of food production which could make a very important contribution to human nutrition throughout the world. Many species of edible fungus are rich in good quality, digestible protein, which could take the place of proteins of animal origin—the production of which is a very wasteful form of land-use—and of proteins derived from pulses, which many people find indigestible. In the West, where diabetes and diseases caused by high blood pressure are serious problems, it is of great significance that Italian research has shown that edible fungi contain substances which reduce the blood-sugar level, while other substances have been discovered which lower blood cholesterol. The vitamin content of edible fungi tends to be high, especially that of vitamin D—the 'sunshine vitamin'—and of vitamin B12, which is found in very few plant foods and the lack of which therefore can be a problem for vegetarians and vegans.

Spawn for the cultivation of certain species of edible fungus can be obtained from a number of European suppliers. The species most appropriate for a forest garden system are 'bracket' fungi and others that can be grown on logs and those that can be grown on humus in the form of compost heaps or in mulches.

Almost all edible fungi need some shade, so sites most suitable for growing them include:

- 'clearings' within the forest garden;
- ground beneath boundary hedges or trellises up which blackberries are trained;
- ground beneath willows or alders on the edge of wetland areas.

For cultivation of wood-inhabiting fungi, freshly sawn logs are half buried, vertically or horizontally, in the ground and inoculated with spawn. This can be done by cutting wedges in the bark, steeping the extracted wood-strips with mycelium and then nailing them back into the logs. Most timbers are suitable, though some fungi prefer conifer, poplar or other woods.

The choicest of all edible fungi is generally considered to be shiitake, which has been extensively cultivated for centuries in the Far East, where it is highly prized as a delicacy and regarded as having therapeutic powers. A wood-fungus, it thrives best on oak.

Other wood-fungi whose spawn can be obtained in Europe include the oyster-mushroom, velvet shank *Agrocybe aegerita* and *Nematoloma*.

Humus-inhabiting fungi include two species which are both delicious in flavour and striking in appearance: the wood blewit, with its mauve cap, and the shaggy ink cap, with its tall white egg-shaped caps which, on disintegrating, emit a fluid similar to Indian ink.

By careful selection of species it is possible to enjoy home-grown fungi in most months.

To create a wetland area, two shallow depressions can be dug out and lined with heavy plastic sheeting. One depression can be filled with water for use as a reedbed, and the other filled with compost, peat or a peat-substitute, such as coir or ericacious compost, and then thoroughly soaked, for use as a bog-garden. The reedbed can be planted with reeds, rushes and other water-plants in plastic containers. These can include plants with edible roots, tubers, stems, leaves or seeds, such as arrowhead, bulrush, flowering rush, galingale, pontederia and reedmace.

The bog can be used for growing *Vaccinium* species such as blueberries and cranberries, and be made attractive with Japanese or Siberian iris, with the wild yellow iris of northern Europe and marsh marigolds, The whole wetland area can be surrounded with a screen of willows or alders, which can be periodically coppiced. If a stream can be incorporated into the wetland area, watercress beds can be made, as they require running water. However, watercress seeds can now be obtained which, it is claimed, do not require moist conditions.

The whole forest garden scheme, with all its constituent parts, should be managed sustainably, so that it can evolve into a unified and closely integrated ecosystem.

The basic principles of management should accord with the Laws of the Forest. These are:

- maximum biological diversity;
- mutual protection and support;
- symbiotic interactions between plants and between plants and fauna;
- multiplicity of function of each plant, where possible;
- economy in use of space;
- total recycling: nothing should be wasted;
- minimal disturbance of soil, to maintain soil structure and circulation systems;

- continuous soil cover, to maintain temperatures and humidity favourable to fertility-promoting organisms;
- provision of niches and attractants for wild-life, especially insects involved in pollination and biological control.

The main work involved—daily during the growing season—is the control of plants, whether 'weeds' or cultivated plants, that encroach on their neighbours.

For a fuller explanation of the principles and practice of forest gardening, see the author's Forest Gardening *(Green Books, 1991), which includes details of recommended species for temperate, tropical and sub-tropical climates.*

Caring for
Switzerland's Forests

ADRIENNE AND PETER JACKSON

ANYONE FLYING into Switzerland from India or Africa must be struck by the verdant scene of forests and green fields topped by the snows of the Alps. It appears as a blessed land, far from the problems of forest destruction, erosion, drought and flood that afflict so many Third World countries.

That may be true today, but a century ago much of Switzerland's forest cover had been destroyed and degraded. Avalanches and landslides swept down on villages, sometimes completely engulfing them. Rivers flooded and carried silt and boulders along their courses, killing people, ruining agricultural and pasture land, sweeping away houses, bridges and cattle, and ruining roads. Rich agricultural soils were eroded.

We live in a small village on the slopes above Lake Geneva. Behind us is a steep hillside thickly forested with pine, larch and chestnut. However, engravings of 100 years ago show just a muddy slope, completely devoid of vegetation. After heavy rains, mud used to sweep down into the village and over the vineyards that were the main support of the people.

In the high Alpine regions the situation was even more disastrous. Dramatic drawings of the period show great slices of mountainside shearing off into the valleys, frantic peasants dragging cattle from the raging waters of the Upper Rhine, and wrecked houses and fields covered by mud and boulders after a flood had passed.

The Swiss Forestry Association, a private body, was the first to suspect that excessive deforestation was to blame and in 1856 petitioned the Federal government to launch an investigation. As so often happens, one man, Professor Elias Landolt, the Association's president, was primarily responsible for goading the government into action. His small band of experts visited all the high areas in the country to study the forests and

The Bougy area over Lac Leman, Switzerland, was denuded
of trees during the last century, as the old engraving shows.
Community planning, cohesion and hard work have restored
these hills and the rest of Switzerland to verdant glory.

geological conditions, while another group concentrated on hydrological questions. Within five years their report lay before the government. Its findings remain valid for many developing countries today:

'Avalanches have become more frequent because of deforestation. They have been experienced in places where they never, or only seldom, occurred. They threaten the security of dwellings, roads and property. Soil fertility has diminished...

'Ill-considered cutting of forests is largely responsible for the numerous areas of land which have become unproductive in the mountains and valleys, considerably diminishing the products of the soil as well as changing the appearance of the landscape...

'The irregularity in the flow of watercourses arises from thoughtless deforestation of the mountains...

'The fertility of alpine meadows has diminished. Their upper limit has come down, and forests have disappeared from the high regions...

'Deforestation in the mountains halts the development of industries and prevents the introduction of those which use wood...

'The forests in part of the regions studied will head towards total ruin if it is not possible to improve the treatment to which they are subjected, and if exploitation is not limited to the amount which they produce.'

Not long after the publication of the report, torrential rains fell in some regions, causing 50 deaths. This demanded serious action by the authorities; but first a political obstacle had to be overcome. Switzerland is a Confederation, where sovereignty rests with the cantons. The constitution of 1848 did not provide for federal action. However, the people, in a referendum, which is one of the basic forms of Swiss democracy, gave the Confederation 'the right of overall surveillance of policy concerning dams and forests in high regions'. On 24 March 1876, the Federal Assembly passed a stringent Forest Law for mountain areas, which in 1902 was extended to cover the whole country. The amended law specifically banned clear felling. Thus was created the foundation on which Switzerland has built the forest wealth so visible today. Switzerland now has 0.9 ha of forest for every inhabitant, more than double the average for Europe.

To rebuild the damaged forests, massive replanting has taken place since the turn of the century. Every canton is now obliged to guarantee the maintenance of forest, both on public and private lands, so that the amount of wooded cover always remains constant, or even increases. Felling has to be compensated by replanting or natural regeneration, with care taken always to have trees at different stages of development. Forests must contain a mix of species suitable to each particular environment. Monocultures are shunned. And all forests must be kept open to the public for leisure and pleasure. Even a private owner may not fence in his woodlands.

The degradation of Swiss forests as a result of exploitation for fuel wood had already begun in the Iron Age, in 800 BC. By the twelfth and thirteenth centuries most of the original forest had been cut back to roughly the extent it covers today. Forest was removed where timber was most needed, around towns and villages, and clearance was also made in the Alps for pasturage and occasionally for mineral exploitation. Even where the forest was not clear-felled, it was ravaged to such an extent that it no longer provided protection against natural disasters. Cattle wandered freely, browsing on young tree shoots and trampling down the soil. Dead leaves were collected for litter, depriving the earth of nutrients.

Industrialisation brought new impetus to the process of destruction. Before the use of coal, wood was needed to fuel the country's iron, glass and tile works, and subsequently for the construction of railways and buildings. In the 30 years from 1855 to 1885, 2,800 kilometres of railroad were built; for every five sleepers a cubic metre of wood, mainly oak, was used. For all these needs, vast tracts of forest were razed to the ground in the eighteenth and nineteenth centuries.

The principal aims of Swiss Forest Law are to manage the forests so as to benefit the people as a whole in four ways:

- to provide protection against the natural elements and against man-made pollution;
- to produce timber in sufficient quantity and quality;
- to contribute aesthetically to the landscape; and
- to offer opportunities for relaxation, particularly in forests near urban and tourist centres.

The law insists that forests should be considered as a sustainable source of supply, of which the capital must be conserved for future generations, with only the interest available for immediate use.

Forests at present cover 1.2 million hectares (12,000 km^2) of Switzerland, more than a quarter of the country. These are not for the most part great expanses of forest, but include manifold woods and coppices scattered throughout the land, the result of centuries of husbandry in which woods on hilly or stony terrain interspersing the fields were left intact, and forest was often maintained around villages to provide fuelwood, berries and game.

It is the basic principle of the Forest Law that the existing wealth of forested cover must not be diminished. This does not mean that for every tree cut, a young plant must take its place. But the loss of any area of forest, for whatever purpose - for the building of roads, factories, public works, housing or ski installations - must be compensated for by the creation of another wooded area of the same dimension. In any case, any removal of forest must have previously been authorised, and the mere fact of offering a plantation in compensation will not of itself give authority to clear the land.

The federal government sets the framework; the cantonal (provincial) governments put it into practice. Cantons are divided into districts, each under the supervision of a forest engineer. In the high mountains, clearings are reforested, barriers constructed to prevent avalanches, cattle banned, and access routes constructed to facilitate management. At lower levels, the emphasis is on the regeneration of the forest and the judicious selection of individual trees to be cut so as the favour the development of young trees to succeed them.

Clear felling, that is, the removal of all or most trees in an area, without allowing for natural regeneration, is prohibited. The amount felled, calculated over a long period, must correspond to the average growth. For example, if growth amounts to 5 m^3 per hectare per year in a forest of 100 ha, the average annual felling will be 500 m^3. In addition, taking a large area into consideration, the forest must have a regular composition by age group. Each stage of development, that is, must occupy about the same extent in the whole of the forest.

Catchment areas of streams must be reforested to prevent an irregular flow of water causing floods. Much reforestation, often combined with works to prevent avalanches, has been carried out over the past century in the Alps and Pre-Alps.

Of the total area of forest in Switzerland, 27% (about 300,000 ha) belongs to private individuals, often farmers, who generally take good care of its maintenance for their own use. The remaining 73% (about 840,000 ha) is in the public domain. It may belong to the confederation, or to the cantons, or most often to towns or villages. In all cases exploitation and maintenance of the forest is regulated by the federal forest law.

To enable the forests to fulfill their manifold functions, they have to be managed and cared for. For this an able forestry service is available, formed of trained forestry engineers, guards and wood-cutters, and of labourers employed in timber exploitation. The forestry engineer has the task of applying the law, of managing as a whole the forests belonging to the canton, and of advising owners on the technical management of public forests. He prepares management plans and projects for access roads and cable railways to remove timber, and for reforestation, and the damming of streams and works against avalanches.

Our local forestry engineer, M. Eric Treboux, tells us that beneath the mantle of greenery above our village of Bougy-Villars lie hidden the extensive works—cables run deep into the rock to anchor the terrain and retaining walls to prevent mud slides—that had to be carried out to hold the hillside in place before reforestation could be undertaken.

Under the supervision of the district forestry engineer, forest guards are responsible for a section of forested land, in which they oversee the application of the law and coordinate exploitation. Such sections may cover several communes and the guard is concerned with all the forests, public or private. Woodcutter-foresters provide the qualified labour under the orders of forest guards, and with the help of untrained labour.

Since observance of the law can involve considerable sacrifices for forest owners, limiting their liberty of action and to some extent their revenue, the government provides some measures of encouragement. Subsidies are allocated for the selection and treatment of forest seeds of good quality. The central government also allows investment credits, particularly to permit some forest owners to pay sums in excess of subsidies received for the construction of forest access roads and other works.

Several new problems have recently begun affecting Swiss forests. Chief among them, as in many industrialised countries, is the damage caused by air pollution. Forests near industrial plants suffer from the emission of noxious gases. But what has been surprising is that whole forests, far from industrial areas, are losing their vitality without any apparent reason. It is presumed that numerous pollutants, such as smoke, soot, heavy metals, and combinations of nitrogen and sulphur, play an important role in this, though it is difficult to prove the connection. Any delay in remedying the situation, however, would be dangerous. Switzerland is therefore carrying out strict measures to reduce all toxic emissions, including those of car exhausts.

Another unexpected challenge to the forests has come from the proliferation of game. Fifty years ago it was rare to encounter any wild animal. But over the 13 years from 1968 to 1981, the number of red deer in the country increased from 12,500 to 20,700, roe deer from 90,000 to 104,000, chamois from 55,000 to 63,000 and ibex from 4,500 to 10,000. The deer browse on the shoots of young trees, preventing them from developing or leaving them deformed. They tear off strips of bark, sometimes baring the trunks. The problem has arisen not just from the increase in numbers of game, but also from the intensification of agriculture which has eliminated hedges and clumps of trees and brought fertilisers and pesticides into use on a massive scale, confining roe deer in the forests where there is no other fodder but the trees.

To recreate the conditions of a natural mixed forest, in which deer cause less damage, care is taken to develop clearings in which smaller trees and shrubs can provide fodder for deer, while the quota of deer allowed to hunters has also been increased.

Another recent experiment has been the reintroduction of lynx, which had been wiped out by the turn of the century, to control deer numbers. More than 100 lynx now inhabit the forests of the Alps and Jura mountains. It is estimated that they kill up to five per cent of the roe deer population each year, a figure well within sustainable limits.

On the basis of its experience in rebuilding and managing its forests, Switzerland now provides technical assistance to developing countries to help them conserve and regenerate their forest land.

People in our part of Switzerland tell a tale about the forest, the source of some discomfiture to our village. According to a tradition of the Middle Ages, the legendary Good Queen Bertha was wandering in the forest one day when she was attacked by brigands. Two woodcutters, one from Bougy and one from neighbouring Fichy, saved her from the robbers. In gratitude, she offered them a choice of gifts—a golden goblet or a tract of forest. The Bougy woodcutter chose the goblet, the Fichy man got the forest. The goblet has long since vanished and Bougy now has only a modest portion of woodland. But the people of Fichy still own a large tract of forest, which for centuries provided a major source of revenue to their village.

Self-Reliance
in Poor Alpine Communities

DAVID PITT

IT IS NOT OFTEN REALISED that there are pockets of poverty, absolute as well as relative, in the Alps. Surveys in Switzerland (a country which has one of the highest per capita income rates in the world) have revealed villages without roads or electricity and families with very little income. Some of these families are more or less totally dependent on charity dispensed through such organisations as the Aide aux Montagnards. But others pursue a self-reliant way of life which, if it does not produce great wealth, ensures a long, healthy and happy life. The last at least is a rare commodity in Swiss cities where there are high rates of suicide, and mental and social problems.

Self-reliance has a long history in the Swiss Alps and was the rule rather than the exception until the World War II. Ancient and medieval farms were self-sufficient. Only a few necessities like salt, spices and the occasional ornament were imported, though the cheese barter trade brought in Mediterranean products, such as wines and olive oil in times of prosperity. Switzerland, at the time of its origins in 1291, and for much of its history, was a heavily wooded country, probably much like modern day Bhutan. The biggest town in 1300, Zurich, had only 6,000 people.

Poverty, however, stimulated co-operative social institutions. The Fruitières of the Jura date from the twelfth century and involved complex sharing of milk and cheese production. Transhumance agriculture, where common land in the high meadow alpages was shared, emerged at this time too, probably as a reaction to a deteriorating climate and the Black Death epidemic. Much commerce was in the form of 'gift' exchanges between mountains and valleys in a context of marriage and the pooling of labour.

Some of these ancient customs survive and have adapted well to the modern capitalistic economy, both providing a living and perhaps more

Living in harmony with nature also means hard work. This
Swiss family living in the remote village of Golzern cut steps
through the snow to take their cows down to the valley.

significantly, a base for an environmentally benign land use. It is no accident that the 'small is beautiful' ideas of Kohl, Schumacher, and others originate in the Austrian Alps, built on the ideas of an ancient Celtic people, the Taurisci. The Celts established a self-sufficient economy in the Alps from about 3,000 BC until the Romans and Germanic tribes drove them out to the Atlantic seaboard. In the millennium before our era, the Celts established a formidable network of trade and culture extending from the Alps (Hallstatt and La Tèric) to Scandinavia, Ethiopia and Asia Minor. The Celts originated the livestock Alpine ceremony and indeed the word Alps itself (meaning high) and the names of the great rivers that flow from the Alps (Danube, Rhine, Rhône) all have proto-Celtic roots. The Taurisci who were at the centre of the Hallstatt phase of this 'empire' (1,000 BC – 500 BC) probably derive their name from the ancient Celtic word for bull, which was a central deity symbolised in the alpha, the first letter of the Indo-European and Semitic alphabets.

Something of this lifestyle can be appreciated from the story of a traditional family in 1992 in the valley of the Maderanertal in the canton of Uri. Here, families follow the cows in a nomadic fashion, as was the custom before transhumance. The system of agriculture is on several 'floors'; that is, there are parcels of land at different altitudes which are exploited. In this valley, the cows are in the mountain pastures in the summer—over 2,400 m—but come down to the high village of Golzern at 1,800 m in September, having eaten out the higher meadows, and descend further as the lower pastures are grazed or grass growth stops. When there is no more grass the cows go back up to Golzern at the beginning of November to live off the hay gathered there in summer. This hay lasts until mid-January. Then the families and cows come back down to stables and hay gathered below. A track is cut through the snow by hand.

The nomadic system is not only efficient and ecological but also socially successful, even though depopulation and the decline of other institutions hardly provides a promising context. The Swiss journalist Bernard Baumann has described Golzern thus (in translation): 'Golzern is really the end of the world. The dominating church, the deserted inn, the wooden chalets with closed shutters, the village plunged in the most absolute silence—there has never been a single car here—is like some scene from an old mountain drama...If it were not for the wisps of smoke from five or six scattered chalets one could believe that the last inhabitant had left dozens of years ago on one of those boats which carried off so many people from Uri to the New World.'

Despite—perhaps because of—the isolation and the absence of modern amenities, the family has survived and is the centre of a vibrant life. Let us visit the Freis family as described by Baumann, in the depths of winter on a crisp January day as they prepare to move down with their cows. The family, which is extended for the move with kin who have climbed up to Golzern from many miles away, assemble in the tiny kitchen of the chalet before dawn. Hot coffee, a huge 'Znuni' (a dish of home-made cheese and smoked bacon), strong schnapps, and hot bread are on the table. The conversation gets more and more animated as the kitchen warms up. There are stories and songs. The party lasts until midday when the sun is at its zenith. By then men, women and children are thoroughly warmed and ready for the tough descent; they move off with the cows in a column following the head of the family and the queen cow down the snow track. In recent years one of the few benefits of climate change has been a lower depth of snow cover which means that the passage and the cutting is quicker. The safety of the village below is therefore reached well before nightfall.

This nomadic agriculture is interesting for many reasons. A romantic art and oral literature has evolved round the seasons, and the tranquillity of life in the snow. Most significant are the ecological dimensions. This is an agriculture without pollution, herbicides, or imported fertilisers, where products are natural, where virtuous cycles support production and daily living, and where many species retain their niche in a relatively undisturbed habitat.

Unfortunately, such valleys are rare now in the Alps. The politicians on the plains have always assumed that mountains were peripheral to national economies and politics, and could be either run down or supported with subsidies. It has been left to NGOs, like Alp Action, to try to save the natural and cultural heritage. Alp Action, chaired by Prince Sadruddin Aga Khan, was launched at the World Economic Forum in Davos in 1990. Alp Action has now 30 projects encouraging sustainable development at the grassroots by promoting reforestation, alternative energy and conservation as well as preserving the best of traditional culture. Alp Action has created a partnership between scientists, businessmen, ecologists and local people to build on the tradition, ambience and energy that is generated around the chalet fire and from the resilient wells of strength in kin and family.

LIVING IN HARMONY: PRACTICAL SOCIAL EXPERIMENTS

Introduction

THROUGHOUT EUROPE, the declining health of villages mirrors that of their surrounding environments. But there are beacons of light in this encroaching darkness: indeed one of these, the Village Action Network in Finland, has been given the Right Livelihood Award for 1993. As **Hillka Pietilä** points out in the next chapter, the Finnish Village Action Network is a great grassroots movement now comprising around 2,800 village communities, who use the old Finnish tradition of voluntary teamwork, 'talkoot,' to work to rebuild their communities into attractive, socially rewarding places to live in. As she says, 'Work substitutes for money, and rewards more than money!' This indeed could be a universal motto for community rebuilding. One of the most touching results of this village action is the new care being taken of the elderly, who find meaning in life by being with children once again.

In a number of earlier chapters, mention has been made of CADISPA (Conservation and Development in Sparsely Populated Areas), an environmental education project developed by WWF in five countries of the European Community. What is CADISPA all about? The project can be defined as an opportunity to bring into contact with one another the inhabitants of areas which, while still being of great natural value, are very fragile, and whose social and economic situation is precarious. The ultimate aim is to promote development which simultaneously provides a solution to the environmental issues in the area and makes use of rational exploitation of natural resources, allowing human communities to grow economically and culturally.

CADISPA was the brainchild of **Peter Martin**, head of education policy for WWF-UK. His philosophy of environmental education can be summed up as follows: 'Trying to give people an education that enables them to make decisions and take actions about the use of the environment with insight and understanding.' Could this concept be expanded to include whole communities? CADISPA started in Scotland in 1989 as a collaboration between WWF-UK and the Jordanhill College, and was extended in the following year to Italy and Spain; most recently, WWF-International initiated the project in new areas of Greece and Portugal. The project is financially supported by WWF and the European Community.

The areas of implementation of CADISPA are the Central and Eastern Pyrenees in Spain, the massif of Aspromonte in Southern Italy, the islands of Uist, Skye and Islay and the Flow Country in Scotland. CADISPA-Greece is being developed in the area of Prespa National Park (Western Macedonia), and a project has just started in the Municipality of Mértola, in the Portuguese region of Alentejo.

These regions of the continent are far from each other, and present many profound differences; nevertheless they were selected according to specific criteria, and all show the common characteristics required by the project. These characteristics are as follows:

• large areas with a wealth of environmental issues, which have for years been at the centre of conservation campaigns waged by environmental groups;
• fragile and precarious environmental balances, damaged by tampering and threatened by further plans which have a negative impact on the environment (dams, roads, bridges, buildings, intensive farming and forestry, destructive tourist development, and hunting);
• a very delicate social and economic situation, and a widespread desire displayed by the population to overcome the present precarious economy through development schemes;
• the presence of local organisations, WWF offices or other local NGOs who are active at a grassroots level and willing to cooperate.

Marco Pagliani, WWF-International's education officer with special responsibility for the CADISPA projects, initiated the Greek and Portuguese extensions of the project. He has this to say: 'I remember when the embryonic CADISPA-International team got together for the first time during a meeting in Madrid in December 1991. People discussed their dreams and schemes for future projects that have since started in Spain and Italy. Everybody returned home enthusiastic and full of goodwill; but slowly, while CADISPA took shape, a thousand unforeseen details and factors emerged, helping to mould the final, precise theoretical plan to help rural areas, which had been born in the urban offices of WWF. On a map we had proudly circled in green the spots chosen as project targets and these abstract hoops were becoming reality. They were filling up with real people with real problems.'

For the Spanish project, located in a number of valleys in the western Pyrenees, WWF decided to develop an environmental education programme built around the symbolic figure of the brown bear, which is on the verge of extinction. A deep-seated problem soon became apparent:

the local people at whom the project was aimed despised the bears, with a hostility that was perhaps no longer justified—a cultural throwback to a time when humans and bears competed for food. This hostility may seem absurd, but it is nevertheless still very much alive.

In any case, there was a first lesson to learn: to present ourselves as defenders of the bear in the Pyrenees, we had to go against the tide of prevailing sentiment. How could we get people to listen to us?

There are no bears left in the Aspromonte region of Italy, but the difficulty and delicacy of the social and economic situation is perhaps unequalled in Europe. Organised crime, with its long history of violence and injustice, poisons relationships, makes the older people cynical, and frustrates the younger generation in their day-to-day endeavours. In this context we talk about nature, environment, quality of life to children who, when they draw pictures, put a police helicopter where the sun should be! It is a tangible and daily presence in their lives.

The CADISPA project, seen as a whole, is the result of a fusion between an ideal and daily field work, an exchange between people of different backgrounds and experiences and, especially, the work of a team which, despite geographical, linguistic, and cultural differences, can work together in effectively promoting the circulation of ideas.

An important lesson learned in the field is that words count less than action. It is right to promote ideals and lifestyles, to try to talk about environmental protection and sustainable development, but it is also necessary to provide real and effective examples and help people put them into practice. To enable an old loom in the Pyrenees to weave again, to promote trekking on the Aspromonte, to support a women's co-operative in Greece, or to restore an old water mill in Mértola, may at first glance seem to be extraneous efforts for a conservation organisation such as WWF. But in fact conservation depends on people's attitudes. You can't expect respect for nature if the livelihood of the locals is sacrificed as a result of conservation activities. Nature and a good standard of living can go hand-in-hand; but it is necessary to demonstrate it, or least try, by working in the field alongside those who live there. This is what we want CADISPA to be: a beautiful idea that works for people. As **Donald MacDonald** reminds us, in his chapter about the project in the north of Scotland: 'These communities are like old roots touched with fresh streams of living water. What other form of renewal is there?'

For contact addresses for the CADISPA projects, please see page 264.

The Villages in Finland Refuse to Die

HILLKA PIETILÄ

THE VILLAGE ACTION MOVEMENT is the biggest authentic people's movement in the last few decades in Finland. There are, at the present moment, almost 3,000 village committees all around the country. In fact they are more common the further away you get from the metropolitan part of the country. The relative number of village committees is highest in Lappland, the most peripheral province with the sparsest population.

How can one speak about villages and village action in an industrialised, urbanised country like Finland? Did not villages as active self-governing committees vanish a long time ago in such countries in the industrial part of the world? Or at least become mere satellites of the cities without any life of their own?

That is exactly the point—that Finnish villages refuse to die. Over thirty thousand people are directly involved in running the week-to-week activities in the villages, and their work has an impact on life and circumstances of about half a million people in the Finnish countryside.

Rapid, intensive industrialisation leads to the growth of cities, and people moving from the countryside to industrial and business centres. Thus the villages and countryside become impoverished, local life declines and migration to the cities accelerates. This is accompanied by erosion of the social structures, people get uprooted, and living links between generations and relatives are broken. People are left at the mercy of labour markets and impersonal public services, and the whole culture becomes transformed from a rural way of living to an urban lifestyle.

Rapid transformation of the society

This process occurred in Finland as elsewhere. In the 1930s and the 1940s it was still primarily an agrarian country. The industrialisation process took place very rapidly at the end of the 1940s and in the 1950s after the rough years of war between 1939 and 1945. War indemnities and

Two dancers from a performance by the Suhina theatre company in Kaivola village, Finland.

reconstruction of the country speeded up the process; in fact they forced Finland to industrialise.

On the other hand, the countryside received significant injections of population right after the war. Finland lost the densely populated south-eastern province of Carelia in the war, and its population of about 400,000 people moved into the remaining part of the country. At that time this was more than 10 per cent of the whole population.

The majority of these people being farmers, they were settled in the countryside to live again by farming. No refugee camps were ever established in Finland during those years. The people were first temporarily accommodated in the houses of those whose homes were intact. For the final settlement extensive land reform was carried out, when the existing land was redistributed to include those who had lost everything.

Interestingly enough, the war years were followed also by a baby boom in the country—historically, perhaps a well-known phenomenon—producing the biggest annual birth-rate of the century. So when industrialisation gained pace, it drew its workers from the people of the boom years. Quite a number of Finns migrated to Sweden at the end of the 1960s and the beginning of the 1970s, in the hope of better earnings and a better standard of living.

Deprivation in the villages
All this was bitterly felt in the villages.

The prevailing atmosphere in the country was the idealisation of industrial development and the material values in life. The lifestyle of the cities was presented as modern and fashionable, and farming was taken as old-fashioned and backward. Mass media, movies, even the text books, and the substance and attitudes of teaching in schools, prepared young people to move into business and industry. The growing industries needed labour and, after all, there was an excess of people in the countryside.

In the 1960s and the beginning of the 1970s, migration from villages was heavy. Young people and couples moved away. The active population declined rapidly, with the consequence that soon schools did not have enough pupils, the village shop didn't have enough customers, and even the post office had too little business.

It was particularly disheartening that often the co-operative shops were the ones to close first, on the orders of the central union. Not much was left of the idealism of the co-operative movement at the beginning of the century, when the villagers themselves had started these co-operative shops.

It was exactly these factors—young people moving away, schools being closed, or at least threatened with closure, shopkeepers leaving and post offices being withdrawn—which alerted people. These were the signals of death of the whole village. For too long they had been waiting for action by the central government and administration—now they had to take their fate into their own hands.

The village movement started from the most remote villages, which were the first ones to be hit by emigration and its consequent effects. And when people once got mobilized, they demonstrated an enormous capacity for creativity and ideas—what to do and how to do it. Since the movement grew from the grassroots, it appeared in different forms in different villages. The situation of the village and the needs of the people were decisive. Thousands of flowers began blooming in the Finnish village action movement.

The first committees were established in 1975. Then the movement started to spread rapidly. In 1976 they got a devoted supporter in Lauri Hautamäki, professor of regional studies at the University of Tampere. He started a research project on villages, and for several years became an important communicator and facilitator between the villages. In 1980 the number of committees already exceeded a thousand. In another five years, another thousand committees were started. The peak has probably been achieved now, and the number of committees is about three thousand!

Two main general aims can be traced in the activities of most villages:

- to stop the migration from the villages by making them attractive, socially rewarding and cosy places to live; and
- to tempt and persuade new people to move in and settle in the villages.

All the other problems could be solved if only these aims could be achieved. But how could it be done?

A general problem in all villages is that whatever they want to do, they have practically no money to do it. But they have skilful and motivated people. They have reactivated as their 'secret weapon' an old Finnish tradition of voluntary teamwork, called *talkoot*. People have devoted millions of hours of work during these years in the villages for the common good, without pay. Work substitutes for money and rewards more than money!

Their reward is the completed task and the pleasure of doing it together; the best ground for good human relations is working together for common goals. As they say, 'Earlier we hardly knew each other in the village, but now we are all friends.'

In the beginning, the village committees received very little financial support from the municipalities or the state. On the contrary, sometimes their activities were so 'productive' that they donated the product of their work—for example, a ready-made lighting system for the village road—to the municipality on the condition that the municipality would donate the electricity back to the community!

Kuustenlatva—a village of 'top-people'

One of the first village committees was in Kuustenlatva, a village of former tenant peasants in the wilderness of the Western Finland forests. They lost their village school in 1974, which alarmed them enough to start village action in 1975. The community has only about 100 inhabitants.

They could not save the school, but they restored the building into a cosy Village House providing a place for meetings and many festivities, as well as three flats for rent for new villagers to settle in. In fact, they had to reconstruct the building twice, because there was a devastating fire right after the first renovation.

They also had to struggle a lot to maintain the village shop, which now seems as though it will survive; the shopkeeper's family has built its own house in the village. They are a couple of multi-talented people, who contribute to the village life in many ways. Here also the village committee organised log-*talkoot*, whereby the forest owners donated several logs each for the shopkeepers to build their house.

One of the long-term dreams of the villagers was completed and inaugurated in 1990 as part of the 15th anniversary celebration of the village committee. It was the Village Home, composed of three buildings around a courtyard, where people of different ages and occupations can live together. There are six flats and service premises for the elderly and other villagers. The old tradition of helping one's neighbour has been revived, and children are playing in the courtyard under the supervision of the elderly. It has become a new village centre, together with the Village House nearby.

During the years of their hardship and ordeals, the people in Kuustenlatva developed their own Latva-kansa ('top-people')* culture, drawing on their very original sense of humour as a means to overcome depression and resist the entertainment industry. This culture expresses itself in all the festivities and celebrations of the village, like Christmas celebrations, and the welcoming of the spring. Often they organise mockery competitions in order to ridicule the enthusiasm for competitions. They invite other villages to participate.

Their original local culture is a strong binding element in the life of

---

*Kuustenlatva stands for top of the spruces; kansa means the people; hence *Latva-kansa* means top-people.

the Kuustenlatva people. No wonder that it has also come out as a modern epic—two-volumes of 'The Vicissitudes of Top-people' have so far been published.

As a result the village is alive, seventeen years after the alarming signals of death. During these years the village has also brought enough publicity to the whole municipality to make it think more favourably about the aspirations and wishes of the villagers.

Welcoming the new and blessing the old inhabitants

Villagers have an endless supply of ideas for persuading new inhabitants to settle in their villages. Some have even directly advertised their village as 'a place far enough from the city for fine living, but close enough to exploit it!' They have bought land and built—or persuaded the municipality to build—the infrastructure, and then sold it at a nominal price as plots for newcomers to build their family houses.

They have sought the names and addresses of people who have moved away from the village, or who have relatives or roots in the village, and written letters inviting them to come back, offering them inexpensive plots and services. And through *talkoot* the villagers have really done an enormous amount of work to improve the roads and lighting, built sports grounds, boat harbours, jogging and skiing tracks, swimming places at the lakes, and maintained the shops, schools, post offices, banks and other services.

Many villages have ridiculed the calculations of school authorities about the future numbers of pupils. For instance in Kuorevaara the calculations said that the school would be closed at the latest by 1990 due to the number of pupils then being below twelve for the third consecutive year. As a result of all the efforts of the village committee and villagers, there were forty-five pupils that autumn and they even got a third teacher in addition to the two existing ones, instead of the school being closed down!

The latest feature of village activity is that of paying increasing attention to the elderly. In Eskola village they first started to provide meals and various activities for the elderly in the Village House (a restored locomotive carriage from the old railway). Then the village committee decided to build a new day-care centre next to the Village House, and houses for the families and employees around it. The catering for the elderly and the day-care children is now combined.

Actually a new village has been born within the old one, with inhabitants of various ages socialising, and enjoying living together. The result is that the old people of Eskola village are no longer increasing the number of clients in the municipal home for the elderly. They have recovered both mentally and physically, and prefer to stay in their own village as long as possible.

In Malkkila village in Savo, the village committee decided to organise 'days of pleasure' for senior citizens twice a month at the old village school. The programme of the day consists of a tasty meal prepared voluntarily by women of the village (in addition to their daily chores with their farms, family, and cattle), and services for pedicure, massage and the like. But the highlight of the day is always the singing and playing together with the pupils of the school and other children of the village. This has become such an important factor to cheer up the elderly and enrich the life of the village, that now the municipality has decided to retain the school, which was about to be closed.

In the villages everybody is needed: children, young and middle-aged, as well as the senior citizens, and this is the way to maintain village life and make it more humane and meaningful for everybody.

Lappland—a 'Third World' in Finland
It is no wonder that Lappland is the most active province of Finland as regards the village action movement. It is the province which has always found itself at the periphery, and is the most exploited part of the country. It has been used as the provider of raw materials—particularly hydro-electric power and timber—for the economic growth of southern Finland.

A project that has been under consideration for years is that of flooding the valley of the Vuotos river as part of a water reservoir for hydro-electricity production. People in the valley have been held in limbo for thirty years, uncertain as to whether they can continue living in their villages, or whether they will be forced to leave.

In 1982 it was decided by Parliament that the plan would definitely be cancelled, and about 30 million Finnish Marks were allocated to develop the villages. In the spring of 1991 the present government re-opened the discussion and condemned the people to uncertainty once again. No wonder they have lost confidence in the establishment in the south of the country.

Lappland was also the first part of the country where the village committees started to organise themselves. Until 1990 there was no national organisation to bring the village committees together and represent their views at the national level.

In the beginning of 1990, however, a new Provincial Council of village committees in Lappland was established on the initiative of the committees themselves. There are altogether about 320 village committees in Lappland. The Council consists of eleven representatives elected by the villages to coordinate their work in Lappland and to represent them to the official bodies of the state and province.

A similar organization has now been initiated in the province of St.

Mickel. Typically, officials had discouraged the village people from establishing their own organisation. This was another example of the attitude of the establishment concerning grassroots activities by village people.

The rural people all over the country are beginning to feel that the countryside is considered as a colony, a provider of basic commodities to industry and city dwellers, and not as the home and way of livelihood for rural people. Self-reliance has been labelled as poverty, and the traditional self-respect and self-confidence of people has been eroded. The people are victims of imported and imposed cultural values and lifestyles.

The latest threat to rural life is the possible membership of Finland in the EC. The Finnish government made their application to Brussels after a mockery of a show of democracy. If the application leads to membership, the whole of Finland may become an outlying area of a new superpower!

Culture as the ground of dignity

Wherever people are seriously threatened they resort to their own culture and traditions, in Finnish villages as well as in the peripheries of so-called developing countries. So it is not by accident that culture has been a strong element in all village activities from the beginning of the movement.

Without doubt the village committees have made an immeasurable contribution during these years to preserve and collect the heritage and traditions of popular culture in Finland. No institute or research system would have been able to do anything comparable, nor would they have had the resources to do so.

The village people have restored their local traditions and heritage in the form of festivals and celebrations, village books and histories, collections of handicrafts, tools, suits and dresses, the restoration and renovation of old buildings and houses, and preparing miniature replicas of their villages in their former state. In many places they have been particularly active in restoring traditional methods of work and tools, traditions related to livelihood and providing for everyday needs. They have restored old buildings, revived weaving, spinning and other handicrafts, organised demonstrations and presentations of traditional methods of sowing, mowing, harvesting, threshing and other farming work. These are often filmed or videotaped, and TV programmes made about them, so they will be kept for the coming generations to see.

Old customs have been revived, and new ones invented. The Carelian custom of bringing *rotinat*, small gifts to a family when a baby is born, makes both the family and the baby feel welcome. This custom is now spreading to other parts of the country.

Finns love the theatre

An authentic cultural feature of Finland is the enthusiasm for amateur theatre. Finns have always loved theatre. Almost a quarter of the villages have their own theatres in summer. The plays are usually written by local people and based on familiar characters and events. The whole village gets involved in preparing the show, as actors, producers, assistants, managers, caterers and so on. And with the income they buy plots of land for newcomers to settle in the village!

Kaivola village in south-western Finland is one example of how a village theatre group became the initiator of village action. A group called Suhina (or sighing, like the wind in the wheels of a mill) was established in 1959 to restore the old windmill that was on the highest hill in the village. Since 1961 Suhina has been running the summer theatre every year, which has provided the money not only for the preservation of the mill but extra income for the whole village. Among other things, they have bought 20 hectares of land for a village house and plots for building new houses.

Typically, urban people are unable to see the importance of culture for rural people. They often take it as conservatism, backwardness, naivety or as plain 'entertainment'. They are only concerned with the economic progress in the villages, as if 'people could live by bread alone'. The people's clinging to culture should rather be seen as an authentic—though often unconscious—countervailing act against the commercialisation, mechanisation and dehumanisation of life, which implies the degradation of rural life and values, the uprooting of people as well as the destruction and exploitation of nature. In this situation people resort to their indigenous culture and traditions in order to preserve their identity and self-respect.

Village Action is clearly a reaction against development which sees progress only in monetary and material terms, and directs all its efforts towards continuous economic growth through industrialisation and commercialisation, without any respect for social and cultural values of life. The village people fight for more balanced and humane progress, and the rights of people to choose their own way of life, and to live in small communities near to their roots and to the beauties of nature.

Nobody has assessed the impact of this movement in Finland in the last few years. One can only wonder how many more people would have left the countryside if Village Action had not emerged. How much more difficult would the structural change in the country have been?

How many of these villages, which are now inhabited by optimistic and self-confident people, would be empty and dead today? And how much worse would be the problems of unemployment and shortage of housing in the cities? How many more people would have migrated to Sweden and competed for jobs there with the migrants from Southern

Europe and Mediterranean countries?

These effects are difficult to assess. One thing is clear, however: that the social structure of Finland would be significantly different today without this movement. The Village Action movement has been able to slow down the migration of people from the villages; and it has also created a return flow to the villages, which not only compensates for the outflow but steadily increases the population in many villages.

Families move back to the countryside in order to provide a better environment and better schools for their children. Many people take early retirement—which has become extremely popular in Finland—and decide to move once more in their lifetime, back to the countryside. Villages in the neighbourhood of urban centres receive inhabitants who prefer living in a village environment, though they work in the cities. The summer season is an important time in rural Finland, because the 'return migration' of temporary citizens can double the population in many villages. So many Finns are rural in their souls!

The enormous work of village committees in collecting and preserving the rich heritage of authentic Finnish popular culture is not done just to fill the museums and archives, but to cherish the genuine roots of the people and help them regain dignity and self-confidence, which has always been so characteristic of the independent peasants in Finland and other Nordic countries.

In spite of all this work, at the moment the future is gloomy for villages, the country and the whole culture. The EC treaty will be ratified, the borders opened, and international trade increased. The consequences are still difficult to see. The world-view of the businessman, and reliance on market forces, is becoming more and more prevalent. It is not promising for the values of human dignity and reverence of life and nature.

The traditions, values and lifestyles in country villages are fragile and vulnerable. So much work and struggle have been required in the last few decades for their preservation. Will Village Action continue? Will people still have strength and stamina to continue? Will it help? Will it be possible to retain the basic values and keep the country and people alive and independent? There are more questions than answers.

Remnants of
Eden

PETER MARTIN

GOING BACK TO where you come from can be a salutary—even traumatic—experience.

Will we 'arrive where we started and know the place for the first time', or will the experience leave us unmoved and indifferent or even grateful for the day we packed our bags and headed off into the sunset?

More by good fortune than by design, I have had a year of revisiting the sort of experiences that fired me with the enthusiasm to become involved in environmentalism.

High points included watching finbacked, humpbacked and minke whales feeding on the Stellwagen Banks off the New England coast, monarch butterflies drifting and gliding along the sand dunes of Cape Cod. In two hours before dusk fifteen thousand alpine swifts and a scattering of Cory's Shearwaters heading north into a stiff wind through the straits between Paxos and the Greek mainland, green turtles laboriously heaving themselves up a steep Karachi beach and digging nesting holes by the light of a fitful midnight moon, mudskippers flipping along the edge of a Nigerian mangrove swamp and 13,000 pairs of puffins on the Scottish Isle of May strutting and chuckling through summer thrift.

These experiences generated a familiar excitement and pleasure, plus the deep respect for the stoical and dogged determination of these animals to survive against all the natural odds of weather, predation and competition. However, this is now imbued with a deepening sense of panic and sadness brought on by the keen awareness of the vulnerability of all these creatures to the unnatural odds foisted on them by the damaging impact of human activity on the environment.

Given such a response to wild creatures, the case for environmental conservation needs no justification. It is easy, therefore to understand why early environmental education focussed very simply on trying to expose as many people as possible to the natural wonders of the world and what would happen to them if we did not mend our ways. If some additional descriptions were included that detailed what might happen to human beings as a result of environmental mismanagement, then surely the argument for conservation could not fail to be persuasive and effective?

The message was fairly straightforward: ours is a beautiful and fascinating world which is important for our minds, our spirits, our bank accounts and our survival, so we must all look after it.

We now know that things are not so simple.

We are now well aware that the interaction between human beings and their environment is determined by a complex array of forces that relate to the practicalities of living, to human history and the creativity and complexity of the human psyche.

Centuries of social evolution have been determined by the physical, ecological and climatic features of the land, the means of acquiring food and shelter, and accidents of history like conquests and inventions. Beliefs, values, economics and politics, have all affected the way we live and the condition and appearance of the places in which we live. We also know that poverty and conflict or affluence and the desire to maintain power can all override what might well be the excellent long-term sense of caring for the environment.

For these reasons any changes needed to overcome current environmental problems will not take place easily or quickly. If they are to take place at all then a prerequisite is a full understanding of the complex forces that determine human behaviour in relation to the environment. Without this any concern for the environment is expressed in descriptive rather than analytical terms—without analysis we cannot understand the causes and without understanding the causes it is difficult if not impossible to identify realistic remedies that will reduce or remove the concerns.

This understanding of the causes and environmental effects of human activity must be seen as fundamental to the basis of education. Not only should this be seen as an 'academic' necessity but it should also be seen as a 'practical' necessity that informs the everyday decisions that we all make and the everyday actions that we all take in the work we do and in the lives we lead, wherever that might be.

Thus an environmental education cannot be something that is tacked on to education, but needs to be seen as a central function of education and that relates directly to the day-to-day functioning of people within the environment they inhabit. Of course for some people this is exactly what happens.

Picture a river in a South American forest. Close to a small settlement a group of adults and children collect nuts and fruits. Upstream, another group is collecting fish stunned by a narcotic derived from forest plants. In the evening both groups may listen to stories of folklore and legend. In this way the young people receive an education that enables them to make sense of their world, how to use it, how to manage it, and shows them their place in society and the environment.

Out there on the last remaining frontiers of wilderness are the cultures and communities that still have a lifestyle to a large extent dominated by a close relationship with the environment. Here we have the last remnants of Eden.

To liken the life of the forest people to Eden, a mythical golden age of innocence, peace and beauty is, we know, an illusion. But once the influence of the outside world impinges on the minds and bodies of the people and on the forest itself then the illusion of Eden becomes converted into a very real Armageddon.

Not only are the natural ecosystems that support the lives of the people destroyed but there is also the inevitable displacement of the perceptions, beliefs and insights that have determined and maintained these environmentally sound lifestyles.

Attempts to help in these circumstances create confusion, conflict and dilemma. These people cannot be deliberately restricted to their seemingly anachronistic time warp to maintain a belief in the dream of Eden. Yet how can all the known benefits of the lifestyles they lead and the environments they inhabit be maintained if they gain rightful access to the benefits that modernity brings, which seem inextricably linked to the socioeconomics and values of the competitive materialism of the industrialised world?

Conservation programmes are set up to attempt to address these dilemmas. However, a few years ago WWF-UK became concerned in particular about the style of education programmes offered as part and parcel of such programmes: the sort of education that is often identified as 'conservation education'. In particular there was concern where these education initiatives related to conservation programmes in isolated rural areas where sparse populations lived in or around areas of high interest to conservationists.

If these interests were to be safeguarded by their designation as 'protected areas', then the conventional wisdom was that the people in and around these areas should be told why the new designation was necessary and how they would have to amend their behaviour to comply with this designation.

This sort of approach seemed rather flimsy.

Some evaluative research into the use of mobile audio-visual units in rural communities in West Africa to promote a conservation message reinforced this criticism. It collected evidence that demonstrated a distinct decrease in public interest in conservation following the visit by one of these units.

In a similar vein, two eminent and well-meaning conservationists got a very poor reception on the Scottish Island of Islay when they tried to intervene in a conflict between conservationists and local farmers over the shooting of barnacle-geese that were eating the farmers' crops—another demonstration of the inappropriateness of this style of conservation interventionism.

There are of course alternative models of intervention, in the main operated through the development agencies, where enlightened community education initiatives help rural people to take part in sustainable and satisfying rural development programmes.

Although the sustainable utilisation of the environment is central to many of these projects, the environment, on the whole, is a resource that is utilised for development. WWF-UK was interested in investigating projects where the satisfactory resolution of environmental concerns and rural development were seen as inseparable; and, in particular, to investigate how all aspects of education could be harnessed to assist in their successful implementation.

And so the idea of CADISPA, Conservation and Development in Sparsely Populated Areas, was born.

Yet why should Scotland be the starting point of this project? It seems nothing like the pristine wilderness of the tropical forest.

In these rural areas of Europe there are distinctive and very real problems that similarly relate to the imposed destruction of traditional and sustainable lifestyles by outside forces. Outside forces that not only impact on the fabric of the environment, but promote social and economic norms regardless of their cultural and environmental suitability.

The Island of Skye, lying off the West coast of the Scottish mainland, is a magical place in May. The sun is beginning to warm the clear, clean air; early purple orchids, bluebells and primroses colour the still-brown grasses, and great northern divers in summer plumage together with crab-searching otters enliven the seaweed- and seal-bedecked sea inlets.

It was in this remnant of Eden that I spent a week's holiday walking, watching sunsets across the Cuillins and reading Findlay Macdonald's trilogy that describes his growing up on one of these beautiful Scottish Islands. In this he reflects on the lives of his family and the people he knows, and describes how his success in school heralds the inevitable departure from his birthplace.

'Here I was leaving now—the first boy of the new village. Molly the first girl had gone. The trickle would grow into a steady stream that would grow bigger and bigger, searching for its own bit of sea somewhere. Streams can grow into rivers for sure; they can reach their sea, or like ours sink into the sand. They rarely flow back because that way the hill is against them.'

The education he received was based on the socioeconomic needs, skills, values and aspirations of a society far removed from the realities of his life. Therefore success meant an inevitable move to where these skills and values could be better utilised. Not that he should have been debarred from all the wealth of wisdom from outside the small world of this island. But surely there should have been the opportunity to reflect on this wisdom within the context of the island, its life and its people, and to give him the option of using his education within that context.

Of course there are other forces that are at work that encourage the flow of people from the wilderness.

There are many problems living in sparsely populated areas. The level of services, schools, health care can be lower than in other communities. The often inhospitable, geographical or climatic features of the region, the distance from centres of commerce or government, poorly developed communications and transport networks all exaggerate these problems, and people often feel the need to escape.

This perceived 'need' to leave is fuelled by a massive promotion of an homogeneous mode of life not only within nations, but across national boundaries.

If the particular social and environmental conditions in some communities make the achievement of these norms impossible, the members of those communities become frustrated, discontented, imbued with apathy and thus uncommitted to the vigorous pursuit of their particular and often specialised lifestyles. This often causes people to leave areas in order to find a life where such norms are, in theory, achievable— this depopulation itself bringing additional problems which continue and accelerate the process. The lowering of the population and the loss of the younger members of society promote the reduction of such services as schools and health care. Combined with a decay of the culture and social life, this encourages further depopulation and inhibits regrowth. The invasion of holiday or retirement residents, stagnating social growth and increasing house prices, is the final nail in the rural coffin.

However, the promotion of alternative ways of life that suit the characteristics of the environment are often viewed as inappropriate. They seem to have overtones of atavism or anachronism, or they relate to peripheral and low-status employment that relegates people to the role of second-class citizens or tourist attractions.

There are also imposed limits to development that are enforced simply because these areas are sparsely populated. In such areas there is often a high incidence of associated wildlife, scenic or amenity interest. Although this may bring various benefits, it may also pose many social and cultural problems by acting as an inhibitor to development, condemning communities to a permanent 'time warp' of non-development—a social martyrdom that preserves the important natural or scenic qualities of the area.

The perceptions of isolated beauty and natural importance that inhibit development are often 'imposed' by authorities or pressure groups from outside the region, and often by other institutions or agencies that represent the views of elements of society that do not, in general, have to endure the problems of isolation and underdevelopment. This is beautifully encapsulated in Melvyn Bragg's book *The Maid of Buttermere*.

'He saw now the valley, the "secret chamber of the Lakes" as he had heard it called, and his old prejudices against nature faded at the memory: the place was a haven. It had bred Mary and kept intact her virtues against the predatory world of Fame and Reports. He could believe now, even though he was as ignorant of detail as ever, to let yourself be supported by Nature and learn from its steady flux was to be strengthened. "And yet," he added, "this does not apply to those who have not the means to be beneficiaries. For them, Nature is no more than the indifferent backdrop in a hostile world." '

With this in mind a project was envisaged which would explore ways in which education could help to resolve these problems by developing the insight and skills to enable local communities to take part in the discussions and decisions that define their future, and, above all, the skills that would enable them to take part in and benefit from any future plans.

It was agreed that the project should address the following questions:

- How can sparsely populated rural communities initiate dynamic development programmes that are environmentally sustainable?
- How can the legitimate interests and needs of the local population be met without damaging the valuable environmental currency?
- What educational initiatives and what teaching/learning resources will be needed to provide communities with the skills and insights to take on active and fulfilling roles in this development?
- What general initiations outside the community will be necessary to provide support for these programmes?

Jordanhill College at Glasgow was given a commission to develop a four-year programme focusing on two remote areas in Scotland: one in the Uists and the other in the Flow Country of Caithness and Sutherland.

The rest of the story belongs to them.

Scotland:
The Flow Country

DONALD MACDONALD

MY GRANDPARENTS, all four of them, were born in the Hebrides, as were my parents and every other older relative, as far back as we can trace into the 1700s. Although British, these people spoke no English until quite recently. Their culture was traditionally self-sufficient, frugal and non-materialist, and only during the second half of the twentieth century has that culture come to be dominated by the ideas of the wider world. Even so, Hebridean society remains such that the islands are one of the few British regions visited regularly by North American social anthropologists. It was from this society that I first came to internalise such values as continuity, reciprocity and respect for the natural environment. Becoming a professional educator, and more specifically a proponent of environmental education, I found it natural to relate the values of my own upbringing to those of biocentrists, from Arne Naess back to Aldo Leopold. And it was by a strange turn of fate that I eventually returned to the islands of my childhood, as a member of the CADISPA study group.

The CADISPA project

In 1988, WWF-UK funded what was a relatively modest project, spanning three years, to investigate local peceptions of environmental issues in Northern Scotland, and to consider ways in which educational programmes might address these issues. The rationale behind the project was that isolated and sparsely populated areas in European countries are often associated with below-average living standards. At the same time, such areas may also be rich in natural amenity, and conflicts result when indigenous people seek to exploit natural resources which external agencies wish to preserve. Conflicts, where they exist, are sometimes exacerbated by the barriers of distance, ethnicity and language which so often separate outlying communities from the main body of society. In the present case, the team which undertook the investigation coined the acronym CADISPA—Conservation and Development in Sparsely

Scotland: the Flow Country.

Populated Areas. In choosing specific locations for the study, we identified a mainland area (the Flow Country of Caithness—Sutherland) and an island area (the Uists, in the Western Isles chain). At the time of making the choice, the Flow Country was the scene of a much publicised environmental conflict between forestry and conservation, while the Uists were affected by a lower-key tension between tourism and religious observance.

Crofting

The two selected areas share many environmental features. Both lie on bedrock which is the oldest and least yielding in Europe. The climate is cloudy, windy and wet. Precipitation far exceeds evaporation, and the surface in these places is perennially sodden, so that freshwater pools abound. Beyond that, there is a common socioeconomic element. A predominant land use in these areas is crofting. A croft is a small landholding of 4–6 hectares, where the occupant also has rights to a much larger tract of rough grazing land, accessible on a common basis to all members of the community. As a style of farming, crofting is one in which low inputs produce low outputs. Although close to self-sufficiency in the earlier 1900s, crofting now contributes little to the Scottish agricultural economy, and most of the foodstuffs consumed on crofts are brought in from Central Scotland or beyond. Since the financial rewards of crofting are small, crofters invariably have other sources of income. As it happens, the seasonal work of crofting dovetails conveniently with other rural activities such as fishing, forestry or fish farming. It can also be combined with salaried employment (as teacher, postman or policeman, for example).

Environmentally friendly behaviour has been a feature of crofting communities down through the years. The small size of holding discouraged mechanisation, and hand implements were widely used until after World War II. As fellow clansman Donald MacDonald, a crofter in Illeray (North Uist), told me: 'In my early days, when we were ploughing with horses, if we came upon a bird's nest, we got the spade, cut out the nest and placed it on one side. As soon as the plough was past that spot, the nest was replaced and a few minutes after that the bird would be sitting on the nest again.' In a less intentional manner, the low-key operations of crofting as a system have been generally benign towards nature. Using few agricultural chemicals, crofters have not wiped out indigenous fauna and flora. Thus one of the most striking sights in the Hebrides is the rich sward of flowering plants and grasses which covers the west coast lowlands in early summer. Behind the sand dunes and marram grasses, for instance, corn marigold, ragwort and seaside pansies spread in vivid array. Indeed, conservation agencies have capitalised on this situation, identifying the coastal zone as an Environmentally Sensitive Area (ESA). Under the terms of the 1986 Agriculture Act, crofters are paid a sum of money, in return for adhering to certain land management conditions. The requirements include controlling the density of sheep grazing the land, avoiding the use of herbicides, using organic mulch (such as seaweed, peat or dung) and not cutting a hay crop until mid-July, to minimise interference with nesting birds. As one official from the Department of Agriculture and Fisheries in Scotland put it: 'What we are looking for is a plan, drawn up by the crofter, relating to an area of land on which positive steps can be taken for environmental conservation.' At the same time, crofters do not always agree with what conservation agencies propose. There is a problem, for example, with regard to greylag geese. Western Scotland is the winter home for a number of goose species, and the presence of these large grazing birds, in flocks numbering several thousand at any one time, means that there is additional pressure on pasture land which crofters would rather use for sheep and cattle. Some crofters might prefer to warn off the geese by employing a range of bird-scaring devices, but are deterred by the costs. Others would be happy to see the goose population reduced by culling. Meanwhile, the National Conservation Agency has tried to find a compromise by paying crofters to raise sacrificial crops which would, at least in part, divert the attention of geese from other crops and pastures.

Compromise in environmental matters is frequently rendered vulnerable by the economic weakness of the Scottish Highlands. To illustrate this point rather more fully, we can consider developments in two constrasting areas: the Flow Country and the Uists.

The Flow Country

The term 'Flow Country' has been widely used by outsiders to describe an area in Caithness and Sutherland where the flat landscape, low evapo-transpiration and poor drainage have combined to produce deep peatbogs, interspersed with countless freshwater pools. The spread of blanket bog has built up over the centuries, from the accumulated plant residues of mosses, sedges and rushes. The cool wet conditions ensure that the breakdown and decay of organic materials is extremely slow. Blanket bogs occur elsewhere in Ireland, Norway, Iceland, Alaska, Labrador and the Falkland Islands. The north of Scotland contains about 0.5 million hectares of this variety of deep peatbog: a significant fraction of the world total. In addition, this wetland environment is the nesting area for certain bird species, including greenshank, dunlin, golden plover and black-throated diver. But opinions vary about the scientific and aesthetic appeal of the blanket bog. The International Mire Conservation group view it as 'unique and globally important'—equivalent, as it were, to the Serengeti of East Africa. By contrast, the columnist Duff Hart-Davis, writing in

The Independent newspaper in 1988, described the area as 'a desolate wilderness, supporting practically no birds or animals'.

What brought the remote Flow Country to the attention of the British public was the growth of commercial forestry in the area. Forestry interests include the Forestry Commission (a government organisation) and various private concerns. It was the latter, encouraged by significant tax concessions being offered for tree planting during the early 1980s, that particularly came to public attention. A curious pattern developed, whereby several rich individuals (including sportsmen, television presenters and pop musicians) were buying extensive tracts of peatland, some of it from the National Nature Conservancy, the body entrusted with the preservation of indigenous ecosystems. In the war of words which followed, between 1983 and 1989, local people living on the edges of virtually uninhibited Flow Country grew increasingly confused, as the verbal broadsides passed over their heads. On the one hand, the forestry interests claimed that the Flow Country was of little value in monetary terms, was much in need of development, and further that the creation of forestry-related jobs could only benefit the surrounding communities. On the other hand, an amazing array of conservation bodies lined up. Some of these, like the RSPB or WWF-UK, were based mainly in England, while others (like the NNC) used a Scottish branch office, staffed as much by English as by Scots. From these conservation organisations came pleas for the protection of one of Britain's last remaining wilderness areas, for the preservation of rare birds and plants, and not least for the development of eco-based tourism in this unique environment. Among local people, reactions to all this were predictably mixed. Some expressed a desire for jobs, regardless of the environmental impact. Others reminded the visiting experts that the so-called wilderness had once been peopled, having only become uninhabited after the Highland Clearances of 1750-1880. Yet again, there were several expressions of surprise that the main protagonists in the debate seemed to be mostly from southern England, rather than from northern Scotland.

It was at this point, in 1988, that Roy Weston took the CADISPA project to the Flow Country, aiming to ascertain the positions held by local inhabitants on environmental issues, and to investigate ways in which education could heighten awareness. Bearing in mind that CADISPA team members were funded for only one day per week throughout the life of the project, it is to Roy's credit that, over a two-year period, he was able to work so effectively from his permanent base in Glasgow. The first of his tasks was to conduct a set of interviews with a sample of 66 local people, chosen carefully to represent different ages, jobs and localities. The majority of these respondents emphasised their high regard for the peaceful and pleasant quality of life in the far North, while agreeing that threats to the natural environment did indeed exist. At the same time, few had any confidence in the ability of externally-based conservation bodies to do much good. Interviewees kept returning to the idea that local crofters were the best people to conserve the Flow Country environment. A second major task was to raise awareness of the need for indigenous voices to join in the nationwide debate. Articles in community and regional newspapers (such as *The Northern Times*) and in national papers (including *The Scotsman*), as well as interviews on BBC Radio Scotland, all contributed towards this aim. Thirdly, Roy Weston conducted a series of conservation-based lessons in primary and secondary schools throughout Caithness and Sutherland. His national standing as a teacher-educator ensured that he had ready access to classrooms, where he sensitised pupils to the variety of plants and animals occupying the peatbog habitat. While the majority of the pupils had, naturally enough, visited the peatlands on foot, they were only too ready to admit their own lack of detailed knowledge and their indifferent attitude towards that apparently empty habitat. Through a sequence of activities, involving recognition and taxonomic exercises, investigations of soil acidity, surveys of life in pools and the construction of mini-peatbogs in boxes, pupils were helped to perceive the Flow Country as a living treasure. Throughout all this, scientific knowledge of the topic was built up, before controversial issues were brought out into open debate.

The Uists

The justification for taking the CADISPA project to the Uists was different from that behind the Flow Country investigation. Here we had an even more remote community, not associated in the public view with any major environmental issue, but by no means free from development. For many years, the Army has been operating a test range on the islands, for medium- and short-range missiles, which are fired westwards into the Atlantic. The 300 service personnel staffing the base constitute a significant intrusion into the life of the Uists, while providing much-appreciated employment to over 200 civilians. A more recent phenomenon is the gradual growth in tourism, which brought in over 11,000 people in 1989, for example.

Visiting the Uists during 1989-90, myself and Jim Dunlop, Director of the CADISPA project in Scotland, paralleled what Roy Weston was doing in the Flow Country. Investigating local perceptions of the environment, we found many contrasts between the two areas. Respondents in the Uists regarded their environment as relatively unthreatened, but agreed nonetheless that conservation deserved a high priority. In particular, scenery, bird life and clean air were justifiably cited as features to be cherished. What also emerged was a concern that cultural elements were probably more threatened than were natural features. Among these cultural menaces, our interviewees identified the presence of the military, and the growth in summer tourism. During the 1980s, there was indeed a recorded increase in the annual number of visitors, which grew by 20 per cent during 1983-88, for instance. Although the total number of visitors remained low, tourist agencies could identify a potential for growth. The Outer Hebrides Tourist Board brochure describes the scenic attractions. 'A rocky east coast of dark rolling hills, trout-filled lochs in the centre, and on the west long beaches of white sand washed by Atlantic rollers' is an accurate summary. In addition, the Celtic traditions of the islands are recognised as offering unique experiences to visitors. In a letter to the weekly *Stornoway Gazette* a correspondent from Sydney (N.S.W.) asserted in October 1988: 'The greatest attraction is the people, and the customs which they maintain.' One of the most deep-seated customs is the observance of Sunday as a day of rest. A result of this tradition is that no air or ferry links were available to the Uists on Sundays. At the time of our study, however, the ferry company was proposing, in the interests of operating efficiency, to provide Sunday sailings. In the ensuing debate, numerous public meetings were held, and considerable media interest was eventually aroused. Local religious leaders were quick to voice their case. John Smith, Church of Scotland minister in Lochmaddy, North Uist, declared: 'We believe that there are values in life which come before mere money-making, and so tourism must be viewed in its proper perspective. It is not for outsiders to impose changes on our way of life for their own commercial gain or convenience.' But various hoteliers and shopkeepers argued that times were changing and that a daily ferry connection was inevitable. So, indeed, it proved to be and the Sunday sailings are now a fact. Yet, for a time, we had an interesting example of cultural tradition acting as a brake on tourism and therefore as an indirect environmental safeguard.

Further north, just beyond our study area, in the large island of Lewis and Harris, a similar cultural conflict appeared in the early 1990s, when the CADISPA fieldwork in Scotland had concluded. Here, tourism and Sunday transport made up one specific issue, while another concerned a plan for Europe's largest quarry. The primeval hills of Harris contain, among other minerals, large quantities of anorthosite which is much in demand for road construction. At the southern tip of Harris, the hill Roineval rises sharply to nearly 500 metres above the nearby sea. Its potential mineral value has been recognised by Redland Aggregates, a company based in the East Midlands of England. In planning to remove Roineval in its entirety, the company had to defuse opposition by suggesting that its quarry would provide a welcome rise in employment. This idea excited some Harris residents, one of whom wrote in early 1992: 'Where there is a choice of real long-term employment, conservation must take a step back.' But other local people took a different view when it became clear that the bulk mineral carriers which would sail regularly from the proposed harbour at Lingerbay, beside Roineval, might occasionally do so on Sundays. Once again, culture seemed about to become the ally of conservation.

Reflections

The CADISPA study area and its communities remain much in our minds, long after the project's focus has moved on to Southern Italy and North-Eastern Spain. What happens by way of so-called development in the Uists and the Flow Country is repeated in other peripheral regions of Europe. The economic weakness of marginal communities means that they are the ones most likely to welcome any employment opportunities which result from local resource exploitation, regardless of long-term environmental consequences. For some people at least, the temptations of technocracy and consumerism are altogether too strong to resist. But, all too often, the promised jobs are less numerous or less secure than originally hoped. What is more, large-scale schemes for rock quarrying or for afforestation with exotic species have a certain irreversibility about them. Their visual and ecological effects continue long after the originators of these schemes have passed into oblivion.

Beyond these important concerns lie even deeper problems. The capitalist system 'is obsessed', as the Belgian writer Thierry Verhelst has put it, 'with productivity, consumerism, and competitiveness', without regard for either environmental integrity or cultural self-determination. It was to these two concepts that the CADISPA team kept returning during the period of the pilot study in Northern Scotland. What was especially obvious to us was the need for a genuine eccentric ethic; a need which is as great in remote rural communities as in major urban centres. In the conurbations, after all, there are green movements and organisations, reacting against the extremes of conservation. Meanwhile, people out on the periphery are still moving towards conservation, and away from the older ethic of collective prudence. Yet it would also be wise to appreciate the strengths which the periphery possesses, quite apart from its pure air, peacefulness and natural beauty. In the North of Scotland, the fact is that some of the traditional values of society remain evident, although considerably diminished. The notion of frugality, for instance, persisted until recently in the recycling of domestic materials (peat fuel ash used as fertiliser, empty bottles re-used as containers). Again, the old idea of self-sufficiency is by no means dead. Crofters routinely do work in plumbing, roofing, vehicle maintenance, boat repairing and sheep shearing, to name but a few tasks. At the same time, the notion of co-operative neighbourliness is another enduring reality, since families from adjacent crofts will usually offer mutual help in such annual operations as potato planting or peat cutting for household fuel. On the islands, rather than on the Scottish mainland, a further two traditional elements serve to knit communities together. The first is religious faith, Catholic on some islands, Calvinist on others. For a significant number of islanders, it is religious faith, rather than the pursuit of materialism, which provides true self-realisation, through identification with God's will. The second element is the Gaelic language, an ancient offshoot from the main Indo-European branch. This language, even in its apparently final decline, acts both as a social cement and also as a key to a rich cultural heritage of poetry, legend and song.

While these cultural elements and value stances persist, their continuance depends upon the presence of gainful activities, generated by community members. It is here that small-scale self-help has a major role to play. The strength of crofting settlements lies in their functional diversity and sustainability. For example, where minor entrepreneurial activities are integrated with croft-related work, hope for the future is stronger, and the attraction of massive alien projects is less. It is therefore encouraging to note the growth of home-based tertiary employment in the north of Scotland, where resident writers, translators and financial consultants can now link with urban offices by telecommunications networks. Similarly, shellfish farming, tourist bed-and-breakfast ventures and self-catering cottages are just some of the varied enterprises into which crofters are diversifying within the CADISPA study area. Alongside that diversity, it is time to recognise the less tangible merits of these communities, where 'joys are determined in terms of quality of life, not standards of living.' These words of Arne Naess have been echoed more recently by Alastair McIntosh of the Centre for Human Ecology at Edinburgh University. Analysing the advantages of small-scale sustainable developments on remote Scottish islands, McIntosh likens these communities to 'old roots touched with fresh streams of living water', and asks: 'What other form of renewal is there?'

Spain: The Pyrenees
Introduction

UNTIL FRANCO'S REGIME sought investments for large-scale plantations to service the lucrative pulp and paper industry, Spain's great forests were covered with deciduous hardwoods, oaks, beech and chestnuts. Fast-growing species now cover over five million hectares, whereas hardwoods cover less than two. The new plantations have led to familiar forest fires. Monocultural practices accompanying this change have brought in pesticides and loss of wildlife. Common land is lost to industrial plantation and farmers are leaving the countryside. This is a familiar process in Third World countries such as India, Chile, Brazil, and Indonesia.

As in the Third World, people's protest movements have remonstrated against such 'forest policies'. Several thousand Galicians are protesting against the setting up of new pulpwood and paper factories. 'In Spain, as elsewhere, the only way for farmers to survive is to abandon traditional techniques, to expand, to specialize and to intensify.'[1] In Extremadura, a sparsely populated area the size of Switzerland, traditional agriculture was developed in harmony with nature. The ancient forests on the mountain slopes maintained soil fertility, prevented erosion, and regulated the micro-climate of the region. The forest supplied the fodder, firewood and cork needs of the rural people, who pruned and protected the trees.

Transhumance of livestock made use of mountain pastures in the summer and lowland ones in the winter. The areas, often communally owned, called *dehesas*, involved careful balances between agriculture, herding and forestry. But plantations have put an end to this way of life. As in the Third World, forest fires may be started by the local people trying to get back their grazing land, or to get more wages for re-planting work. High-quality food products from the *dehesas* have lost markets to industrially produced cheaper foodstuffs.

Poverty and depopulation in these areas is not tackled by trying to revitalise the old way of life within new settings, but by 'planners schooled only in straight-line solutions who see no alternative other than to stamp upon complex patterns of rural habitat the rectilinear grid of industrial agribusiness: motorway systems, high-speed rail links, strings of pylons, canalized rivers, checkerboard forests and square fenced fields. In such a regime there will be scant opportunity for the small independent farmer. The few who flourish will emerge as large-scale agribusinesses pursuing the prescribed monoculture, dependent upon a battery of chemicals and employing highly mechanized contractors.'[2] This could be the description of the so-called 'green revolution' scenario of a Third World country! As CEPA, a regional federation of small voluntary groups in Extremadura put it: 'The reciprocal relationship between humanity and nature is replaced with a blind economic reality.'

It is within such a grim, inexorable scenario that the CADISPA project was founded to see if a few can make a difference, if they can motivate the many. In fact this kind of courage and vision exemplifies all the people involved in whichever country. Can a balance be found between the best of the old community way of life and the undoubted pulls of the modern world? A fine line has to be drawn if developments are to be practical, to avoid romantic notions of the past, and to actively challenge the life styles of European urban centres. But this struggle is not only a CADISPA struggle, or even a European one. Not only do many cultures , here in Europe and in far away Third World countries, face the same threats, by the same mechanisms, but even the flavour of life that is vanishing in Europe is strangely redolent of similar moments elsewhere. It is strange to read the delightful memories of the old Pyrenean highlander, **Maximo Palacio Allue** (see p159) and feel you are almost in Asia. He talks about how wise women who could cure with herbs were considered witches; he talks about the damp of narrow weaver rooms; about how people nowadays make money, but they do not cooperate as they used to and this works against nature herself. These are opinions that could come from anywhere in the world; they come from voices that are ceasing to be heard, unless the committed and the visionary can bring a revival of the community spirit.

Pyrenees – Catalonia

ENRIQUE SEGOVIA

THE AREA IN WHICH the CADISPA project is carried out is located in the Pyrenees between the Noguera Ribagorgana valleys to the west, and the Alto Segre to the east. To the north it is bounded by the French border, and the southern boundary is in the Sierra del Montsec. This extensive area, made up of four large valleys (Noguera Ribagorgana, Noguera Palleresa and Segre, in the Ebro basin, and the Garona which is the only Atlantic valley), covers different regions or *comarcas*.

The regions of Pallars Jussá, Pallars Sobirá, Alta Ribagorça and the Valle de Aran, covering 3,717 sq. km, with a population of over 28,000, form the main area in which the project is carried out. Some activities are carried out in the periphery *comarcas* of the Alt Urgell, Cerdanya and Solsonés, extending to villages in the Aragonese strip of the Ribagorza.

Although this is an extensive region, the heart of the Alto Pyrenees and the foothills are interrelated biologically and socially. There are seasonal migrations of wildlife from one area to another: for example vultures, which nest in the Prepyrenees foothills but feed in the Alto Pyrenees in the summer. Farmers take herds of cattle from stables in the piedmont to the highland pastures.

The north-south orientation of the main valleys—except that of the Valle de Aran—also has an influence as it determines the transport and communication lines along the bottom of the valleys.

Alpine areas rise to over 3,000 metres, and have narrow glacial valleys, giving cold winters and mild summers. Rainfall is around 1,500-2,000 mm per year. The Prepyrenean foothills are separated by interior sierras, which rise to over 2,500 metres along the main river valleys. The Prepyrenean mountainous strips reaching the plains of Lérida are of medium height, full of great rocky chalky walls.

This area is the largest mountain region of Catalonia. It is still in a good state of conservation, due to its isolation. Many parts are classed as areas of European natural interest. However, it is undergoing great change due to the rise in large-scale ski tourism and the building of resort areas.

The vegetation is very diverse. The alpine zone is the highest area, with beautiful meadows. Below this is the subalpine zone, with extensive coniferous forests of Swiss pine, Scots pine, and fir. The mountain zone is the land of oak, beech and pine groves. In the southernmost part, the Mediterranean zone, the most characteristic woods are of continental ilex or holm oak, as well as submediterranean oaks, with withered leaves.

Wildlife in the open spaces of the high mountains includes changing populations of ptarmigan, brown partridge and the pale eaglet. There are also species in danger of extinction, such as the lammergeier, the Egyptian vulture, and other birds of prey. There are still a few of the mythical brown bears and also the marten, woodland grouse, Tengmalm owl and wildcat. Otters, trout and rock loach are found in the streams, which are also important areas for the breeding and hibernation of water birds.

The average population density of 7.7 inhabitants per sq.km illustrates the depopulation problem in these areas. Detailed analysis of the settlements shows that the majority of the population is concentrated in a few settlements in the valley bottoms and along the lines of communication. The areas away from these lines of communication in the bottom of the main valley, which are usually poorly served, are characterised by high depopulation and isolation. Large-scale emigration over the last fifty years has removed half the people in medium-sized villages, and almost all in more rural settlements. Only in the Alto Valle de Aran, due to its tourist industry and the ski resorts, has this trend reversed. In the high mountain areas such as the Alto Valle de Aran, the Pallars Sobirá and the Alta Ribagorça the service sector employs over 50% of the population, less than 30% in the primary sector and 5% in industry, while in the *comarcas* further to the south, which are better served, 40% are involved in the secondary sector, 40% in services and up to 10% in industry. The dialect spoken by the people is principally Catalan, but Aranese in the Valle de Aran.

The most important traditional activities have always been agriculture, livestock farming and forestry. Sheep, cattle and horse rearing have been the only way of using the huge highland meadows in summer. The livestock is brought to the lowlands in winter when the cold and snow prevent them from staying on the high plains. This was the main source of wealth in the Pyrenean valleys as the climate and uneven relief limited farming possibilities, allowing them only to cultivate some land on the valley bottom and some slopes. The small livestock farmers who did not carry out transhumance needed to supplement their income with other activities, cultivating cereals in some fields, and through market gardening, forestry, wood collection, and in some cases handicrafts in winter. Forestry is also quite important, despite the steep slopes which in many places prevented exploitation.

In the Prepyrenean outer mountains, the widespread lack of summer pasture promoted the growth of small cattle, which made use of the fallow land and private or communal mountain land. Farming in the parts of the Pyrenees with a more favourable climate was essentially based on cereals. Orchards of almonds and olives were adapted to drought and poor soils in mountain areas. These were the main reasons for poverty in these areas, which led to accelerated emigration.

Life here was hard and, with the rise of the industrial and urban culture at the beginning of the twentieth century, the complex farming systems of the mountains, adapted to the limitations of the environment, could not adapt fast enough to rapid change from the outside; and the villages crumbled into ruin. As a result people left in search of better incomes. The terraces, which they had worked so hard to build, became ruined and the crops were lost. The fall in population caused by the disorganisation of their social structures lured in outside investment and speculation.

Hydroelectric companies built huge dams everywhere, taking advantage of the power of the water to generate electricity. The profits from the energy generated do not benefit the region as they are sent mainly to the large industrial centres and cities. However, the flooding of the valley bottoms not only destroys the best land for agriculture, but also ruins livestock management in an area far greater than that covered by the water, as land exploitation by livestock demands a balance between use of the large highland pastures and that of the valley lowland. These imbalances have accelerated the rural exodus. In addition, the uncontrolled retention of water has meant that some parts of the rivers have dried up or flow irregularly, destroying life in the river and also the potential for fishing.

Tourism is one of the most important activities at the present time, both in winter and in summer. The area has begun to receive visitors from the large cities. Since the large investment that the infrastructure requires also comes from outside, the income goes out in the same way that it comes in. So few mountain people participate in this supposed development. In traditionally tourist areas such as the Valle de Aran, it has been observed that when the young come into contact with urban thinking they are uprooted from their traditional culture, and choose to emigrate.

Mass tourism, which requires large-scale housing developments, has a severe impact on the ecology and landscape of the fragile mountain regions, increasing the risk of erosion. However, it must be added that in recent years the lack of snow has opened the eyes of local people, and they now see a region's economy cannot be based, like a banana republic, on a single industry such as ski-tourism.

Miquel Rafa and
DEPANA

INTERVIEW BY ENRIQUE SEGOVIA

MIGUEL RAFA IS A twenty-five year-old biologist, born in Barcelona. From a very early age his hobby has been the observation and study of nature. In 1982 he joined the conservation association DEPANA, where he began working on different topics all related to the protection of nature. In 1987 he became General Secretary of DEPANA until the organisation grew larger, when the post was changed to that of Executive Director. At present he is the CADISPA-Catalonia Project's coordinator.

Miguel Rafa talks about his relationship with the world of conservation.

'My parents have always been very keen on excursions, which has meant that since I was very small I have had direct contact with nature, especially in the mountains. When I was only three months old my parents took me, in the middle of winter, to a peak 2500 metres up in the Pyrenees; I suppose it was my first ascent. After that I carried on making many excursions with my club, the Catalonian Excursionist Club. All this has made me appreciate and love nature. When I was ten years old I went on some camps organised by DEPANA and I bought my first pair of binoculars. From then on, this relationship became an obsession. I read everything I could lay my hands on about ecology, all about birds and mammals. The fact that it was very easy for me to get to the countryside—we lived in La Molina, an area in the Eastern Pyrenees, for two years—made it easier for me to get to know the Catalonian environment. And from this knowledge, which was based on being seduced by the wild beauty of nature, I became aware of the destruction of it all. When you are a young adolescent, changing the world does not seem so difficult.

'DEPANA, the League for Natural Heritage Defence (Lliga per a la Defensa del Patrimoni Natural), is the most important and well-known ecological association in Catalonia. It was founded in 1976 and is, therefore, one of the oldest ecological associations in Spain. Until five years ago, with barely 300 members, it had very little capacity to influence.

'There was then a change in the management, and a new team of younger and more dynamic people took over. We began training a team of people who only worked for the organisation, who worked professionally for conservation. I was the first, which meant a great responsibility for me and additional effort, since I was trying to finish my biology degree.

'DEPANA has worked above all for the conservation of the last natural spaces of Catalonia. The industrialisation of this area, as well as the tourist boom along the coast in the sixties and the seventies has caused numerous ecological problems. Founded at the same time as the renewal of democracy in Spain, DEPANA has also worked on the preparation of new laws and basic regulations about environmental protection and planning for its territory, and has been linked closely with Catalonia's autonomous government. It must be said that this has not always been a good or an easy relationship. Other topics which have been worked on have been biodiversity protection, forestry resources, the environmental impact of roads, reservoirs, and tourist facilities.

'One of the main topics for DEPANA has been environmental education: camps—like the ones I went to as a child—courses, day courses, lectures and nature excursions. The magazine we publish quarterly has also been important for this function, as well as to attract more members. We have worried about our image. A few years ago it became clear it was necessary to break with the "ecological image of long-hair and utopia", and give a positive image, of seriousness and sound ideas.

'I think that we have now achieved this. The design of ecological projects on a scientific basis has reached the point of being able to achieve success. And at the same time our economic resources have multiplied. At present, DEPANA is made up of about 4,000 members; there are eight people on the staff, and our finances are under control. All this allows us to tackle many more topics, which previously we had to pass up.

'Most important for us are the conservation projects. DEPANA has carried out projects such as "Pollo Blava", the reintroduction of Purple Gallinules in the wild, which are reproducing naturally. Another important project which is under way is the Delta del Llobregat Project, where we are trying to retrieve and protect the last marshes of this greatly damaged area, which lies right next to Barcelona. The project is based on the creation of reserves which are equipped to be a Nature School, for a million school children who live less than twenty minutes from the area. The building of an observatory has already started. Another project which we finished this Spring, consisted of the restoration of a wood on the banks of the river Llobregat. Next Autumn we will begin another wood restoration project on the banks of the beautiful Banyoles lake to the north of Catalonia. And, of course, there is also the CADISPA project.

'What happened was that DEPANA had been collaborating with

ADENA-WWF España on several different conservation projects in the Pyrenees through a great friend of mine, Pablo Xandri. We had worked together, for example, to conserve a feeding haunt of eagles and lammergeiers, which is very important for the latter species, as well as to report on the felling of some forest areas, the construction of a dam in a virgin alpine lake to make artificial snow, etc. One day we met in Zaragoza to talk about the possibility of developing an environmental education project in the Catalonian Pyrenees, in accordance with the proposal that had reached ADENA through the Education Department. A few meetings later, the CADISPA-Catalonia project was under way.

'The Pyrenees is the last great natural zone of Catalonia, and the north of the Iberian Peninsula. Ski resorts and urban developments are being built which have a serious impact on the fragile ecosystems of the mountain tops. At the same time, the rural population is losing its identity. With a population which is getting older and older, many have left the small villages to live miserably in flats in the city or in the bigger towns in the valley. In this area, ecologists have until now only denounced serious ecological damage, or the loss of another species. Such statements were rejected by the rural population, sometimes manipulated by the mayors and local bosses. During 1989-1990 there was a great controversy caused by the cutting back of the protected areas of the National Park of Aigües Tortes, with the aim of expanding ski resorts. The conservation-development debate erupted in a serious way. DEPANA headed the opposition. This gave us the opportunity to see that it was essential to have a change of strategy in our nature protection work, to make the local people the main leaders interested in conservation in the Pyrenees. To do this it was—and still is—essential that the necessary information reaches people; in short, to carry out environmental education. And it was clear that the public administration system would not do this by itself.

'To start with, it is not easy in an area where very little environmental education has been carried out. But an important factor has been the freedom and the flexibility ADENA-WWF España gave us to design the project according to our own criteria and knowledge of the area. Another essential point was that almost from the first minute we got in touch with Joan Vazquez and the "Escola de Natura L'Arc de Sant Martí". They have had many years of experience working in a mountainous rural area, and it has basically been they who have prepared the proposals, materials and, later, carried out the activities. They have worked very hard, in an environment which does not always give easy rewards. There were also financial difficulties, but these were finally overcome. Best of all, throughout the formative period of the Project we have been gaining experience, learning from our mistakes, from the difficulties, doing new things (for example, we had never made a film before) and also learning to work with new people in the Pyrenees, and in the other CADISPA teams. In the end this is the best reward.'

Has there been any improvement thanks to CADISPA?

'This year we are carrying out an external evaluation study of the actitivies. We will be able to see how to continue. The feeling is that we must carry on working. We knew this from the beginning: environmental education cannot be achieved in a few months. Another thing which we can see is that it is necessary to provide materials and training for those who are teaching, so that they themselves work with the young people. On the other hand, specific development proposals must be got under way: the adult population needs to check the feasibility of the messages, to see beyond the words—to see that the ecologists "build" something which is visible and tangible. This will be our future challenge. Now small groups are beginning to form in some villages, ideas about protection of nature have become incorporated into local politicians' speeches. This is visible improvement.'

Tourism: A Sustainable Future, or Destruction of the Pyrenees?

MIQUEL RAFA

LIFE IN THE PYRENEES was never easy. Forty or fifty years ago it was not unusual to be cut off for weeks due to a heavy fall of snow. However, people survived then with their livestock, agriculture and forestry resources. Now they find it extremely difficult to do so. Everything has changed, and change is needed for survival. It is not easy for the population of the Pyrenees, which is getting older and older. You cannot ask an ageing shepherd or farmer to change what he has done all his life; and the young people have moved to the city to study, or to look for work. Most of them do not want to go back to living and working in the mountains.

The main cause is the new economic situation, especially Spain's integration into the EC. Mountain livestock is mainly cattle; the farmers cannot compete with central European producers, with their industrial-ised production systems. Mountain agriculture is in a similar situation. Only a radical change, making it easy to produce quality products, could make a difference. But in order to do this, co-operatives must be formed, and markets must be found—which is very difficult to do if there are no young people willing to begin the process. The forestry sector is also going through similar problems: compared to the French market, prices for wood are not competitive.

Furthermore, tourism is becoming the sole industry in the area. Over the last twenty years, alpine skiing has been virtually the only leitmotif of tourism in the Pyrenees. At present, in the Catalonian Pyrenees alone there are twelve ski resorts, most of which were built recently. All of them have been created by private enterprise speculators, usually by urban-planning promoters from Barcelona or Madrid. Around the ski resorts tourist complexes have been built: apartment blocks, terraces of houses, top-quality chalets and shopping centres. These areas are located at the bottom of the ski slopes, are usually at some distance from the villages, which are located lower down in the bottom of the valleys. Indeed the ski resorts' economic profitability comes from the sale of urban complexes, and apartments, rather than from the sports facilities. Land for buildings has been purchased at very low prices, since the local inhabitants had no better prospects. The capital gains generated were very tempting for investors who did not come from the mountains. The local inhabitants have, of course, not become rich, nor gained any benefit from the situation.

Naturally the environmental impact of these resorts is very great. There is no sewage purifying system in any of these ski resorts, although they become full of temporary residents. Below the level of the ski resorts the mountain streams become polluted, and the water sources above dry out when the water is used to supply these artificial villages. The subalpine forest areas where these urban developments are usually found are affected by the building of new ski slopes and access roads. Important forest fauna is disturbed and disappears from the area, such as the Tengmalm owl, the black woodpecker, the pine marten and the bear. The great birds of prey also disappear, or die from hitting the ski lift cables. The ski slopes, built over alpine meadows, drive out ptarmigan, linnets and the ibex, and ultimately destroy the meadows by erosion.

This destruction of nature is very similar to what happened along most of the Spanish Mediterranean coastline. The tourist 'boom' of the 1960s and 1970s destroyed the coast, and it also destroyed the tourism possibilities of the 1990s. Present day tourism demands a higher environmental and scenic quality: clean water, natural areas, wild animals, and villages which haven't been corrupted by tourism. This comparison is very valid; the actual inhabitants of the Pyrenees know that they must not fall into this trap, but they still cannot clearly see other possibilities which do not involve the great infrastructures of tourism.

In any case, things are changing. Snow is a very variable factor according to the seasons and it can be catastrophic when the entire year's profits depend on it. Lately, artificial snow cannons have saved the situation somewhat, although they add another ecological problem: the water catchments destroy the alpine lakes and mountain streams. But not everything can be based on ski resorts, especially if in this way we are mortgaging for ever the countryside and wildlife of this valley. In any case, not all of the Pyrenees can be used for skiing, especially some areas in the southernmost mountain ranges.

Another increasingly important tourist activity is adventure sports. In the highest area of the Noguera Pallars river, rafting and thaw-water riding of the rapids have become a great industry. From the start, the impact is much less, given that these sports do not require special facilities, although the amount of people who are beginning to practise these sports could endanger some areas along the river banks. Other activities of this type, such as abseiling, mountain cycling and pony trekking, also have similar characteristics: if the numbers are kept down they can be compatible with conservation—the very nature of these sports implies the need to preserve the countryside and wildlife.

As for accommodation, the Pyrenees are ideal for developing farmhouse residences in which visitors can stay with the local people. This allows the farmer to get a supplement to what he earns from agriculture, thus helping the family economy. This rural tourism involves visits and trips of a cultural nature, to Roman hermitages, traditional fiestas, and nature walks to national parks. Without doubt, this type of tourism is what best represents the integration of development and conservation, but there are still very few enterprises which offer this. One of the problems is the investment which the farmers must undertake to improve rooms in their houses. Another is the lack of knowledge about managing hotels, which complicates the setting up of this kind of tourism.

Without doubt tourism, together with the production of high-quality food products, must be the path to follow to allow sustainable development to take place in the Pyrenees. The question is to see if this will happen in time. CADISPA has to work through educational programmes, and support those practical enterprises that could be used as models for eco-development projects.

Life in the Pyrenees: My Personal Experience by Maximo Palacio Allue (age 67)

INTERVIEW BY RICARDO AZÓN AND DOMINGO GÓMEZ

TRADITIONALLY, LIFE IN THE PYRENEES has been based on a self-sufficient economy. We tried to produce everything we needed. There was no money to buy things. Food was scarce. We made *farinetas* from maize, flour with milk and potatoes, there was *chorizo*, spicy sausages, eggs, meat, cheese and potatoes. We also had vegetables and some legumes during the summer, which were grown in the garden. Clothing was very poor, and was patched time and time again—until you did military service no one knew what a suit was. Boots or leather shoes were rarely worn; sandals and canvas shoes were used.

The social unit was the home, whose members gathered around the hearth. The grandparents were the most important, and while they were alive they were the owners, then the house was passed down to the eldest child.

The traditional economy was ruled by various local institutional obligations which worked perfectly and everyone took turns in taking charge—this was obligatory and could not be avoided. These institutions managed the livestock, the mountain, the irrigation and the local works. Most of the work was carried out by the inhabitants who, according to their estate, had to put in a certain number of hours of work.

They gathered what the land provided them in summer, and in winter, when there was little work, they emigrated to France to buy something they needed for the house: a sewing machine, wall clocks, mules, bicycles, cowbells.

In my house, as in most at that time, we were short of money and so the young used to work as day labourers for the large farms. A typical job for the people of Biescas was to go and scythe or mow grass in the Valle de Tena. In fact, my first job was mowing grass in Piedrafita de Tena. I also worked with timber: cutting it and storing it for the timber dealers to send elsewhere.

There was a time when the hydro-electric companies started to carry out works, and we realised that this was a good way to earn some steady wages. We were country men without any training and they sent us wherever they needed us: many went to work in the tunnels (to lay the water pipes to the power stations) as they thought they would earn more money. Boring through mountains was hard, dangerous work. Every day one's life was at risk—no one appreciated that at all.

Life greatly improved in the village with the arrival of work. For example, during the immediate post-war years not one single new house was built, due to the lack of money. Later, building and investment in works began—all this coincided with the boom in the 1960s, which was a time of much growth, and one could see a lot of money floating around. Everyone was very anxious to work and to save, as there had never been so many things to spend one's money on before. You wouldn't believe it, but the village meetings were held around a radio listening to *cante jondo* (a type of flamenco singing) on Radio Madrid.

When the work of the hydro-electric power stations was coming to an end, people began to look for other work; this coincided with the flourishing of industry in Sabiñanigo. They chose a few people who knew their way around the mountains to maintain the dams in the high mountain. A brigade of about fifteen people was set up, in which I was one; from October to June, we had to live in camps and walk round the mountain repairing the dams. They sent up food and other necessities by mules once a week. From 1980 onwards they did this by helicopter and we could go down to the village at weekends.

It was a strange life spending so much time up in the mountains with nature; in such a situation a man becomes bestialised and irritable, and living together becomes more and more difficult, and towards the end of the period you almost end up fighting with each other.

One consequence of life spent in the high mountain is that it awakens interests which were probably there before but which were dormant. Being in constant touch with nature, you begin to notice many things which were right in front of your nose before, but which you didn't even look at. I became interested in animals and plants, and started learning their names.

When I was young I had seen otters in the Rio Gallego, between Biescas and Bubal. They were abundant. The last one I saw was in 1960. They disappeared with the construction of the dams, as otters need a lot of water and they like it turbulent. The poachers hunted them in the grilles of the channels.

I also witnessed the appearance of the marmot in the Pyrenees in the 1950s. They started to be seen in the high mountain in the Valle de Tena which went into France.

When you are alone in the mountain and you look back into your memory, you recall the former way of life, tradition, and the customs, how you lived as children. You recall your native language, the old dialect—the aragonese *fabla*—the vernacular names of the plants and animals—the names formerly used, which you cannot remember when you are back in civilisation.

As a result I rediscovered my grandparent's language. When we were young we thought they spoke very badly, but they knew the dialect of their land, and they spoke it; they barely knew any other language.

My interest in medicinal plants developed because I knew a whole range of vernacular names but I did not know what they corresponded to—the *cardonera* means *acebo* (holly), *taxo* means *tejo* (yew), *mochera* means *los serbales* (service tree), etc. Then you begin to learn the Latin and the Spanish names, and you discover that many used to be used to cure various illnesses and wounds. I used to scour the Biescas area, which is full of curative plants which were formerly known and used. While doing this I realised something very curious: that all those who had a reputation as witches were those who knew the medicinal plants and cured with them. However, it was the majority of people who were the real witches as they were ignorant and uneducated.

There is a lot of legend surrounding witches, but they really did exist. I still know two people who have a reputation for being witches, and who lead a very solitary life, and who cure with plants. I also know two young people who have this knowledge but who are afraid to say anything in case they are taken for witches.

There is a lot of superstition surrounding these subjects. For instance it is believed that if you hang a bear's or boar's foot, or 'witches' thistle' (*Carlina acaulis*) in the door you will be safe from witches.

A special stone or 'espantabrujas' (scarewitches) is placed on the chimneys; according to the experts, this is to stop the witches leaving the house, once they have come in by the door. Many people used hallucinatory plants, whose effects were little understood, in order to escape and to dream, so giving rise to the so-called witches' sabbath. They rubbed them on, because they were afraid, and could feel drowsy for up to 48 hours or dream that they were flying. They used aconite, foxglove (in very small amounts), stinking hellebore, etc.

I will speak a little about the weaving mills, a traditional industry which has been lost in Biescas but was in former times very important to the economy.

Their origin goes back a long time: data exist indicating that there were mills in the year 1300. At first the cloth was very rough, but it soon began to be produced for export and a wide infrastructure was developed: it was sent to Italy, the south of France, Valencia and Navarra. They managed to use 10,000 *arrobas* (115,000 kg) of wool a year in Biescas. The quality gradually improved, and there was a body which checked the quality of the mills in accordance with the rules.

A new occupation was created: the *pelaires* or wool manufacturers, and today the people from Biescas are still referred to as 'Pelaires' by people in the rest of the region. There were closed, hierarchical family clans which must have been rich and powerful: Aragon's strength in the Middle Ages was based on wool exports.

The mills developed greatly and they began to weave silk with wool, and the famous 'strip' bedspreads of Biescas arose from this, of which a few pieces still exist.

In the eighteenth century there was a severe decline, I believe because of the plague. In the San Pedro district of Biescas, there were only seventeen houses left out of sixty-four; in the census one can see that in fifteen years there were virtually no births. There was a terrible decline in everything.

Another reason was the deterioration in the weaving industry due to certain privileges. The weavers were protected by the Crown of Aragon and they did not pay any taxes or do military service. As armies were needed, the Crown offered the title of master weaver to anyone who went to war. As a result people who did not know the occupation began to work, and so the quality worsened and the markets disappeared and they could not compete with Catalan or French weavers.

The mills were in small, damp places, with little ventilation or light, and they used premises which could not be used for anything else. It must have been a fairly unhealthy occupation. There is a saying '*hombre alto y de mal color, tejedor*' (a tall, pale man must be a weaver).

Dyes were prepared using people's knowledge about the plants in the area. At least forty or fifty plants were used for this job. There was an important dyeing industry and large premises were needed to house the enormous vats and the necessary water. There were three principal dyers' shops as well as six or seven families engaged in the business, either working on their own or as employees.

Related to the textile industry were the fulling-mills, which took advantage of the water's power to prepare flax and hemp, beating the material with huge mallets, but which was also used for finished fabrics such as blankets, etc. There were at least three or four places with fulling-mills, although documents are now appearing which cite others.

There were many other craftsmen, such as silversmiths, harness makers, blacksmiths, saddle-pad makers, carpenters, etc. There were even female craftsmen such as cobblers and carpenters, who worked for several generations in the same house.

Today they are nothing but shades of the past. Life has evolved in such a way that the crafts are lost. The most important ones, such as the saddle-pad makers and the harness makers, disappeared when the use of mules succumbed to mechanisation. The blacksmiths turned to carpentry using metal and the numerous carpenters disappeared with the arrival of machinery; one new workshop had more work than all the craftsmen.

The mills completely disappeared in 1950. In 1936 there were four weaving houses: Casa Bernadino, Casa Brecas, Casa Mercader, and I think Casa Latas. They had little work; they only made sacks for the country and covers to collect the grass. With the arrival of mechanisation in the country and the change in the farm implements they were lost for good.

The craft tools were lost in the post-war period: people came and they exchanged for fruit the tools they had in their homes—the rest were burnt. People showed no interest in them as they thought they were of no use.

Other occupations disappeared with the mills: there were dyers in the village until 1936, at which time there were still two families, one of which still has all the associated infrastructure.

The beginner's course in textile crafts, organised by the CADISPA-Aragon project and Biescas Council, was a good idea and the people's response has been positive. We have discovered various things: that there were itinerant weavers, who used to go round the villages preparing the material to be weaved later. There was also a craftsman called a bedspread maker, who during the last century, made bedspreads to order when there were weddings, but we do not know what these bedspreads were like.

The weaving course has awoken a lot of interest, and many people have remembered things that they knew when they were younger and which they had forgotten. It is waking people up and opening up a way to bring back the textile traditions of the village. I am sure that we will manage to revive local crafts—young people are becoming interested in them.

Publicity is needed in order to carry on with this; once people start to learn well, a weaving school could be set up. However, if quality is not obtained, it is not going to be very successful economically. We need good teachers, to teach the young and for organising summer schools.

They are thinking of setting up a museum, but they need somewhere to put it. This could provide someone in the village with a job, and a crafts workshop could be established in the lower floors in order to promote and foster the museum itself and the mills.

I believe that the greatest change in the way of life in recent years has arisen from disillusionment. The highlander has come to the conclusion that one should work less and live better. He is trying to earn more money and spend it, but by working the least possible, attempting to work in the summer and in winter claim unemployment benefit.

People today lack initiative: they do not want to set up companies or businesses, they want to be employed, be paid and not have to worry about anything. This means that people from outside come and invest in the area, and this is dangerous because in the long term the important things are in their hands: the camp sites, petrol stations, hotels, restaurants. When local people begin to invest the market is flooded. Tourism is not doing well because prices have risen and the quality of the developments, food and service have dropped.

In addition, we have become used to asking the authorities for everything and they are inundated; perhaps that is why they only make short-term plans, without attacking the root of the problem.

In the past, the customs and traditions kept a certain order which we could all follow because our subsistence depended on it. Doing things on an individual basis does not work: we have seen how the present-day individualism has led to a breakdown in society as a whole, a society which has existed for centuries. Everyone just earns money—co-operation with others is missing, and this works to the detriment of the environment.

Formerly inhabitants got together to repair paths, a practice which should be revived today—you can get to many places with cars but you cannot enjoy the mountain. Also, there are places which lose their charm if you drive there. I would put chains along the tracks to prevent cars using them, thus completely banning tourists from them, only allowing them to be used for forestry and livestock needs.

The future of the Pyrenean culture will be lost if we do not manage to lead a modern life but at the same time conserve traditions. We must educate and raise the awareness of the population, and do this quickly, before there no longer remain people who know this culture. Today we lead hurried lives and we get many things, but we are not happy and relaxed. People worry little about our culture; we should bring back the traditional *estamentos* (a legislative body in Aragon), communal work, the old posts of responsibility, such as that of the *mayoral* (head of a district), who was responsible for maintaining and defending the traditions.

Portugal: Mértola
Introduction

CLOSE TO THE ALGARVE, where north European tourists flock in their numbers to take the sun and sand, stands the ancient town of Mértola, once the centre of Moorish culture in Portugal, and the home of a colourful and gifted people. Mértola and its people face not an invasion from the outside—the fate of many unfortunate people elsewhere in the world—but its equally destructive opposite force—the sucking away of its future, its young people. Village after village in its region have been 'closed down' by the authorities, as people leave for Lisbon, for the prosperous north, or elsewhere. Its famous river, the Guadiana, a beautiful waterway which carried the region's crafts and produce, which linked its people, and which brought fish and birds to its waters, now carries mostly a burden of pollution from industries to the north, and in Spain. Nearby stand the ruins of Mina de San Domingos, turned into a poisoned, bleak wasteland by the British mining company, where the old jobless miners are waiting 'for death to come and take them'.

The story of Mértola is not even newsworthy, because there are so many such places all over the world where modern industry, after having taken what the land had to offer, and made it unfit for the old way of life, then takes away the young to its centres, to help repeat the process of destruction elsewhere. What is newsworthy is what the people are doing to revive their town and their culture. For **Jorge Revez**, president of ADPM, Mértola's leading NGO in the struggle to recover, the main fight is against social injustice—though he has also brought the birds back to his Guadiana. For **Claudio Torres**, archaeologist, who has abandoned university cloisters to come to live in Mértola, reviving the culture of the town and finding jobs for people are all part of living archaeology, since the strong link with social reality brings true knowledge. Here we find a synthesis of science, social action for the benefit of others, and a social investigation into the structure of knowledge! For **Senhora Adélia**, the old weaver, who has now taught a younger generation of girls a dying art, it is enough to find meaning in work that so many people, both the locals and a constant stream of visitors, consider good and beautiful.

Jorge Revez
President of ADPM

INTERVIEWED BY PAULO FARIA

JORGE REVEZ IS THE President of ADPM, The Association for the Defence of Mértola's Heritage. The key question is what must be preserved, and for whom?

'Obviously, what must be preserved is what exists—the natural resources, including the fauna, the flora, geological resources, and even our cultural values. These things must be preserved in a dynamic way.

'For whom? First of all, for the local people, in order to serve those who live here, who are born here, who die here, who are part of this community. Secondly, we must preserve in order to develop, and this is important mainly for those who visit the country. In fact, Mértola possesses a very important heritage which can trigger its economic development. Preservation must benefit both the residents and the visitors.'

The issue of conservation raises another very important question: Mértola has suffered depopulation. This can be seen as a result of the lack of a sound economy, which would enable people to stay here. Will the preservation of Mértola's heritage hinder economic investments within the county? Instead of development, isn't it possible that conservation will contribute to economic stagnation, and consequently accelerate the process of depopulation?

'Obviously, we are taking that risk. But, if we want to develop an area (here or anywhere else), there is a choice to be made: either we take the path that guarantees success—which is what has been happening all over Portugal and even all over the Western World. This is the path of producing mass consumer products and uniformity (for example, clothing and food industries are always profitable). Or we take some risks and choose an alternative path, relying on the fact that people in our society are increasingly searching for different and genuine products. Obviously, this path takes longer to bear fruit. But, although it is a long-term process, we in Mértola have decidedly chosen it—and we have already, I think, tasted the first fruits.

'We must also remember that this area, the so-called poor lands of

Guadiana, was totally abandoned for a long, long time. The few activities that remained also contributed to the desertification, both physical and human. Any effort to reverse this process could never be successful in a short period of time. It takes many more than ten or fifteen years (and that is the 'age' of our project here) in order to fight successfully against the effects of fifty years of complete abandonment. We have been, since the 25th of April (on 25th April the revolution overthrew the fascist regime in Portugal), making up for the lack of development of the previous five or six decades, but the 'positive' outputs are yet to come.'

One of Perez's main aims is to reach external markets, both with products, and also with tourism.

'Indeed it is so. We do not own Mértola County (what a thought!), so we must not act in a feudal way towards its culture and heritage. The Batalha Monaster (a very famous medieval Portuguese monument), for example, does not belong only to the people of Batalha—every Portuguese has the right to visit it; and the same is true of Mértola. Everyone has the right to enjoy all the good things, wherever they are. Our role here is to take advantage of this universal right of enjoyment in order to make Mértola profit from it, always assuring that this right does not become destructive.'

Guadiana
ADPM's project follows several trends—ecological improvement is obviously one of them. For instance, the Guadiana river is nowadays heavily polluted, and the human activities linked with it are being lost; there are fewer and fewer fishermen in it. Can ADPM save the river and the people and communities that depend on it?

'Our development project is a global one, in the sense that it involves all the living forces, social partners and resources of the county—and this is the only way to make it work. Our global aim is to enable all the ten thousand inhabitants of Mértola to participate in this vast and rich living eco-museum. And the Guadiana river will be a fundamental feature of this living eco-museum. The river has always been important. It was the first 'road' linking the county with the outside world. Lately, people had turned their backs on it. But now its potential as a development factor is again being recognised. ADPM wants, first of all, to create a protected area that will cover the Guadiana valley.

'Obviously, we think of the Guadiana as a whole. But we must start by protecting the areas which are still more or less pristine (in terms of their fauna and flora) and so have economic potential. One of these areas is the

Guadiana valley within Mértola county. Only eight days ago a deer was killed near the Guadiana: this means that we can still find here rare species which can certainly attract tourists. But we must be careful. As we promote the natural beauties of Mértola, we may well be sealing its doom. We do not want Mértola turned into a new Algarve. So we are fighting to get the authorities to create a protected area in the Guadiana valley, which would enable us to control tourism. If this is not done, we are at the mercy of all kinds of aggression: touristic investments, eucalyptus planting, oil presses, pulp and paper factories and domestic sewers polluting the Guadiana. And there are no laws to prevent this pollution.'

The majority of causes contributing to the destruction of the Guadiana are situated outside the county. What can ADPM do outside the county to save the river? The Guadiana has its source in Spain; it receives the domestic sewage from Badajoz, Mérida and other Spanish and Portuguese cities and towns. ADPM's message must reach these people to get some results.

'First of all, we had to create a public image to enable us to make ourselves heard by the authorities and the local people. Only by getting people's recognition can we aim to tackle such a vast problem as the preservation of the Guadiana. Once we became known, we could face the authorities and make our demands. We started by making a documentary film on the Guadiana, showing it from its source to the mouth, illustrating two aspects: the pollution sources and their destructive effects, but also the fact that there are still long reaches of the river that have been preserved. So if the pollution stops, the Guadiana can be a source of economic development for this border region between Spain and Portugal.

'Furthermore, we have worked with all the schools situated near the river on the Portuguese side. We have had meetings with the local authorities, both Portuguese and Spanish, trying to enforce the revision of the hydrographic agreement between Spain and Portugal, because it does not mention the pollution problems or the using of rivers as sources of economic development. We are sensitising the populations when nothing else can be done, and acting on a legal level when possible.'

Using the river as a source of development is an important feature of ADPM's work. As a result of this, ADPM and the Municipality of Mértola are investing money on the building of a traditional boat that will operate on the Guadiana.

'It's a project that has two main aspects: in the first place, the boat will be used to make programmed excursions on the river between Mértola and Vila Real de Santo Antonio (at the mouth of the river) and back. This will mean the promotion of the river on touristic terms. Secondly, this boat will be an educational vehicle, allowing us to link the marketing of tourism with the sensitising of the visitors and of residents to the conservation of our heritage.

Ecology and economics

While the project is being recognised in Portugal and even abroad, how far does the local population participate in it? In 1987 Revez launched a big campaign for the preservation of the Montagu's harrier (Circus pygargus).

'Three years after launching the campaign, the Montague's harrier population of the county had more than doubled (beforehand they were facing extinction). Of course, we can't be absolutely sure this happened because of the campaign. But the fact is that in the last few years not only the Montague's harrier population has increased—the same has happened with the griffon (*Gyps fuluus*), the white stork (*Ciconia ciconia*), the black stork (*Ciconia nigra*), and also other species from the Guadiana, mainly the lamprey and the eel—we have been trying to sensitise the fishermen in order to avoid intensive catches of these species, and things are changing.'

But the fishermen need to absorb the economic loss of not catching large numbers of lamprey and very young eels. Are they prepared to make this sacrifice?

'Not yet, because this problem goes beyond us. There are still about fifty families in Mértola county that depend directly on the river, scattered through the various villages near it. We know that the belly comes first, and culture comes only second. We cannot ask a fisherman to choose between his survival and the conservation of the environment, national or local.

'Furthermore, this is a problem that has to do with the action of intermediaries. They come here and buy all the fish that local fishermen can catch, and the more the better. Then they sell the fish at a high price in the big cities, and earn large amounts of money—but not the fishermen. The intermediaries affecting the Guadiana are exactly the same ones that destroyed the life in the Minho river (in the north of Portugal). When there was nothing else to catch there, they moved here. We have tried to convince the authorities to act, but they don't—mainly because Portuguese legislation in these matters is not clear.

'So this is another example of how fragile this project is, and how it depends on the politics adopted by the Government for the development of these regions. The Government must choose the kind of development which is adequate for each region, and reinforce it. It must not try to bring together totally different ways of living in the same area, because that doesn't work. For example, the whole of our project can go down the drain if the shooting-range for the army is installed here.'

Eco-tourism
The project involves tourism. But the tourists may prefer the seaside and the beaches, instead of going to Mértola, where the only fresh air comes from the polluted river...

'Right now tourists still prefer the beach, as opposed to coming to the countryside, to more under-developed areas—here, a tourist still can't find a private bathroom in his hotel. But a new kind of tourist is now beginning to come here seeking high-quality products, cultural products. We are not interested in the same tourists that go every summer to the Algarve, and use Mértola only as a road to reach the seaside. We want fewer tourists, but ones who are interested in our culture.'

Do not the people of Mértola feel awkward when people come from abroad to look at them, their habits and way of living, as if they were an endangered species? Don't they feel 'invaded'—even if this invasion is good in economic terms?

'We are aware of that problem. That is why we involve local people in this project. It is up to them to decide how far tourism can go, how many people they can stand visiting their homes or their churches or mosques— twenty per month or two hundred per month? They must be the ones to decide how far this can go without their feeling that this land is no longer their home, without their feeling invaded and uprooted.

'Whenever it is possible, we involve local people in the project. When there are young people from Mértola working in the project, local participation is automatically ensured. Because not only the youngsters get involved: their families, friends and neighbours know what is going on, and what are our aims. That is why we say it's important to turn Mértola into a living eco-museum. When that is done, everyone's opinions will matter, and the people themselves will come to us, telling us how far this process can go and when they have had enough. Of course, we are aware that we are taking risks...'

More jobs and fewer jobs
ADPM needs to create new jobs, to prevent people from leaving Mértola...

'Obviously I feel very unhappy when I see people from my family, my friends and my acquaintances—here we all know each other—leave the county because they cannot find good jobs. But we must behave like the mother that does not give rich gifts to her daughter when she is a child, in order to save the money to buy her a nice trousseau. Probably, some young people from the county will have to be 'sacrificed'—meaning they'll have to leave—in order to preserve the heritage of Mértola.

'Whatever development pattern we chose, some of them would have to leave anyway. It's the price we must pay for not having a Ford plant here, for example, that would give jobs to everyone but would also destroy a sustainable way of life.

'As for ADPM's role in this issue, we are trying to create jobs. How? By facilitating the rebirth of traditional activities, like weaving, that had almost vanished until we created a co-operative to teach new weavers and sell the traditional coarse-woven woollen blankets. Other traditional activities, like house-building using lath and plaster (which is typical of Alentejo), the goldsmith's art, traditional cooking techniques, pot-making—all these are slowly beginning to employ people, mainly young women, who are the most affected by the unemployment. Already dozens are employed in this way.'

The women's weaving co-operative

One of ADPM's investments is in the weaving co-operative, whose members are women. The board of ADPM also includes a lot of women, despite Portuguese society being traditionally macho.

'There is a lack of jobs in Mértola, and those able to leave do so. These are mostly the men—they have the chance to emigrate, or to go and work in industries in Lisbon, Sétubal, or in house-building in Algarve. It is much more difficult for the women to leave, for cultural reasons, and also for practical reasons—men go to Lisbon and sleep in rooms, or stay in barracks with 15 other men—it is not quite so with women, of course. So women tend to stay behind, and any project in Mértola will obviously involve more women than men. This makes things more difficult for us, because it is harder to convince women to get out of their homes and get involved.'

The fight for social justice

Revez talks about sensitising the people, principally those of Mértola county, where he was born. Has his position towards environmental issues been strongly influenced by the fact that he was born there? In other words, is defending Mértola's heritage a matter of defending his home, or are there universal values behind his position?

'Both. First of all, I've already said that everyone should have the right to use the good and beautiful things on Earth, wherever they exist—if, of course, they don't destroy them—so ADPM acts in order to defend this universal right of humankind. But I do not hide the fact that my everyday

work here has not only its material side, but also its emotional side.
Whether we like it or not, those who are born in a place 'feel it' in a
different way than those who come from abroad. Obviously, if a person
lives here for many years, after some time a complementarity is generated
between urban points of view and rural ways of thinking. But for myself,
I am still strongly influenced by the fact that relatives of mine still don't
know how to read or write; their culture is an oral culture, and I lived
with them for a long time. So all these matters regarding our heritage, I
feel about in a very strong way. For example, when the issue of Alqueva
(a large dam to be built in Alentejo, in order to irrigate the dry lands of
this region) is raised, we are perhaps the only Portuguese NGO that is in
favour of this project. It will submerge important natural areas, but it is
essential for the development of Alentejo. Besides the values of
conservation and heritage there are the social and human values, and these
are the ones that matter ultimately.

'We feel something has changed in the last few years: not only in terms
of economic development, but also in the minds of people. The way
youngsters see their homeland is now quite different from their parents'
view; they feel proud to see Mértola's name in the newspapers and on
TV, and sometimes they feel the need to tell others that they were born
in Mértola—even if they hide the fact that their parents and uncles don't
know how to write or read.'

*Perez talks passionately about this project. For him this is the project of a lifetime.
But why such passion? Is there an 'economic' reason?*

'As for the economic side of the question, all of us who are working on
this project could be earning much more money if we had chosen to do
something else, or if we had chosen to leave Mértola and move to an urban
centre. Those that stay and work on this project do so because they love
what they are fighting for. Many of them have received better offers from
elsewhere, and yet they have stayed. This is because we are not only working
and fighting on behalf of others, but also for ourselves. The more I work
here, the better I feel, both professionally and on a personal basis. That is
why we work day and night, on weekends, on vacation—all the time.

'I have been involved since I was seventeen, that is since eleven years
ago. I have had many offers, like the others involved in this project. The
fact that I keep refusing is due to the upbringing I had as a child, and the
opportunity I had to become aware, as I grew, of the injustices of the
society we live in: it is a society where some have the possibility to enjoy
life and satisfy all their needs and wishes, while others have nothing at all.
And the latter are given no possibility to change this state of affairs. It is

only just, humane and logical that those who have the possibility to change this pursue such a change. Not as a favour to the disinherited, but as an act of justice and as a duty towards the community and those that it gave birth to. When I was studying, I sometimes spent on books the money my parents gave me for food; I also recall that I couldn't enter the University because my parents couldn't afford it. I only managed to enter the University later, when I had earned the money myself. I was able to do so, but many of the young people of Mértola cannot. So, it is my duty to ensure that in the future others will have such opportunities.

'Beyond all doubt, the main issue is to fight against social injustice. This kind of project tends to be drowned by centralised development schemes; the decision-makers want the Gross Internal Product of Portugal to grow, even if it grows unequally; in fact, it is growing very fast in the urban centres and in the *litoral*, but not at all in the interior of the country. So this project is undoubtedly politico-cultural.'

Claudio Torres
Head of Archaeology, Mértola (CAM)

INTERVIEWED BY PAULO FARIA

MÉRTOLA IS ONE OF the poorest regions of Portugal. In less than thirty years, the county's population has been reduced to less than 10,000 inhabitants, from 36,000 thirty years ago. The process seems relentless. And yet it is here that one of the most important human science projects in Portugal is being developed.

'This project was formed after a series of chance occurrences. It led to the coming together of a group of interested people who were willing to work here. A lot of work has been done here continuously over the last few years, and our aims are now beginning to be attained. At first, we were well received by the local population, but there was no interest at all in our work: we were seen as some guys who liked to dig out pieces of broken pottery, and people didn't see any development possibility in our activity. Today things are different. There is mutual understanding, and local people have understood that this is not a mere local project: it is already one of the best archaeological investigation centres in Portugal. Now on one side, local people demand better results, and they are right to do so; and on the other side, we try to diversify our efforts, by attracting young people to work with us. In the beginning, our work was merely to rediscover a civilisation which has almost disappeared; today our field of action is more diverse. We have teams working on cultural and ethnological issues; on environmental problems; on issues related to regional development. Obviously, we keep on doing specific archaeological work, recovering monuments, working on museum projects and so on.

'A start was made with people coming from the outside. But from the beginning people from Mértola took part in this project. We made a point of that. Some of the youngsters who worked with us from the start are still with us, and others are working as Cultural Animators in the Municipality.

'Those that came here to work on the archaeological sites were people from the University of Lisbon. During my lessons there, I prepared these people (who were my pupils), choosing the ones that were to come and telling them what this work was all about. In order to make them more acceptable to the local people, it was necessary for them to understand the realities they were going to find here.'

The universities do not worry about the economic and social problems of the population of the poor areas. How does someone who was a teacher in a university come to be at the head of the Alentejo project, whose aim is not merely the scientific study of a piece of land? A project which reflects deep worries about the social and economic realities of the area which is being studied?

'I was born in the north, that is true, and in fact people tend to return to the place where they were born. But I was exiled in foreign countries for fourteen years, and my linkage with the place I was born in was broken. So when I returned to Portugal after the revolution of 1974, I plunged into the urban sphere of Lisbon and, by then, my divorce with my birthplace was already complete. That was a time of intense political activity, of the revival of the ideas of May 1968, and little by little this gave rise, in my mind, to the idea of a project of political intervention outside the big city.'

By why Mértola? Why the Alentejo? Is this not political identification with the south and not with the north?

'In Lisbon, in the years after the 25th of April, Alentejo was seen as a myth, as a lost Paradise, or a Paradise rediscovered—it depends on your point of view. Anyway, it was a place worth visiting and knowing about. So Alentejo was highly attractive to me. Also, as long as I can remember my scientific interests have always been in the late Roman and Islamic civilisations, and that also tended to draw my attention to the south of Portugal, where these civilisations left more traces. All these factors converged when I met a man called Serrao Martins, who was the President of the Municipality of Mértola, and who was also my pupil in the University. He brought me and others here to show us his beautiful homeland, and a year later this project started, initially with archaeological excavations.

'The Municipality quickly understood that this project was not only about digging up pots, but could also regenerate the economic development of this region, perhaps in a more fruitful way than anything else.'

The Islamic occupation of Portuguese territory has been scarcely studied by the universities and yet you are investing your life's work in this. Was this a calculated risk?

'When I took my degree at the university I was already interested in the historical period of Islamic occupation, centred in this region of Europe, the Mediterranean. What I lacked was experience in terms of archaeological field-work. I was a young student in Lisbon, and I wanted to know more about Islam in Portugal—an authentic 'black hole' for several centuries in our history, so little was known about it. Curiosity allowed me, through archaeology, to seek the roots of the past.

'Did the university accept this? Well, there was a strong reaction on its part because this remaking of history through archaeology was, in a way, innovative. Until a few years ago archaeology and archaeologists were one thing, history was something quite different. Let's say that the historian sometimes used, if he wanted to, some of the data provided by the archaeologist. Now, the idea of 'building' history of an entire period almost solely on archaeological data was difficult to accept. Of course, the history of the Roman Empire was written using lots of archaeological data, but it is a 'heavy archaeology', based on big monuments, big cities. The Islamic period of the Iberian Peninsula, on the contrary, is one of a rural society, little urbanised, and the answers provided by the archaeology of this period are obviously different.

'For example, when reading a text by an Islamic writer of this period, we must keep in mind that when he is speaking of a 'rich house', he is speaking of a place where he himself lives or that he has visited—if he knows how to write, then he is part of an élite, both intellectual and economic. But part of the excavations of this 'rich house' reveal to us great poverty, in contrast to the literary description of its chambers. These are the pieces of the puzzle that archaeology gives us—the ways of living of the poor, those that could not write, and so left no written traces—in a word, the people.

'We started excavating on the site of the old Moorish village centre, near the castle. Little by little, for various reasons, our intervention was requested in several spots within Mértola. We were asked to give advice, to excavate ancient ruins that were revealed. Little by little, our work was extended to all over the town. By then, we had realised that it was not possible to reverse the trend of depopulation that this region was suffering without reinforcing Mértola as its unifying pole. The only way to stop people leaving was to turn Mértola into a very strong cultural nucleus for this region, able to compete with the more distant urban centres, in terms of what the immediate culture could offer. This was our aim.

'Within the town of Mértola we have, gradually, won scientific 'control' over the urban scene, by assuming that archaeology is not only subterranean, but is also done on the surface; to understand the structure of the house we are excavating, we must understand the houses built nowadays by the local people. Finally, we realised that all Mértola is part of our archaeological project. So, we have placed, along the touristic pathways within the town, several 'Museological Nuclei'—homely little museums of local culture—that induce the tourists to walk through Mértola.'

Torres is obviously worried about the economic development of this region. The project has the aim of bringing tourists to Mértola...

'First of all, I and the other persons working on this project now live permanently in Mértola. We have moved here, which means that we must be able to survive by our own means—the Municipality is no longer able to sustain the project. So alternative sources of income must be found for it, and these must be sought outside the boundaries of the county, through scholarships, investigation projects financed by official bodies, etc.

'On the other hand, we know that, in the long term, the economic development generated by this project will eventually sustain this group of scientific investigators.

'So we and the other investigators are more and more dependent on this community. We are convinced that a certain kind of tourism development will be needed for the economic strengthening of Mértola. This region has some exceptional values in terms of its landscape, so it is possible, by keeping an eye on the mistakes committed in the Algarve (for example) and avoiding them, to follow an alternative trend of tourism development—one that would allow the survival of community structures, and also allow the young people to stay in the county.'

But do the politicians of the Municipality realise that a model like the one followed in the Algarve can compromise, in the long term, Mértola's development?

'We have been working for quite some years now in perfect harmony with the Municipality, and that's what gives this project such great strength. We could not have achieved what we have without their cooperation, and the truth is that Mértola wouldn't be what it is today without our cooperation and effort. So, there is mutual cooperation. The same happens with ADPM, which is the third party involved in this Mértola project.

'S. Domingos is not the only problem of the county—there are almost three hundred villages in the county presently abandoned by their populations. Every year, another village is 'closed', because all its inhabitants have died or left for good. So all efforts outside the town of Mértola sometimes seem to be fruitless. For example, we go to a village, we study its architectural heritage, we design a project to recover its buildings, and the next year that village is 'closed'. Sometimes this happens in a very sudden way. There may still be ten or fifteen persons living in a village, but if two or three key members of that little community die, the others leave and the village is 'closed'. Some extremely beautiful architectural buildings are in this way left to destruction, and with them a whole culture is lost.

'So what must be done right now—and the Municipality has already started doing it—is to select the villages that are the most able to resist this trend, and to invest in them endowing them with electricity, running water, and so on. This is, obviously, a very difficult choice—if an investment is made in one village, and the same is not done in another village nearby, the latter is sentenced to death. In this climate with the kind of building materials used, an abandoned house falls to ruins in a few years.

'So, the county of Mértola—apart from the town of Mértola itself—is a world in danger of extinction, suffering from the terrible agricultural mistakes of the past two centuries and of recent decades. Within this dramatic perspective, the Mina de S. Domingos is in an even more dramatic situation than the rest, because it is a village where a lot of old miners wait for death to come and take them. It is a big town—once 6,000 people lived there, although now there are only 800—still owned by a British company that has no mining interests, that does not want to spend money there; and so everyone has been waiting for the last twenty years for a miracle that will save S. Domingos.

'For the last six or seven years the Municipality has tried to get in touch with the company that owns S. Domingos. We must also remember that this mining complex has an 'extension' towards the river—the port of Pomarao. Lately, the Pomarao has begun to be coveted by some tourist agents from the Algarve. So, we decided to act. First, we tried to obtain the classification by the central government of all of the mining complex as a Monument of Public Value—and that has been achieved. This will prevent (or at least control) speculation that may happen in the future. Secondly, the Municipality has contracted a group of architects to make a plan for the safeguarding of the whole mining complex; this has also been prepared. It is now possible to negotiate with the owners of the land, so that the plan will be able to be implemented.

'There is a risk in this kind of intervention—the risk of depression, and also of complete exhaustion at the end of the day or at the end of the week. But there are great advantages: nowadays it is impossible to do good scientific work, even if it is very important, without messing with all these issues—sociological, ethnological and anthropological. It was not by accident that one of the first projects developed by CAM was the study of the patterns, materials and techniques involved in the production of coarse woollen blankets in the county—which has nothing to do with 'direct' archaeology—and yet I consider this work to be one of the most important studies in the field of medieval archaeology, because the patterns and techniques of weaving have been kept unchanged since the Middle Ages! This work culminated in the recovering of traditional weaving, through a women's co-operative that has been formed.'

Could Torres reconcile his work at the University with his intervention in Mértola? Or was it impossible?

'I hope this example will help other colleagues of mine to get rid of the powerful traditions of university work, which is almost exclusively based on book knowledge. You can see, right next door to us in Spain, lots of regional centres of investigation which have recently been created, keeping pace with the 'explosion' of nationalities that has occurred there. And we can see that nowadays history as a discipline is already closely linked with anthropology, with social reality, and with other fields of knowledge. So they have been able to reverse the trend that had been followed for so long, which is the analysis and discussion of the same written documents, over and over again, done by successive generations of researchers. And the results they are obtaining are spectacular!'

Torres' work has recently been recognised by the award of the 'Pessoa Prize' in 1991, which is given each year to the Portuguese citizen who contributes the most to the deepening of Portuguese culture. It is named after Fernando Pessoa, the great Portuguese poet.

Senhora Adélia: a member of the traditional weaving co-operative of Mértola

INTERVIEWED BY PAULO FARIA

'MY NAME IS ADÉLIA. I am fifty-four years old. I have worked with looms since I was very young—I learned the technique from one of my sisters, when I was eleven. I worked until I was eighteen. Then I abandoned this activity, because it wasn't profitable, and almost no one did it any more in the county.

'The profit we made from coarse-woven blankets was very small: we worked for ten, twelve or even fifteen hours a day—not for eight hours a day! We worked from sunrise until sunset to make a coarse-woven blanket, and in exchange we earned twenty escudos and two loaves of bread. The bread was included in the price. The client gave us the raw material, the wool, for us to work, and the twenty escudos plus the bread was meant to pay for our work.

'After I abandoned weaving at eighteen I was a sewing-woman and made embroideries. Later on I married. Then one day, twenty-three years after I had last woven a blanket, two people knocked at my door to ask what I knew about weaving, why I had abandoned it and so on. I told them I knew how to weave, even if I hadn't done it for a long time. Those persons were Jorge Revez and a girl from Lisbon called Xana. I sold them one weaving loom, and they asked me if I would like to teach others how to weave, and I told them, yes. Later they returned to my home, asking me to come to Mértola, to teach others how to weave. And this workshop was publicly opened six years ago, on the 25th of April, the anniversary of the Portuguese revolution of 1974.

'The first training course began on the 6th May of that year and it lasted until December. Later, three other courses followed, attended by eighteen or twenty girls. Many of these girls didn't even know that this activity existed, and they had never seen a loom—at least the first ones that attended the courses. Later one girl came whose mother had been a weaver. All the rest of the girls didn't know how to weave—they applied to join the course and came to learn.

'The majority of them got bored, but some stayed. So the only way to keep this activity going when the courses ended was to get together and form a women's co-operative. This was done three years ago. The girls weave, and I do the final work on the coarse-woven blankets, the saddle-bags, the tablecloths. I also help the girls whenever they have difficulties with the weaving.

'The door of my workshop is open and the people that come to visit Mértola come here also, to visit me and see me working. I sense an interest on the part of the visitors because we do things like in the past; the majority of people nowadays don't know anything about these looms and these traditional products, and so they are interested and value our work. They think this is good and beautiful. For example, the coarse-woven blankets are the most expensive products we sell here, but they are the ones we sell the most of—they catch people's attention.

'They see the old looms, and they appreciate that there is a difference between our products and those they are used to. Our looms are 200 or 300 years old. They were scattered all over the county. Many weavers who no longer worked had kept their looms in their homes, and these were recovered for this weaving school. Some parts of them had to be repaired, but they are still the original ones.

'The wool is the most expensive of the raw materials, so these blankets are the most expensive products. We also make tablecloths of linen, but it is very difficult to find good linen nowadays—so most of the time we have to use cotton.

'We publicise our work by taking part in exhibitions. Every month we send our products to an exhibition somewhere. We also attend art and craft fairs, in Lisbon and in the north of Portugal. Our products are very popular at these fairs.

'If there had been no co-operative I would have been in my home, sewing and making embroideries, which was what I did during the twenty-three years when I didn't weave. You know, there were many, many weavers in the county—but these products tend to be very expensive and the work is so very hard that most of them don't weave any more.

'That is why the weaving school was created, to avoid the loss of this activity in Mértola County. Because, you see, apart from these girls who learned how to weave quite recently, there is no other weaver in the county younger than myself, and I am already 54 years old. So, if this workshop closes, the weaving activity will end in Mértola, because no one does it any more apart from us.

'Young girls don't learn it any more, because it is hard work for little profit, and the raw materials are hard to find. Without the co-operative this craft will completely die out.'

Italy: Aspromonte
Introduction

THE CADISPA PROJECT IN ASPROMONTE has been undertaken to help conservation in the region; to improve the livelihoods of local people and link jobs to nature; to increase awareness of local culture through exciting school projects; to help youth organise eco-tourism judiciously; to restore local crafts, such as weaving, in order to help find work for women; and to involve the community in an eco-development plan for the region.

While many projects are being started by interested people all over the area, here are brief details of a few of them, which give a sense of local enthusiasm.

In the beginning, there will be small pilot projects for the Eco-Development Plan, to explore eco-compatible social and economic development. The planning group will also act as consultants to government on various issues, while seeking funds themselves to encourage artisan activities and the revival of local culture.

The people of San Luca have established a cultural museum. The museum will also be a visitors' centre for the Aspromonte National Park, and a starting point for excursions.

The Caraffa Young People's group is one of a few that could develop into a co-operative to promote eco-tourism, as being done by the already established New Frontiers Co-operative.

Above all, the 'Let's Shape the Future' theme in education is bringing enthusiasm for learning and hope for the future to the area's young people. The theme involves getting students to identify how their communities can live in harmony with nature; how to run community meetings; how to use schools after hours; how to make the most of the facilities at the San Luca museum; and how they, the young people, can contribute to the region's eco-development plan.

The Aspromonte Region

GIORGIO NERI

When seen from above, the gravelly river beds, which descend from Aspromonte down to the sea, look like sinuous snakes lying in broad sunny valleys, making the most of each bend and fold, in striking contrast with the green of the mountain, which reaches out tentacle-like towards the sea. The eastern Aspromonte is all like this: harsh, deeply furrowed— visual signs of hard struggle, marked by time and destiny, and by the force and determination of nature, which has always conditioned every choice and change. An incredible world, where each fold in the mountains encloses unimaginable traces of history and culture. But also a world ruled by contradictions and obvious problems, where many tiny universes exist, which it would be difficult—and superficial—to interpret with generalisations.

These facts alone explain why this area was chosen for the CADISPA project; it is an area of over 530 square kilometres, 451 sq. km of which are in the mountains; a region where a total of 40,777 people live in fifteen administrative areas, with 28,000 of them in mountain districts. It is an area for passing through, but also a meeting point for the various cultures which looked on to the Mediterranean from both the east and the west. This process started in the eighth century, when the first Greek peoples landed on the coasts of Calabria and founded the first colonies in Magna Graecia.

These peoples had a profound respect for the land in which they settled, and had a deep belief that interrupting the delicate balances of nature would threaten the very existence of their cities. There are clear references to this idea in classical literature, in which, for example, the stately beauty of the vast 'Silva Brutia', which at that time included Aspromonte, is celebrated. In his descriptions, Dionysius of Halicarnassus, historian and geographer, describes the mountain rivers as if they were more constant and slower than now, and could be used for transportation, at least in the lower reaches. Some Greek writers even spoke of river ports in Calabria, though this could not have referred to all of the rivers in the region. The only certainty is there was an ever-decreasing quantity of water in the rivers, over and above seasonal variations—a tendency which has become ever more marked, and which is due to human activity.

But the history of Calabria is not made up only of literary allusions. It was also held to be of considerable strategic importance, and a source of inexhaustible riches. From this point of view, the region assumes a tragic role, having undergone devastating despoliation and become the target for countless attempts at expansion and conquest. The first consequences of man's intervention in the delicate balances between the mountains and the rivers can be dated back to the period of Roman domination, when widespread deforestation was carried out in Calabria. The natural equilibrium was disturbed, causing the gradual disappearance of farming and grazing inland, and the spread of deadly epidemics on the coast. Foreign rule further aggravated these problems, and fierce raiding by Muslims and pirates, who for decades plagued the coast, led to the abandoning and ruin of many coastal settlements. This in turn explains the founding of small mountain communities, which were never large enough to provide a starting point for a fresh, more incisive phase of development.

In addition, it should be remembered that the region has always been isolated (especially the part looking on to the Ionian Sea), and cut off from all communication, partly as a result of the violent pillaging which lasted for centuries. Meanwhile the region was shaken by uncontrollable landslides and earth movements, which also forced the population to abandon the flourishing cities.

The last twenty years have shown that the natural environment is as volatile as in the past. Lake Constantine was formed very recently, on 31st December 1972. On that day, after more than ten days of heavy, uninterrupted rainfall, an exceptionally large landslide occurred. Sixteen million cubic metres of earth and rock fell into the River Bonamico, blocking its flow in Oleandri, in the district of San Luca. The force of its fall was so great that it impacted into a perfect natural dam. The side of a mountain had fallen from a height of over 1,200 metres to the valley floor. In two days, a lake of almost 10 million cubic metres of water formed behind the dam; this lake, by its very nature, will disappear in a few years because of constant silting, which is rasing the level of the lake bed.

The influence of history on this troubled land can be seen in the poverty of the region. The classification of administrative areas according to per capita income shows three areas of the eastern Aspromonte mountain community as falling among the lowest six. The poorest is Plati', with a per capita income of 6,990,000 lira per annum—ridiculously low, being a third of that in the provincial capital, Reggio Calabria.

This is the largest area in the province of Reggio Calabria, and that which includes the largest mountain area. Most of it falls within the boundary of the future Aspromonte National Park, which at over 100,000 hectares will be one of the largest and most important parks in Europe.

Here, the agricultural economy based on crop cultivation and grazing has generally given way, over the last twenty years, to government-assisted forestry work.

The poor water situation and geological instability have for years necessitated large-scale intervention. This has led to an uncontrollable expansion of the workforce, operating in numerous syndicates and bodies authorised by the local government, for the study and implementation of intervention plans for the area. There has also been interference by political interests, which for electoral and domestic reasons have promoted the creation and growth of a short-lived boom in employment and development. The overall result of all this has been a general moving away from sustainable kinds of activity. This is a familiar picture, the cause of the current social and economic problems of the area, which have been worsened by the lack of any kind of proper planning, either industrial or agricultural.

It also explains the lack of new business or entrepreneurial initiative, apart from the few businesses operating in the tertiary sector, and also the almost total disappearance of the local craftsmen, who worked with ceramics, wood, and fabrics. A new National Park could represent a turning point to the trends of both the distant and recent past. But for this to happen, social and cultural awareness needs to be stimulated, together with economic and environmental consciousness, in a programme to teach the local people how to exploit their resources differently, and more productively.

The natural setting of Aspromonte is very attractive—enhanced by the presence of rare animals and plants. But rather than speaking of Aspromonte in general, one would do better to speak of the different areas making up the whole, which vary according to altitude and orientation, with different physical features and different plant and animal life forms.

Eastern Aspromonte is the most beautiful and wildest part of the whole mountain area. Its inaccessibility, the deep ravines, and the abundant vegetation make it seem like a wild garden. Going inland from the coast, orange and lemon groves give way to hillside vineyards, and almond and olive trees, followed by the broad belt of mediterranean moorland, rising towards the large forests, which are still untouched in the innermost and highest parts of the mountains. Oak and ilex groves and enormous chestnuts, larch and white fir give way to the occasional yew, birch or a kind of aspen, which can grow up to 30 metres tall, and which is called *candelisi* in this area. The vegetation is different if one follows the course of a dry, white river bed. Here the landscape is almost lunar, with wonderful tufts of oleander, which in late spring are completely covered with bitter-smelling pink flowers, or the rarer lagano (*Vitex agnus-castus*), a resiny bush with compound leaves. These are the sole forms of plant life which can adapt to, and resist, the sudden movements of the river bed substratum.

The animal life in the region gives rise to debate, with contradictory opinions being expressed about the regal Bonelli eagle: some people believe it still nests here, while others are sure it hasn't been seen for a long time. The black woodpecker, has recently come back to the Calabrian Apennines. Here one finds the Driomio, a small mouselike rodent, still almost unknown outside its native Aspromonte, and apart from here found only in the eastern Alps. The reappearance of the Apennine wolf, has undoubtedly been the most important event in the last few years. The wild boar shouldn't be forgotten, along with the wild cat and the eagle-owl, the most important nocturnal bird of prey in the area. There are many foxes, martens, badgers, hares and squirrels in the mountains. The birds include buzzards, sparrow-hawks, kestrels and hawks migrating from Africa to northern Europe. The reptiles present here are the adder, the leopard snake, and the salamander (*Salamandra gigliolii*), a sub-species which is mainly yellow and black, and is common in southern Italy. It has been chosen as the symbol of the new Aspromonte National Park, and is featured on CADISPA stickers. At Ferraina, in the centre of the National Park, just upstream from Lake Constantine, a few otters have been spotted, undoubtedly because of the numerous streams, which are full of large trout.

It is an exceptional area, where splendour and simplicity, culture and folklore, history and legend are to be found side by side; an area threatened not by occupation and exploitation, evils resulting from modernisation and progress, but by isolation, depopulation, and the bad reputation it has been given, often by its own inhabitants.

It is said that Calabria is the land of olive trees and vineyards, and this is certainly true. Extensive olive groves, with some majestic specimens more than 100 years old, surround the Aspromonte mountain range, while the vineyards cling to terraces on steep hillsides, or stretch across the slopes which descend from the mountains, summits to the coast. Then there are the citrus trees, especially in the province of Reggio, which colour the countryside on the Ionian and Tyrrhenian coasts. Here there are also the native bergamot trees (*Citrus bergamia*), which only grow at the tip of Calabria. The fruit is used in the production of citric acid, while the outer part of the peel is used as the basic ingredient for liqueurs, sweets and perfume.

Here too, Aspromonte is generous in her gifts. There are also problems, however, which have always been present. Although this is a region where there is still very limited industrial development, agriculture is not highly intensive; indeed, Calabria is characterised by a subsistence agriculture. The peasants in each area traditionally produced just enough for the family,

and intensive cultivation to produce goods for sale was rare. This was a type of diversified agriculture, which ensured self-suffiency and goods for the local market without much specialisation. It was common for the productive unit to be one family, as a self-sufficient peasant unit. This type of ownership accounted for almost 50% of the land in cultivation, and was able to survive thanks to reciprocal help and support which were typical of the way of life.

The crops that are commonly grown in Calabria were developed not by choice, but as the result of national and international pressures. Thus the olive trees, for example, which are now a common sight throughout Calabria, were the result of population pressures during the second half of the eighteenth century. At that time, the production of olive oil was almost at the same level as that of Apulia. This was due to several reasons, the first being high demand in the markets outside Calabria, because of the increasing population during this period. Another was the common belief that olive trees did not require much work or investment, and so were highly profitable. During the late eighteenth century the foothills of Aspromonte were gradually turned over to olive trees.

Rapid growth in the plain of Gioia Tauro and Rosarno led to the extension of the olive trees to the mountainsides, a decisive move for the whole area. However, on Aspromonte itself there were no great changes. It was excluded from any kind of development because of its isolation, which maintained its very low standard of living, and began to set it apart from richer areas. Each of the three forest areas of Calabria developed its own characteristics. Aspromonte was a land of olive trees; Sila of wheat and grazing; and the Serras of wood and iron—in the Mongiana area there were considerable deposits of iron, which were highly exploited during this period. A relationship between the people of Calabria and those of the mountains started to develop, which had never happened before. The description 'mountain Calabrians' became current from that time.

Despite the remarkable development of the olive groves, and the conviction that they represented the winning card for the development of the Calabrian economy, this type of farming remained backward. Neither the large landowners, nor the many religious bodies which had large tracts under their management, thought it profitable to employ men and money on improvements. Indeed, they rarely intervened in the direct management of the land, preferring to pass the fruit on to third parties, year after year. Naturally, the quality was very low. To eliminate the costs of harvesting, it was customary to wait until the olives were overripe, or

Above: flower-picking.
Below: pride in the local community is being revived through
projects such as this, where students are painting a giant mural.

even dried up, so that they would fall to the ground and could be collected more easily. Large quantities lay on the ground for many days, and produced acid, which was not considered a bad thing—more often than not the olives were left to start producing oil naturally. It should be added that the farm machinery used was entirely inadequate.

The olives were pressed in old, crude presses, and the whole process of transformation from fruit to liquid was carried out without stringent controls. It was therefore inevitable that the oil from Calabria, traditionally with a high level of acidity, was only reluctantly used in Italian cuisine. In contrast, it was widely used industrially and for 'cutting' other oils. The olive managed to maintain the region's links with national and international markets. In contrast, the regional economy was damaged by crises in the silk and mulberry industry, upon which until this time it had depended.

Citrus cultivation was already flourishing at this time, especially in the province of Reggio. The groves 'began almost on the coast', as stated in reports of the time, and were tended carefully and attentively. Oranges and lemons, certainly, but more significantly citrons, bergamots and limes, were to be found 'among the houses of Reggio, and the many, often rich, villas along the coast'. It was a landscape that was already 'much to be admired', with alternating citrus groves and vineyards which pushed up to the nearby slopes of the backbone of Aspromonte. The produce was treated and sold in Reggio. From the citrus fruits, especially bergamots, lemons and limes, oils and essences were extracted for export, to be used industrially for perfumes, medicines, dried fruit, sweets and liqueurs. Large quantities of goods reached international markets, and gave the city a notable amount of business, ably managed by the local nobility. In the second half of the nineteenth century bergamot became more significant, when the qualities of its essence began to be appreciated. Even today, we do not know when it was introduced into Calabria.

The essence *acqua admirabilis*, known as Eau de Cologne, was discovered in 1676 in Cologne by the Italian Paolo Femi, and was destined to be a huge success in the perfume market from the beginning of the nineteenth century. Between 1850 and 1905, the number of hectares under bergamot increased from 200 to over 3,300, and led to production that was fully able to satisfy the world market. Secondary economic activity, dependent on the citrus sector, became an economic field in its own right. Most important, of course, was the treating of bergamot, with processes for extracting the essence, and the preparation of the juices from which alcohol and citric acid were extracted; this was followed by the processing of oranges, and to a lesser extent, lemons and mandarins.

In contrast with this considerable progress in the citrus sector, in the middle of the nineteenth century the cultivation of olives was still suffering from the traditional bad management. The olives were, as in the past, treated badly. The fruit were still gathered from the ground, and processing was unchanged: old-fashioned and crude. Not until the 1840s, with the introduction of the Genoan press, were there any encouraging improvements. Only towards the end of the century, after the setting up of a model oil press works at Palmi, financed by the Ministry of Agriculture, did new methods of production take hold and spread among owners and tenants in the area. Years of vintage production followed, leading to a significant increase in prices. This was a period of interest in vines, too, but grape-picking and wine-making methods were very old-fashioned and inefficient. At the same time brigands became more common—an endemic problem in Calabria during the nineteenth century, caused by many factors and favoured by the many hideaways offered by the wild, rugged nature of the area. This created a problem which was highly detrimental to agriculture: it was difficult to reach the areas under cultivation, and trees and animals had to be protected from theft and revenge raids.

But Calabria's biggest problems have always been its distance from the trade routes for international markets, and its lack of ports. It should be remembered that from the second half of the nineteenth century, Gioia Tauro was already one of the most important centres for embarking oil from the south of Italy. At the beginning of the twentieth century, the loading was still done by any local boats available. This was due to the economic policies of the large shipping companies, which preferred to reduce to a minimum the number of stops en route. Even though Reggio at that time was more than ever oriented towards the international markets of northern Europe, stretching from Marseille to Liverpool, from London to Odessa, it still did not have a direct shipping line to Genoa. The only link was through Naples. First the goods had to go there (or to Messina, which had started to become more important), and then they would be forwarded to the other large ports.

Significant quantities of export goods left Calabria at the beginning of the century: olive oil, citrus fruit, chestnut wood and silk. As regards oil, the productivity of the Calabrian trees was not far from the record for that period. There was no specific scientific knowledge of the olive, which at the beginning of this century had been little studied. But the problem was not that of quality or quantity. The isolation of the region was the important factor, especially with the introduction of railway transportation for citrus fruit in the north of Italy and in northern Europe, resulting in transport costs which meant that the price of the produce had doubled by the time it reached its destination—an enormous handicap for Calabrian producers.

Even fixed prices, guaranteed by the state, were of no avail. The lack of ports and railways, plus depression on an international scale at the end of the nineteenth and beginning of the twentieth centuries, marked the end of a prosperous period for Calabria, a period which had begun at least 20 years before Italian unification. There was no longer a continual passage of British and French ships which loaded barrels of oil from off Gioia Tauro. In the most dynamic sectors, there were some attempts at facing the new situation. But times had changed, and this was a particularly unhappy period for Reggio, not only because of the lack of outlets on to the market, but also because of repeated falls in production due to diseases which struck the olive trees, particularly at the end of the nineteenth century.

In addition, demand from France decreased as more olive trees were planted in many areas looking on to the Mediterranean, especially in Provence. Trading practice, in response to market needs, was such that the producers had to accept the conditions dictated by unscrupulous middlemen. As a result, oil produced in Calabria was sold in Italy, or exported, under the best-known national brand names. This process meant that the producers of Reggio were excluded from any kind of direct contact with the large markets. Calabrian production was influenced greatly by the years of fascism. First the devaluation of the lira in 1927, and then the crisis of 1929, led to regression in agriculture, which worsened after the outbreak of World War II. At the end of the war, conditions in the region were generally worse. Moreover, the natural outlets of the past no longer existed, and Calabria now had to face competition from other countries in the south and east Mediterranean.

This was the background for a clear break with past trading patterns on a regional level. Calabrian products, inevitably, were increasingly excluded from capitalist markets; this situation was worsened by the attempt at land reform, which was utterly unable to renew agriculture in the area. Organised crime also had its influence, acting in some cases to endanger productive development, local economies and markets. But the final blow was the massive emigration which took place over the 1950s and 1960s, which finally brought the region's agriculture to its knees. In 1961, villages with more than 2 per cent migration per year included more than 90 per cent of all those in the province of Cosenza, 63 per cent of those in Catanzaro, and 74 per cent of those in Reggio.

This was a hard blow for Calabrian agriculture. Previously, many processes had depended on large amounts of low-cost labour. Now this had become unavailable. Machinery was therefore introduced into some sectors, while others collapsed once and for all, partly because of a lack of suitable technology. Large numbers of people moved into the towns, abandoning the countryside. All these factors forced agriculture to adapt quickly and continuously; methods of production have been completely transformed. In addition, outside pressures became significant: changes in Calabrian agriculture were no longer determined by local choice, but in accordance with factors which lay outside the sector and the region. Even today, the general outlook for Calabrian agriculture, linked as it is to its traditional produce, olives and citrus fruit, is not good. Lack of infrastructure and isolation weigh heavily on the region, which despite the expected benefits of economic unification, risks being even more isolated than it has been in its recent and not so recent past.

New Frontiers Co-operative

GIORGIO NERI

MANY PEOPLE STILL FIND it hard to envisage hordes of tourists walking through the torrid, tormented valleys of the Aspromonte rivers, climbing the steep paths along mountain ridges. Perhaps this is what inspired Alfonso Picone, the chairman of the New Frontiers Co-operative, based in Reggio Calabria, which provides services for the tourist industry. He is the real 'explorer' of Aspromonte, and, at the present time, the area's most fervent marketing manager. His idea, and the founding of New Frontiers, cannot be separated from his sensitivity and love for the mountains, or rather for Aspromonte. His expeditions, long treks at high altitude among forests and ravines, rocks and ruins, getting to know the real Aspromonte, gave him the idea of starting the first, and as yet the only, Calabrian business concerned with mountain expeditions and trekking.

It should be remembered that Calabria is not all seaside, despite its 800 km of fabulous beaches. In fact mountain areas make up 90% of the region. As Alfonso Picone got to know the area he gradually appreciated the enormous historical and natural importance of Aspromonte, especially the eastern part, which has been designated a National Park. It is a vast stretch of land, where natural beauty is enhanced by valuable historical remains. From here, moving east, the so-called Valley of the Large Stones opens up, a natural pathway which climbs past the beauty of Pietra Cappa, Pietra Castello and Pietra Lunga. These are characteristic rock formations, created by erosion and natural and meteoric forces. The pathway encapsulates Aspromonte's glorious and mystic past, from the ruins of ancient Potamia, near San Luca, to the remains of remote huts, churches and convents, where monks and ascetics lived in the eleventh century, especially during the Arab domination of Sicily. They came here in search of solitude, praying and fasting, and making Aspromonte a 'holy mountain'. Expeditions and treks seem to go beyond an invisible frontier, beyond city life, progress and the rat race.

The aim was to better understand and publicise this 'new world'. Certainly not an easy task, when one considers the prejudices which abound even now regarding Aspromonte. There was a widespread negative mentality which saw Aspromonte as a land of kidnappings, bandits' hideaways, a refuge for wanted criminals—inhospitable, and not recommended for visitors. But due to the determination of Alfonso and his friends who share his passion, an awareness of the true character and beauty of Aspromonte is spreading, especially in Reggio. A following has been born, which is growing rapidly and which confirms an extraordinary fact: Aspromonte is unknown even to the people of Reggio, who live only a few kilometres away.

The first expeditions to be promoted outside his close circle of friends inspired and involved many young people. The moment came when this passion, which was becoming a collective phenomenon, deserved a name: the expedition group called People in Aspromonte was born. The name is taken from the most famous novel by a writer from San Luca, Corrado Alvaro. As Alvaro says in the book's opening lines, 'The shepherds' life is not easy in Aspromonte in winter, when the dark torrents race to the sea, and the land seems to float on the waters.' He fully recognises the tensions and contrasts which originate in the enormous mountain, which Alvaro considered as a live, throbbing being. This sentence has often been quoted by Alfonso and his friends in the association's publications and brochures, as if to transmit the breadth of their idea with the help of these few words.

A long and profitable period of practical experience began, which will enable the young people involved in People in Aspromonte to discover areas of wild and striking beauty. The group promotes many outings and short trekking trips. These activities confirm the fact that the lovers of the mountain are far from few, and more and more people are amazed and enraptured by the beauty of Aspromonte, especially thousands of youngsters from Reggio who have gone to Aspromonte for the first time, discovering its true character and real image. The mountain's fame began to spread beyond the city and region. Alfonso Picone has taken part in national meetings and conferences, explaining that Aspromonte is not just what we see in the news: police searches, kidnappings, wanted criminals. It is also an area which is unique and extrordinary in its natural beauty. Many people are unaware that a part of it is a National Park. Alfonso and friends feel that they are the official guardians of their land.

The members of People in Aspromonte started contacting the local and national mass media to generate newspaper and television articles on Aspromonte. This was their first real success. As a result of this coverage, many nature-lovers showed an interest in this mountain in the centre of the Mediterranean area. It was decided to start the co-operative, offering 'green' tourist facilities on a professional scale. It wasn't such an unusual idea—in other parts of Italy, similar enterprises had already clearly shown that careful marketing of inland areas could lead to economic development

and more employment. This type of enterprise was also favoured by current legislation, some of which was specifically aimed at this kind of business.

However, it was not easy to start: the idea was not favourably received, or rather, was not fully appreciated. There were the politicians, who had never shown any appreciation of the Calabrian mountain. They were not interested in the unique, unspoilt nature of Aspromonte, but only in monumental projects which could be sited there: roads and dams costing billions of lira, as opposed to projects involving a few million for the upkeep of paths and mountain shelters as the basis of real development more in keeping with the surroundings.

As a result most young people in Calabria didn't believe in the possibility of economic development based on the natural surroundings. The members of New Frontiers had therefore to invent a new professionalism from team effort, which was able to make them feel to some degree the redeemers of their land. Today New Frontiers is alive and well. Founded in 1987, it has been active in various sectors in promoting and marketing green tourism in Calabria. But the most important victory has been gained in involving young people who live at the foothills of Aspromonte, in San Luca, and other villages on the east side of the mountain. This is where it has been proved that there is work to be found in the environment and surroundings, without dramatic change, which means that these places should be defended, cared for and conserved, as indeed they are being, because there are people who want to go there, who are willing to pay for the pleasure of appreciating and admiring the area.

The co-operative has promoted many activities over the years. Slides and films have been shown in many parts of Italy, during trade fairs, meetings and conferences. Schools, universities and associations have been involved in many educational activities, such as that organized by the University of Reggio Calabria: a programme of twenty-four expeditions, in which almost 2,000 students were involved, over a single year. The co-operative has also worked on scientific and historical research with the Artistic and Archaeological Heritage Department of Calabria and other state bodies. It has produced brochures on tourism and the environment, and taken part in many conferences, one of which was organised by New Frontiers in November 1990. 'An Italian Path: From Aspromonte, a Step Towards Europe' was the name of the conference, an attempt to erase the stereotyped image of the inaccessibility of the sadly notorious Calabrian mountain. New Frontiers is involved in three projects, financed by the

Above: cultural revival in Aspromonte involves dance and music festivals.
Below: a footbridge over a mountain stream.

government and the EC. The first concerns the promotion and marketing of green tourism in Calabria, with a funding of 192 million lira from the Council for the Development of Youth Enterprise. The second is the census of tourist facilities in the area of the mountain community overlooking the Straits, with funding of 720 million lira from the Ministry of Employment, which is employing 100 unemployed young people for 12 months. The last project involves the setting up of a centre for promoting and marketing Reggio Calabria, financed with 480 million lira by the EC.

The most significant aspect of this whole endeavour has been the contact between New Frontiers and some promising youngsters from San Luca, one of the best-known centres in Aspromonte, but also one most closely tied to the stereotyped image of violence which the mountain evokes. At the present time some of them are involved in a project which is contributing to the area, financed by the Ministry of Employment and managed by the co-operative, maintaining and marking the mountain paths. Additionally, they have for some time been working on the setting up of a visitors' centre, also called 'People in Aspromonte'. A small museum will be linked to the centre. The author Corrado Alvaro was born here, among these steep, narrow lanes, in the same landscape which opens out towards the sea along the River Bonamico.

Alfonso Picone is optimistic about the future. 'The results we have had in Calabria', he says, 'are worth twice as much as they would be in a normal situation: we have been swimming against the stream. People have always seen the mountain as blocking progress, have always left the area, and this flow is still continuing. It's obvious that against this background, the mountain does not offer opportunities for the future and is not considered a resource to be protected and conserved. The Aspromonte National Park will certainly help, but we still have a long way to go. At the moment, mountain trekking is considered a kind of low-cost tourism, which does not attract large numbers of people or much capital. The co-operative has recently started working with the regional Tourist Board, and we will expand our routes and activities to other mountain areas in the region: Sila, Pollino, Serre and Orsomarso. And it would be nice to be able to market our activities abroad.'

Teaching in Plati'

GIORGIO NERI

THE MIDDLE SCHOOL in Plati' isn't the best one could hope for. A visitor sees depressing grey concrete walls and small, unwelcoming classrooms, in a building which is even more miserable and bare. The pale glimmer of a lightbulb is lost in the shadows. Only the light from a window shows just how small the room is: a short, narrow space where an untidy group of boys and girls are seated. It is difficult to talk about maths, physics, geography or Italian here. These subjects seem remote from the harsh realities of the village—unemployment, a lack of facilities, and one of the lowest income groups in Europe.

But despite all this it is not really an unpleasant place. The village is surrounded by a ring of mountains that seem to protect it, every prospect being lit up by the bright colours of the natural vegetation. It is one of the most beautiful and wildest areas of the Aspromonte, and Plati' is the settlement furthest inland in the eastern part of the mountains. It has just under 3,500 inhabitants—it has been dramatically depopulated by emigration, which has affected this area more than others. Even so, there are signs of well-being—one of the characteristic contrasts to be found in Plati'. On the one side there are the rewards of years of hard work brought home by returning emigrants—emigration being the only way to realise the simple ambitions of a humble life: a decent place to live, and a little piece of land to cultivate—just the bare requirements for a family. On the other side, less common but more noticeable, are the fruits of criminal activity, which are shocking against the simple background of the village and which offend the entire region. Aspromonte, because of its wildness and inaccessibility, is considered (wrongly) the silent accomplice of criminal misdeeds, an impenetrable hiding place for kidnap victims and wanted criminals.

Against this background, any kind of new initiative or project instantly takes on the significance of 'a challenge'. A challenge against hopelessness, ignorance and isolation. Pina Fotia, a teacher, uses these words to express her initial reaction to the opportunity offered by the CADISPA project to take part in an environmental awareness programme. She's not worried about her relationship with the pupils, who are often 'over-enthusiastic', and can cause her some problems. Rather, she's fed up with the indifference shown by the other teachers, with their prejudices and unwillingness to consider any kind of original idea.

Giuseppina Fotia, maths and science teacher, was born and grew up in Plati', and perhaps embodies the stubbornness which is typical of the people from this area. She's the exact opposite of many of her colleagues. She is excited and optimistic about the project, and the results can already be seen—it takes special energy here to get anything done. The young people at the school have few opportunities—street games, short walks just beyond the houses—but nothing more.

Obviously, we are no longer living in the world portrayed by Corrado Alvaro in his novel '*Gente in Aspromonte*', in which the daily problems and worries of the farmers and shepherds seemed preordained by a cruel destiny, which no-one, least of all the poor, could escape. An evolution has taken place and overturned the old social structures which that world was based upon. But nevertheless, that world had its own values, hidden riches, which were expressed in many small ways—reciprocal support, concern, respect—which underlay everyday social relationships. And these relationships seemed to be acted out repeatedly in accordance with some script created for the comedy of life, against the backdrop of the piazzas, the houses, the fields, the workplaces.

The young people of today need to experience a transformation, a rebirth, fulfillment. But how can they be made to discover the village where they were born, where they've always lived, and which has been abandoned by so many because there's no work? How can a place where they know every stone, every branch, every path, be made interesting? What's so special about it?

Pina Fotia is clear about this. She explains: 'Plati' still has these values. They've only been clouded by the insistent, repetitive, superficial messages transmitted by television and the radio, which attract the youngsters but which are devoid of any human or social meaning.' This determined teacher seems to suggest that the future depends on choices which are unrelated to the mirages of progress and industrialisation.

These ideas have been expressed, repeated and discredited many times in Calabria. But she has insisted on the only possible valid approach for this area: an increased appreciation of the natural heritage, the correct use of it, and the protection and stimulation of folk traditions.

'Here,' she says, 'the school has not been able to overcome the gap, the opposition, that there has always been between pupils and staff. This split has frustrated any attempt at communication or a new approach by the teachers or the pupils—a situation determined by the teachers, often without motivation, based on superficial prejudices and misconceptions.

Obviously,' she adds, 'there are problems; it would be silly to deny that there are real difficulties. The youngsters here are bright, very bright, but often have to face problems which are too much for them. These are usually family problems—often the father-figure is missing, because he has emigrated to find work or is wanted by the police. So they need to find a substitute in the teacher, who in this way is given the difficult role of someone to confide in.'

As Pina comes from Plati' herself, she knows the problems. After graduating, she spent many years teaching in the industrialised plains of northern Italy, and so has a better perspective of the differences. Time has shown that she is right. The results from the project at Plati' have been much more rewarding than elsewhere, because they were obtained in spite of the real difficulties that the village faces. The pupils carried out research into their surroundings, finding out about the land, its history, cultural heritage and traditions, and realised that they are part of a reality to be proud of. This was the central, and probably most important aspect of the project: rediscovery of one's own surroundings from a different point of view, more natural, honest and less aggressive. It was reflected in the youngsters' drawings, which didn't just show the historical and natural features, but gave a realistic, up-to-date view. Through this process, the children abandoned their uneasiness with their land. The pictures showed a helicopter—the police helicopter, which is always hovering nearby looking for criminals and kidnappers—which for the children is a brand on the village, a curse, to which they feel inextricably bound.

The crowning of the teacher's work with her pupils is the fact that these efforts have not gone unnoticed—many people have become aware of the project. Pina Fotia knew this would happen. She knew exactly what she was doing, and has been rewarded, both by the pupils at her school, and the people from her native Plati'; the former, by the care and attention they put into their work, and the latter by the help and support they gave the children, with their recollections, reports, personal stories—and their deep wish to take part, both actively and as spectators, in their own story, as the children acted out the lives of the people of fifty years ago.

Grandmother Angela's Loom

GIORGIO NERI

ANGELA ZURZOLO COULD BE CALLED the founder of the 'Loom of Samo' co-operative, in the sense that she had the idea, along with some other girls from the village, of creating jobs around one of the oldest and most attractive Italo-Greek traditions of the area, that of weaving.

Samo is in Calabria, on a hill in the eastern Aspromonte area overlooking the La Verde river, and has a population of almost 1,500. It has always been considered the home of hand loom weaving. Tradition has it that it is the birthplace of Pithagoras the sculptor, but this claim to fame has never been proved. However, the ascription gives an idea of the historic origins of Samo, which are lost in the mists of time. People have come from far afield to the village to buy the beautiful fabrics produced locally. There was a thriving cottage industry based on fabric production which developed naturally, since having a loom and spinning and weaving linen, broom fibre, and silk were commonplace activities for meeting the needs of the family, especially for preparing the dowries of daughters of marriageable age.

All the fabric patterns reflected the Greek heritage of this area, but this was not their only peculiarity: they were the result of a complete local production cycle, starting with the treatment of the broom used for the the 'rag' pieces, the linen used for towels with fringes (and traditional geometric designs which none of the weavers would have been able to explain), and silk, which in the past formed the basis of one of the most flourishing industries in Calabria.

Angela herself has a large number of bedspreads, blankets, towels, tablecloths and sheets—they are her dowry, produced on her family's looms by her mother Girolama and her grandmother Angela, both skilled weavers. Angela can weave too—she learnt from her mother and grandmother. She loves her grandmother's 150-year-old loom—for Angela, the most precious of the family heirlooms. But not only the loom

The wildly romantic terrain of the rugged Aspromonte region
offers great scope for eco-tourism, which can also bring much
needed money into the area.

ties her to her family's past; there are the childhood memories as well. She remembers her grandmother as an 'incubator': to make the silk cocoons open earlier, she used to keep them warm in her bosom. Grandmother Angela would use only the silk from the mulberry tree in her garden for weaving articles for her grand-daughter. Angela also remembers the many hours her mother spent working on the wonderful dowry she produced for her daughter—skilled embroidery, delicate laces, patterns and colours from classical myths and legends.

With all these recollections in mind, Angela had the idea of setting up the co-operative. She was twenty, and wanted to start work, but there were no opportunities in Samo, apart from leaving home and finding work in another town—which is hard when you have to leave your friends for an unknown and impersonal outside workplace. So Angela decided to try something based in Samo itself. She spoke about her idea with a few friends—girls of more or less her own age. 'What do you think about setting up a co-operative to produce and sell Samo fabrics?' she asked. Fifteen of them were enthusiastic, and the idea was welcomed by the rest of the village. So the girls set up their co-operative, under the name of The Art of Hand Loom Weaving in Samo.

The first problem, says Angela, was buying thread (linen and silk) for starting production. Setting up a loom, carding, warp and weft, is a costly business, and opening the co-operative had already absorbed the girls' limited resources. Angela had the idea to start producing something simple which could be sold straight away—little wool dolls, the same as those she had made for fun in the past with a crochet hook. Selling them would bring in some funds, and each of the girls could put in a small sum of money to buy some wool. This was the start of a very busy period, each member of the co-operative having a weekly target of wool dolls to meet. Angela herself was a student at the time, and had to work at night to keep up. But the idea was a success; the sale of the dolls, through friends' shops, worked very well, and encouraged the girls to go on.

At long last the first pieces of fabric were produced on the co-operative's looms—the two looms of Angela's childhood, her grandmother's and her mother's. They were brought back into use with the help of some of the village women. Setting up a loom requires expert hands, and Angela and her friends asked their grandmothers, mothers, relatives and neighbours, all of whom are experienced with warp, reed, shuttle and lay. The work started in the narrow alleys of Samo, where the threads were strung out, prepared and wound ready for the loom. If one walks through these alleyways, it seems that a traditional ceremony is taking place, with warp and weft forming ritualistic patterns along the walls. Every passage has its group of women working on the long skeins of thread, stretched across the walls or between low buildings with their little doorways. Many hands are needed for this phase of the work, and the women help each other set up the looms, brightening the alleys with the striking colours. The next step can be done indoors, on the looms—the pieces are set up, with their spools of different coloured threads. The ends are tied to the treadles, which raise and lower the heddles, and the shuttle passes through, following the pattern to be woven. Angela remembers how her mother spent her days in the family butcher's shop, and came home and worked at the loom on her daughter's dowry at night.

It wasn't difficult to decide what colours and patterns to use on the fabrics. They were, and still are, part of the cultural heritage of Samo and the Aspromonte area. In addition, each girl has her dowry, which she can draw on for inspiration—delicate patterns woven into the linen, wonderful designs on bedspreads and tablecloths or cushions. Then there are the rag pieces—traditional fabrics from an Italo-Greek heritage—with simple patterns, or the traditional 'bottle', 'rag flower', or 'garland' designs, all reproduced in the original colours and weavings—an inexhaustible supply of ideas.

In the past, the loom had its own place in the house, just like a washing machine or a fridge today. The looms were not factory-built, but produced by skilled carpenters, following the traditional designs handed down from generation to generation. The basic structure is very strong, made of beech, the only wood which can stand up to the strains and repeated movements of the weaving process. The individual craftsman left his mark in the finishing of the loom—with patterns and inlays from local tradition, or historical pictograms.

Angela knows that the most valuable pieces are the blankets, the silk towels, the embroidered sheets, the bedspreads and the cushions. According to an old tradition, a pair of cushions are bought for every bride and groom for their new house. Production has to be regular, and of good quality. Angela hopes one day to build the co-operative into a small factory with ten to fifteen looms, employing many people from the village. But she needs a market to justify increased production and new investment.

Although she is determined, and so far has been rewarded, it would be hard to say that everything is going well. She says that the group manages to keep going, despite ups and downs. She has persuaded her father to let her use a building the family owns for the co-operative, because they cannot afford to pay rent, and in the meanwhile is trying to obtain grants from the state and regional government, but so far to no avail.

Every now and then something happens to keep their hopes up. The first chance they got was taking their work to the truffle fair in Alba, in Piedmont. 'Very expensive, but a huge success', says Angela. 'At first, people didn't believe we were from Samo, from Aspromonte, right down in Calabria—and they weren't convinced that we had done the weaving, which they found very beautiful and unusual. The first few days, the public came to our stand, admired our work, and then went away. Only the other exhibitors, who appreciated the quality of our fabrics, wanted to buy everything, at the end of the fair. By then we were feeling pretty discouraged, but in the last few days we managed to sell nearly everything.'

This encouraging experience led the girls on to try other outlets, such as the summer exhibition in a large town on the coast, where they went for two years running. This was a huge success with the holidaymakers, and people back for the summer from work places far afield. Nevertheless, the co-operative is still a long way from being well-established in Angela's eyes. Many of the original members have given up, and others have joined to take their place. There are now nine members. Some of the work is done by part-timers, and Angela says it's often difficult to pay them. But she is determined to realise her dream of reviving Samo's heritage and creating jobs for the people in this area.

Greece: Prespa
Introduction

AT PRESPA, THE LIVELIHOOD of people used to be woven into the very fabric of nature. They bred hardy cattle, and grazed them on the reed beds; this permitted the fish to spawn near the foreshore, which is now choked with weeds. The hillsides were carefully terraced for a variety of vegetables and cereals and irrigated by mountain streams. Their self-reliant way of life demanded social cohesion and cooperation, traditional in such societies. The wars and the pull of modern cities have swept away these communities. Their present reliance on intensive cultivation of beans for outside markets leaves them at the mercy of price fluctuations; and young people continue to leave. The cattle are almost gone, the reeds have multiplied, fish cannot spawn any more, and the fishermen have lost their living also. The situation is all too familiar.

CADISPA–Prespa has just started. It will, it is hoped, promote traditional economic activities and local culture, until now looked down upon. People may get back to building houses in the traditional way and breeding their tough cattle. Fishing could come back. A women's co-operative will market local crafts and produce. These projects will be shaped after discussions with the local people. It should succeed, though political problems remain, and the get-rich-quick hopes still linger with a few. Prespa should live again, even as villages in similar situations are beginning to revive in Portugal, Spain, Italy, and far-away Scotland.

Prespa:
The Loss of a Sustainable Past

MYRSINI MALAKOU & GIORGOS CATSADORAKIS

PRESPA IS SITUATED at the north-western corner of Greece (Western Macedonia) at the borders between Yugoslavia and Albania. It is an area of 30,000 hectares lying on a mountainous plateau at an average of 1,000 metres above sea level. The area consists of two lakes, Mikri Prespa and Megali Prespa (4,850 and 28,000 ha respectively) and the surrounding forested mountain slopes. Prespa is characterised by outstanding natural beauty, great biodiversity and rich natural resources.

Isolated among the mountains and far from big urban centres, the inhabitants of Prespa maintained until the mid 1960s an almost self-reliant way of life, in harmony with nature. But it demanded specific social and family structures and relationships, cohesion and self-help activities.

Before World War II, 12,000 people lived in Prespa in eighteen villages. Owing to the War, and the civil war (1944-1949), the population fell to fewer than 1,500 people, six villages being entirely abandoned.

Up to the mid-1960s, the economy of the area was based exclusively on livestock raising, farming a variety of crops, and fishing. Agricultural land was of limited extent and was mainly located at the periphery of the lakes. It included a patchwork of croplands, pastures, hay fields, natural hedges and a lot of trees, interspersed with tracts of natural riparian woodlands. Mountain slopes were also cultivated with cereals up to an altitude of 1,800 metres, perhaps the highest croplands in Greece. In order to cultivate the steep and rocky slopes, it was necessary to level a piece of land, remove all the stones and build up stone-walls, to stabilise the soil and prevent erosion. The terraced fields were cultivated mainly with cereals, rye and barley and vineyards. Irrigation was carried out using natural streams, with the help of gravity flow, through a network of small ditches. In irrigated fields, vegetables and trees were planted. Oxen and horses were used for ploughing and horses, mules and donkeys for transport. Sheep, goats, pigs and cattle were used for the production of meat, milk and other food products, as well as wool. The cattle were a local breed, characterised by its small size but with great toughness and endurance.

The local people also used many products of the wetlands—reeds were used as animal fodder during winter. They were also used for thatching, for constructing walls with clay, and for fences and fish-traps. Other plants of the wetlands, such as rushes, were used for the construction of baskets, mattresses and 'carpets'. Because of these activities, the expansion of reedbeds was controlled, and wet meadows were kept open for grazing by domestic animals. These were excellent spawning grounds for fish, and feeding areas for wading and aquatic birds. Pelicans, cormorants, herons, spoonbills and glossy ibises were breeding in large numbers, giving Prespa the greatest diversity of large aquatic birds in Europe.

Because of the high altitude, winter at Prespa lasts for seven months; the local people developed many techniques for surviving this hard time of year. These techniques included several methods of storing food: salting meat, preserving meat in fat, milk in sheepskins, and drying vegetables, fruits and salted fish. Trade was practically unknown. People obtained necessities that they could not produce themselves through the exchange of goods. Among the few things they bought were petrol for their lamps, and salt. Fat was used instead of oil, and honey instead of sugar.

People in the villages worked co-operatively, grazing sheep or cows, in house construction, and farming. Families consisted of many people, of all ages. That is why many of the traditional houses of the area were large and with a special arrangement of rooms. When a new house was to be built, all the people in the village helped in the construction. Some cut timber from the forest, others transported it to the spot. Some were unearthing stones and carrying them and others cut them. Some were cutting, carrying and matting reeds, and others were providing clay for the masons who were building the house. This close cooperation in every day life was an unwritten law, and had never been made official—although a certain number of co-operatives had appeared before the war.

Religion, strong family bonds and cooperation all played important roles in social organisation and life. Sustainable use and wise management of land and natural resources was a necessary prerequisite for living.

The importance of sustainable use of natural resources was widely accepted, although the underlying mechanisms were rarely understood. For example, fishermen ceased fishing activities on their own initiative during the fish spawning period. The beneficial effects of the harvesting, burning and grazing of reeds on fish spawn was thoroughly appreciated.

Owing to both isolation and the low degree of contact with the outside world, the local people created a culture related to the available resources. Many elements of this culture are unique to Greece—for example, a fishing method involving juniper branches and funnel-shaped traps.

Population changes as well as changes in the way of life influenced, gradually but decisively, the situation at Prespa. During the 1960s many people started to emigrate to foreign countries. During the same period, the Greek state financed the construction of an irrigation network utilising the waters of the lake. In order to construct this network, parts of the wet meadows and inundated areas were drained, and this had a dramatically negative impact upon aquatic birds.

The following decades marked the transition between the old way of life and the new way of life, bringing in industrialisation to Prespa and resulting in changes in all aspects of everyday life, and the cultural values.

During the 1980s more and more families, especially young people, gradually abandoned their old way of life, which was based on a diversity of activities, and became farmers, cultivating beans in an intensive way. In a few years the number of people occupied with animal raising and fishing decreased substantially. The completion of the irrigation network and the shift to bean monoculture gradually changed the appearance of the agricultural zone: it became more monotonous and unattractive to wildlife. At present, Prespa is still one of the most important bird breeding areas in Europe. But the glossy ibis does not breed here any more and the breeding populations of waterbirds have decreased significantly.

Isolation and self-management determined local society, especially in its relationship with the modern world. Nowadays, according to modern perceptions, local society can be said to have a low level of education, and to be having difficulties in practising new activities.

On the other hand, the abrupt change from practising diverse activities to the specialisation in one activity impoverished the culture of the local society. A feeling of social isolation and a crisis in their cultural identity prevails, despite the fact that communications and mass media seem to give such areas the chance to abolish isolation. In practice, at the local level, the exchange of information is one-way—from the modern world towards the local society. The way to promote, publicise, evaluate, appreciate and use the knowledge of these people, who lived in nature and managed sustainably their natural resources, has not yet been found.

At present, the livelihood of each family depends on the State and EC policy. Politics play an important role in the decisions of the local people. Personal interests and politics have destroyed the cohesion and social cooperation within the local communities. Almost all the initiatives for the establishment of co-operatives failed because of political conflicts and a lack of experience in understanding market conditions.

The Women's Agrotouristic Co-operative, which was established in 1987, was an effort to break through the situation described above. Women have a downgraded role in local society, but this initiative was supported by their families—mainly for political reasons. The Co-operative started with the running of tourist lodgings in Ag. Germanos, and was supported by the State. Fourteen women, from all Prespa villages, participated in the co-operative, but soon many internal problems appeared: lack of experience in this new activity, low incomes and political pressures. Nowadays co-operatives mean something completely different to the self-help activities of the past. Although in theory all the members of a co-operative have the same rights and obligations, in practice everything depends on the decisions of the leader. Thus, the relationship of the members with the co-operative becomes a strictly financial matter.

At present, the management of the environment, conservation and the economic development of the area depends on decisions taken by planners based in Athens. Unfortunately these decisions have often proved useless or disastrous to the environment and the economy of Prespa. Activities related to better management of the natural resources slowly die away. For example, reed management and grazing in the wet meadows have stopped because most of the local people are occupied exclusively with farming. The wet meadows which constitute spawning grounds for fish and feeding areas for birds are encroached upon by a continuously expanding reedbed. A decrease in fish production of the lake, and a similar decrease in the populations of wading waterbirds, has been observed.

In addition, though much money (especially from the EC) has been spent on its development, Prespa is facing an economic and social crisis. Bean production has increased enormously, but recently trading is problematic, mainly due to overall EC agricultural policies. Young people do not know how to develop other activities: certain potentially profitable ones, such as livestock raising, lack social approval and thus are neglected.

In recent decades, plans for the development of Prespa have followed a conventional pattern: the increase of productivity without any consideration for the protection of natural resources. The proposals of conservationists often represent a narrow view, being concerned almost exclusively with the protection of nature, or of certain species, without any consideration of the culture of the local people, and the importance of existing human activities for the management of the environment. Discussions on the protection of nature often become bargains about the economic development of the area, and alternative proposals, such as eco-tourism, are usually put forward to resist the intensification of agriculture. However, tourism is not understood by the local people—they lack experience. At Prespa, it is evident that not only animal and bird species are threatened with extinction, but culture itself, which was based upon the sustainable exploitation of natural resources. Most of the wildlife that remains in Europe is the result of a co-evolution of human activities and nature. In certain areas, such as Prespa, not only do people owe a lot to wildlife, but also wildlife owes a lot to people. In the last analysis conservation requires the integration of human beings and nature in every way.

PART THREE

HABITAT AND COMMUNITAS

Though hundreds of thousands had done their very best to disfigure the small piece of land on which they were crowded together, paving the ground with stones, scraping away every sprouting blade of grass, lopping off the branches of trees, driving away birds and bees, filling the air with the smoke of coal and oil—still spring was spring, even in the town.

Leo Tolstoy, from *Resurrection*

HABITAT AND COMMUNITAS

Introduction

'SPRING WAS STILL SPRING, even in the city,' said Tolstoy at the beginning of *The Resurrection*. But for **Christa Dettwiler**, activist and thinker, the poetry of the city has become an insane noise. What kind of Spring is it if blackbirds refuse to sing in cities—even in Swiss cities? Birds may be able to fly away, but the poor are trapped in their concrete jungles, as effectively as they would be in jail. In the next chapter, Christa writes with great passion about the popular movements in Switzerland and elsewhere that are trying to reclaim the cities for the people who live there.

The City is a great human creation, a creative organisation of all human activities where ideally the aesthetic, the material and the spiritual extensions of our nature can all seek identity. The metaphor St. Augustine chose to describe perfect creation was the City of God. Jerusalem remains a centre for people of three faiths. William Blake called on Englishmen to replace their dark satanic mills with a New Jerusalem. Unfortunately, it is the mills that have survived. Ur, the capital of Sumer, the oldest city in the world, called itself simply the City. How can we restore the special significance of this word, its true meaning of the material abode of the community's spiritual aspirations? The only clue we have is that the concept of a community must come alive once again.

John F.C. Turner is one of the foremost thinkers working within urban communities in practical ways to make them of human scale. He defines pollution not only as dirtying its surroundings but defiling nature and desecrating life's meaning. The turning of homes into commercial products for passive consumers is a form of pollution for Turner, and a threat to nature and to human existence. The future and the hope lies in people's unique 'vernacular' knowledge of their own situations, their needs, expectations, and priorities. Failing to understand the critical difference between complex machines with simple functions, and simple systems (such as housing) with complex functions, professional developers alienate people from the design and production of the houses they will be living in. Personal fulfilment is inhibited as surely as real learning is by the institutionalised school system. In the Hesketh Street Co-operative of Liverpool, the architects were grilled by the tenants: 'What was the worst mistake you ever made?' With real people's participation, and everyone contributing 'sweat equity', the estate has turned out to be a well-preserved, pleasant residential area, with good neighbour relationships. The most important element in the development was 'power to the people.'

Turner certainly is not alone, but few have catalysed local initiatives in housing as he as. There are many effective grassroots efforts going on within the United Kingdom, where people are being squeezed by one of the worst recessions of modern times into suffocating living conditions produced by rash 'modernistic' housing policies of the post-war period. The notorious Tower Hill estate at Kirkby near Liverpool has been compared to Beirut on a bad day. Built early in the 1970s for a population of 10,000, its blocks were already being condemned by the 1980s. Between 1987 and 1989, the recession cost Kirkby 13,735 jobs. One person in three has no job, and four-fifths of all school-leavers have no hope of getting one.

Abandoned by government and ignored by big business, the people have pioneered the Tower Hill Community Trust to give education and training and encourage local small business development. A well-funded housing co-operative has come into being. A council depot is being transformed into over a hundred managed workplaces, to provide around 300 jobs in the next three years. Steve Dumbell, chairman of the trust, was unemployed for eight years: 'I'm much stronger for the fact that economically I was a non-person. I was down, so I had to fight back. I had to stand my ground. The most important result of the initiative has been a revival of the community spirit.' Jack Jones, the secretary of the trust says: 'If we can do it, just ordinary people from the area, then surely other people can get off their backsides and have a go.'[1]

The greater Pilton area, with a population of 30,000, is the unknown part of Edinburgh, internationally famous for its Festival, its Castle and Holyrood Palace. Pilton's housing has been called the worst in Western Europe, and likened to a refugee camp. In the 1980s, the City Council proposed the demolition of Pilton and the sale of its public park. With this threat hanging over them, various tenants' organisations under the leadership of the Moderator of the Presbytery of Edinburgh himself produced the 'Pilton—It's Now or Never Plan' and forced councillors to hold consultations 'with ignorant slum dwellers'. In the words of the Reverend Alan McDonald, Pilton Community Minister, 'There was no miracle, but the demonic, vicious downward spiral of a whole neighbourhood had been ended.'[2]

Another response by local people to inner city disasters has been to go away and re-create the community somewhere else. The best-known example of such a movement is the Findhorn Foundation, on the Moray coast of Scotland, east of Inverness. Founded in 1962, it became famous for the kindliness of its spiritual community and its 'magical vegetables'. It offers a New Age refuge to over 200 people of all spiritual beliefs. In the words of one of its community, people go there 'because cities don't work—communities do.'[3]

Sue Austin tells us how a small, thoughtful, quiet community of Swedish middle-class people came together in Tuggelite, to form what is now Sweden's oldest 'eco-village'. Detailed planning and community-based democratic decisions, as well as people's participation in manual labour, have created ecological and energy-saving houses which cost a third less to run than conventional housing. Tuggelite's future really depends on its community and its children. The children benefit from the warmth of social relationships, as do the adults. But the adults have taken care not to be too radical, or different from others, 'as it is a mistake to try to go too far too fast.' A resident says: 'We have created an efficient and sustainable community which can be seen to be working. I feel needed and valued here, but I also feel we are acting responsibly towards the environment.' Another admits that they are a community of middle-class professionals, but says that if they had not been in tune with each other in the first place, Tuggelite might not have survived. 'What is exciting is the children are starting to tell us what to do to protect the environment!'

These examples of the resurgence of the community spirit among people living in densely populated areas of Europe show their need to re-create life within their communities, and to retake control over their lives . It is the wave of the future—not just a backwash from those left behind.

Loveless, Speechless, High-speed... Cities?

CHRISTA DETTWILER

SHE USED TO BE shy, living in seclusion, intent on having sufficient space and maximum flight distance. Life in the city changed her. Instead of close to the ground, the urban blackbird builds in airy heights, metropolitan-like with a density of up to twenty-five bird territories on twenty-five acres, not two, as in the country. The flight distance has shrunk to a tenth. And when the blackbird lets its song rise up between concrete and construction, when it floats with heartbreaking sweetness above traffic and frustration, man stands still, touched and almost indignant.

The cities—centres of social experiments that once attracted those intent on taking their chance to be a part of, to contribute to, the creation of something new and different—have become so monotonous that the blackbird's song bewilders. Instead of centres for living together, modern metropolises have degraded into arenas where people, ideas, and lifestyles crash into one another. Political and intellectual minds become encrusted; there are shop windows instead of living spaces, massively protected by the police. At night, life only happens where there are sex and games; the rest of the city is left to the hungry and the angry and those who don't belong. One of the reasons is the automobile—an overwhelming element by day and by night, and with it the cold, grey asphalt tracks, traffic noise rolling ceaselessly on, interrupting sleep and clear thinking; there are noxious fumes for breakfast; cars left carelessly on the scarce empty spaces. All this is aggressive, and depressing.

The quality of life in inner cities has literally been run down by traffic. And Steppenwolf lives in many hearts when he dreams of pedestrians hunting down those fat, well-dressed, perfumed drivers with their large, growling, snarling automobiles. Even the architecture of cities has changed with the narrow view through the windscreen. Highly ornamented, finely detailed façades which people—pedestrians mostly— took time to look at, have given way to a loveless and speechless high-speed architecture.

Cars devour living space, quality of life, and the joy of life. Streets are

'Green' pedestrians stop automobiles in Zurich to make the point that the cities are for people, not machines.

enemy country instead of places of encounter and movement. And it is for precisely this reason that all along those life-threatening, breathtaking race tracks and amidst the wall-to-wall concrete, resistance starts to crop up like flowers through cracks in the asphalt. The citizens in many western European cities and towns are tired of being stranded on one side of the street with hardly a hope of getting home again, and have seen enough maiming and killing by those in gleaming armour. Resistance often begins with women, mothers in particular, who cannot bear to see what the mobile mania does to their children—either by violence or by poisoning the air.

In Switzerland, citizen groups putting up active resistance against the burgeoning traffic are spreading like wildfire. Hundreds of groups with thousands of members are forming spontaneously, remain active for some time, dissolve, reform. Some throw flowerpots at drivers racing through residential quarters, some swarm out under the cover of darkness to open valves on tyres, leaving flyers saying: 'We just wanted to let ozone into your tyres, but what do you know: air came out!' Some block a busy commuter road with chained-up bicycle parts to turn it into a playground for grown-ups and kids, others block the road with official-looking barriers and go to town with jackhammers and picks. All are men and women who are tired of the noise and the stench, bitter about the countless victims, and disappointed by the politicians. They have begun to put the brakes on the ever-growing, ever more destructive stream of automobiles.

It's like an apparition: from the Weidengasse thirty figures emerge all wearing yellow hats. They carry stop signs—and they carry carpets. They march towards the pedestrian crossing. It's five p.m., with the rush hour in full swing. The strange-looking figures have come to assist pedestrians in exercising their rights: the right to cross the street in relative peace and safety. The group, who call themselves 'Reconquering of the Zurichstreet', stop the cars and roll out the red carpet for those on foot. Leaflets ask the 'dear commuter' to think, that 'without you here it would be almost as nice as at your place'.

It's hot in the city on this day in July, and the ozone levels are accordingly high. The limit, that should only be broken once a year, has been surpassed for the seventh day in a row. People are casually strolling up the street, looking perfectly normal, were it not for the deck chairs and paddling pools they are carrying. At the Neumarkt, the place with the sea of parking spaces, the men and women set down their chairs, and draw water from a nearby fountain to fill their plastic ponds. Children jump in, screaming happily. Where there is normally a wasteland of parked cars there is now a lively, joyous family scene.

It's still early in the morning when farmer Karl-Heinrich Kohl takes his brand new tractor out of the shed, rolls slowly down the country road and joins a group of several dozen others sitting in the middle of the street crossing. For two hours the farmers and their wives sit chatting over coffee and cake.

Wherever these scenes unfold, cars are stopped in their tracks, drivers are invited to think. To reflect on the necessity of that one journey and the next one and the next. These acts are not done by trained activists, nor by rowdies or subversives—they are done by women and men who normally respect the laws of the land and move within the accepted social boundaries. Driven to use unusual means by the terrorism of individual motorised mobility, they may even overstep the law. But their concern in those moments is not primarily legality, but legitimacy. Their legitimate right—as citizens, as mothers and fathers, as children, and as old folk—to a sane environment.

And the citizens are not alone. They find more and more sympathy with creative planners and far-sighted politicians. More and more European cities are coming to the conclusion that cars and living in inner cities just do not go together. Bologna in Italy and Lübeck in Germany have closed the inner cities to traffic. And in Frankfurt, the era of construction purely for profit seems to be over. The uses of street space and the surrounding environment are now considered in the planning for new high-rise buildings—ecologically thought-out multi-functional buildings for working and shopping and entertainment, complete with winter-gardens and water fountains, bring back life into the comatose city centre. City ecology at its best.

It is of vital importance that cities are remade into places for people and not for machines, and urban centres are re-animated. Ideas like 'soft mobility' or 'city of short distances' have become part of traffic concepts and the vocabulary of politicians. But still too little is actually done. Those responsible ought to read the philosopher and author Peter Sloterdijk, who writes: 'Above all, it seems to me, that European cities can only make a true decision to survive, if they have the strength to confront individual transport. Cities have entered over the last two or three decades into a raging sado-masochistic affair with automobilisation, out of which they can—as one must have known for quite some time now—only emerge in ruins.'

The euphoria of Le Corbusier, for whom the city of speed was the city of success, and who fell into verbal ecstasy watching the traffic streams of the Champs Elysée, has yielded to sobriety. Instead of giving in to the rush of speed, we count the dead and wounded. We acquaint ourselves with chemical compounds like CO_2 and NOx and O_3, and evaluate the quality of air by how much poison it contains.

But there are people who remember the city as a living space, built by human hands—a marvellous and fascinating experiment. They have not forgotten that the nature of a city is inspired by people, is brought to life by their knowledge and abilities. It has lured the birds out of the forest. Let us reconquer the city.

The Community Base of Sustainable Development

JOHN F. C. TURNER

WORLD LEADERS PUT 'sustainable development' at the top of the political agenda for the 1992 Earth Summit in Brazil.[1] The hard fact is that the world's minority of high consumers cannot for much longer maintain their wasteful lifestyle at the expense of an increasingly impoverished majority and an accelerated rape of nature. If human life does not end with a nuclear bang it will end with an entropic whimper—unless the high polluters soon learn to do much more with much less.

Most materials and energy are used in and for homes and neighbourhoods, especially in the most highly industrialised countries. Global economy and sustainable development largely depend, therefore, on the knowledge and responsible care of locally used resources by people who are free, able and willing to do so. The necessity of greater economy in the use of resources is now officially recognised and accepted; its dependence on greatly increased local self-management, however, is only beginning to be understood.

Countries with low-income populations provide many pointers to sustainable development. As their governments have very low per capita budgets, their economies depend heavily on local, community-based production—the so-called 'informal economy'. In many supposedly 'developing' countries this third sector produces more than the public and corporate private sectors combined. Faced with these realities, many low-income countries are pioneering partnerships between the three sectors on which resource economy depend.[2] These trend-setting changes are more urgently needed, however, in the minority of high-income countries which use most capital resources and generate most polluting waste.

This urgent need for policies that support and enable local self-management is illustrated by two inner-city case histories of publicly owned housing in Britain—the pioneer of urban-industrialism, and the first to seriously erode its community base, so vital to sustainable

Partnership with people builds community and hopes that last.

development. The Trowbridge Estate in the East End of London is one
of many failed redevelopment projects of the 1960s. The *re*-redevelopment
of Trowbridge, now planned, follows examples illustrated by the second
case: the Hesketh Street Co-operative in Liverpool. This case shows how
three-way partnerships can rebuild the community base while making
immediate contributions to sustainable development.

Maldevelopment: The Trowbridge estate[3]

Trowbridge is a public housing project in the Inner London Borough of
Hackney. The original scheme has contributed to the loss of faith in
urban-industrial progress. It vividly illustrates the triple meaning of
pollution as defined by the Oxford English Dictionary: not only dirtying
its surroundings but defiling nature and desecrating life's meaning—the
inevitable result of excessive industrialisation, institutionalisation and
professionalisation. Happily, Trowbridge is currently undergoing transformation through community action supported by newly emerging policies.

The Trowbridge Estate (as public housing projects are quaintly called
in Britain) was designed in the 1960s to re-house the residents of Victorian
terraced houses which had been designated as slums for clearance by the
local authority. This decision, along with the planning and building design
standards and forms, complied with the then current central government
policy for funding. Policy was based on the unquestioned belief that bigger
and faster was better, housing being no exception. Plans were drawn up
in the fashion of the times: large buildings and heavy technologies, with
their high visibility for politicians and high profits for professionals and
contractors. Seven fourteen-storey tower blocks were completed in 1972
with one- and two-storey houses and flats in the spaces between the tower
blocks—a physically attractive and seemingly economic use of land where
high buildings are widely spaced in order to avoid overshadowing and the
creation of high winds at ground level.

In 1968, even before Trowbridge was built, the image of this type of
housing development was tarnished by the partial collapse of Ronan Point,
a systems-built tower block, following a minor gas explosion in a kitchen.
But by then, the Trowbridge project was too far down the bureaucratic
pipeline to be changed. By 1980, technical and social problems were so
acute that the tower-block residents demanded demolition of their blocks
and that they be rehoused. The tower-block residents outnumbered the
satisfied tenants of the one- and two-storey houses and flats, so the residents
were split into two rival factions. The combination of the cost of making
the blocks safe and habitable, the increasing costs of management and
maintenance, the difficulty of renting high-rise flats, and pressures from
the majority of the tenants, led to the decision to demolish and rebuild

the entire scheme. The *re*-redevelopment proposed closely resembled the original 'slum': two-storey terraced houses with small gardens together with flats in small three-storey blocks. The new project would have reduced the total number of dwellings by little more than 10 per cent. The surviving Victorian terraced houses just outside the project perimeter have meanwhile been in continuous occupation, mostly improved and all with greatly enhanced value.

Three of the original seven tower blocks were blown up in 1986 and 1987—occasions for local celebrations and family picnics to view the spectacle. Further demolitions were suspended following central government policy changes accompanied by drastic reductions of public housing budgets. With little or no prospect of major government expenditure on public housing, together with the related increase of government support for tenant management, the new development scheme was abandoned. The position of the one- and two-storey house and flat dwellers' association strengthened as the tower-block tenants' group was weakened by a greatly reduced membership. At the same time government policy now supported the introduction of tenant management for public housing. The population of the towers had declined even before the demolition of three of the original seven; by 1992 many flats in the remaining four were vacant and two-thirds of those were occupied by squatters, many of them young people with no long-term commitment to the neighbourhood.[4] At the time of writing, this combination of circumstances and successful precedents elsewhere for commercial rehabilitation of tower blocks by private developers, has led to a new redevelopment scheme being prepared. In close consultation with the low-rise tenants' association, a scheme of 120 new single-family homes and low-rise flats on the sites of the three demolished blocks is being prepared.[5]

Sustainable development: the Hesketh Street Co-operative

In February 1979, Hesketh Street Co-operative, Liverpool's second housing co-operative, was set up following the City Corporation's (the local authority's) drive to complete clearance of the remaining unimprovable Victorian terrace (row) houses; these were built to a much lower standard than those cleared for the Trowbridge Estate. The Co-operative was formed by two groups of families with young children and pensioner couples, mostly former tenants of dilapidated, privately owned terraces from adjacent inner-city areas. Many had been neighbours before the Corporation rehoused them in random locations all over the city. One group were the former residents of houses cleared from Hesketh Street, the site of the new development. The Council offered the site to Co-operative Development

Services (CDS, a Housing Association in British law), a non-governmental organisation for channelling central government funds into low and moderate income rental housing. CDS is one of the few Housing Associations that has used its powers to act as a secondary co-operative, that is, as a sponsor and enabler of independent housing co-operatives. For reasons discussed below, later projects which followed the Hesketh Street Co-op were modified to virtually eliminate tenant participation in design and construction. The first CDS Co-op, Weller Streets, was set up in August 1977 and fully occupied in October 1982. CDS introduced the two Hesketh Street groups, reserved the site for their use and assisted them with the formation of their own housing co-operative.

The relationship between CDS and Hesketh Street Co-op deserves emphasis. The Co-op employed CDS as their advisor. Assisted by CDS, the Co-op selected their own architect. This took place after the Co-op members carried out their own field research, making coach trips to inspect different housing schemes, including some designed by the candidate architects. These were subjected to gruelling interviews by Co-op members who asked questions such as: 'What was the worst mistake you ever made?' Their selected architects worked closely with an elected Design Committee, most members of which were women. Periodic general meetings with all 40 member households allowed the architects and committee members to collaborate on the development layout, the house designs (allowing for individual variations of interior layout), landscaping and planting. Dr. Tony Gibson's 'Planning for Real' method, an invaluable technique for overcoming the communication gap between lay people and professionals, including the local authority, was used for planning and design.[5] (This 'us and them' gap was a major contributor to the Trowbridge disaster described earlier.) Co-op members also chose the building contractors, whose work they likewise inspected closely as well as subjecting them to similarly tough interviews.

Layout planning, building design and construction were subject to strict limits imposed on the use of public funds. The Co-op preferred to maximise the quality of materials, workmanship and architectural design, cutting back on items that could be improved later—unlike the more usual sacrifice of 'the architecture' which is so often treated as an optional add-on. According to Hugh Anderson's appraisal: 'The planning is good at both site and detailed level, the workmanship is excellent and the choice of materials suggests genuine quality. Once inside the scheme it has an air of naturalness and straightforwardness, suggesting that the "vernacular" is more than just an image and may indeed grow to fit with its surroundings.'[6]

Overhead costs for the development process, with the exception of a small grant to CDS for the Co-op members' education, were limited to

2.2 per cent of the total construction and land purchase costs. The first costs of co-operative housing are a little more expensive than other more conventional ways, due mainly to the substantial amount of additional work with the tenants. Much of this was borne by the architects for whom no allowance was made in the fees paid, usually in arrears. Even where this additional but under-estimated cost is not offset by 'sweat equity' earned through self-help building, as in this case, the pay-off through the tenants' 'enterprise (or management) equity' is considerable—but all too often blocked by the priority which short-term results have over long-term gains.

By 1984 Elaine Dutton, a design committee member, felt secure in predicting that '...in ten years' time [the Co-op] will still look nice. It's because the people who hold the purse-strings are also the people who live here... Corporation [local authority] estates start off looking nice but in ten years they look awful because people see plants being destroyed and bricks being taken out of walls and say, "It's nothing to do with us".' By 1992 this confidence had been fully justified: the development is very well preserved and maintained while physically similar projects built and managed by the Corporation, even after the completion of the Co-op's scheme, have deteriorated and are seriously vandalised. The membership has remained stable along with the good neighbour relationships developed during the process of organisation, design and construction.

An essential difference

According to Hesketh Street Co-op's first chairman, Alan Hoyte: 'The most important thing about [the process] is the power to the people bit. In general in Liverpool, people are told what they are getting, not asked what they want. But once we had established our viability by being accepted by the [central] government for funding, we determined everything; the way we lived, and who we employed to run our affairs. We did not succumb to bureaucracy.' As Sophy Krajewska, the journalist from whose article much of this information is drawn, put it: 'We are not talking here of an exercise in participation [in the sense] of delegating selected crumbs of decision-making powers to tenants to use in consultations. Rather it is a complete reversal of the traditional power relationships inherent in our paternalistic system of housing provision.' These are illustrated by the earlier, unreformed Trowbridge redevelopment.

The 'power relationships' changed through projects of the Hesketh Street kind are illustrated by another Co-op member. Mary Waring, a member of the design committee, said: 'We all got to know David and Peter [the architects] like friends. We never felt they talked down to us, it's never been "them" and "us".' Elaine Dutton, another member, added: 'Even the builders were our friends as we had regular site visits. Because they cared about us I think they might have got to enjoy their work more.' Personal relationships with CDS staff were and remain cordial although there have been times of disagreement and even heated discussion between Co-op members and other responsible individuals as well as between members themselves—a normal and generally necessary condition for honest and lasting co-operation.

Whether the change of power relationships is a key economic and, therefore, an environmental factor, depends on what underlies Elaine Dutton's observation that: '...when you live [in the place] you know what the money needs to be spent on. Money gets wasted by the Corporation [the local authority]. They say: "Let's put in a children's playground on every single estate [project]" whether the people want one or not, so thousands of pounds get wasted.' This suggests that the vast waste of materials, energy and living space resulting from the original Trowbridge scheme resulted from ignoring people's own personal and local resources: their experience and knowledge of their own personal and local situations and priorities; their skills and initiative; and their capacity for commitment and caring, whether latent or conscious and practised.

Towards an explanation
The reports on the Trowbridge Estate and Hesketh Street Co-operative add to the large and growing worldwide body of evidence confirming that:

'When dwellers control the major decisions and are free to make their own contributions in the design, construction or management of their housing, both this process and the environment produced stimulate individual and social well-being. When people have no control over nor responsibility for key decisions in the housing process, on the other hand, dwelling environments may instead become a barrier to personal fulfilment and a burden on the economy.'[7]

This widely accepted and often-quoted statement implies but does not explain the connection between local self-management and material economy. It also begs the question of relevance to activities other than housing and, therefore, the scope and significance of autonomy.

Much has been seen, said and written about community-based or 'bottom-up' initiative in many fields and in all contexts during the twenty years since the 'freedom to build' proposition above was written. Discussion of community-based initiative and its relationship with state-based powers and corporate market-based forces is generally confused by the 'private sector' label which lumps both corporate and community-based non-governmental sectors together. This helps to maintain the grossly distorted conventional view of society which ignores the 'third sector' or system on which the caring and responsible use of resources mainly depends. Attempts to enable local initiative are often misdirected, at least partly because its economic potential is grossly underestimated or even ignored. The 'third sector' is treated as an adjunct to, or a part of, the 'private' sector in 'free-market' economies and of the public sector in the remaining 'command economies'. The lie is given to both these views most dramatically in low-income, rapidly urbanising countries where the productivity of the so-called 'informal economy' is clearly greater than that of the other two sectors combined—not only in housing as noted above but in most other productive activities.[8] In low-income countries this has been obvious in 'housing' or home and neighbourhood building for decades. It is now becoming clear that the economic as well as the social roles people play in this sphere, especially, is far greater than generally assumed in highly institutionalised, high-income countries as well. As the above cases confirm, the existence of homes and neighbourhoods, physically as well as socially, depends mainly on the care residents take. Over time, any initial divisions between production and use blurr and disappear as users' contributions overtake those of the original builders. This economically necessary process is clearly accelerated as well as ensured by user-producer partnership from the beginning. When resources invested in home and neighbourhood building and use are assessed, the relative economic power that people have, apart from that of the state and the market, is clearly massive: homes and neighbourhoods occupy a high proportion of built-up land; most of one's lifetime is spent there (in addition to time spent elsewhere earning money to pay for it); a significant proportion of all manufactured materials are used for building and equipping homes and neighbourhoods, and they consume more energy than any other area or activity.[9]

Misconceptions about the variously and confusingly misnamed 'third sector' will continue until the vital difference between activities that are necessarily personal and local and those that are necessarily large scale and impersonal is generally understood. Home and neighbourhood building and learning are clearly different from, for instance, inter-continental transportation. The former are not only essential for normal life; they also provide opportunities for personal fulfilment and cultural development through active participation. The latter provide opportunities for specialised producers and personnel only. Consciously or unconsciously, actively or passively, everyone who has a home and lives in a neighbourhood is involved in their 'production'; as noted above, the useful life of dwellings, and of their surroundings to varying degrees, depends as much on the users as it does on the original builders—and more so as time passes. Learning depends, of course, on the learner as much as or more than on the teacher—indeed, in vernacular English the word 'learn' also means 'teach'.

As the all-too-common experience of the Trowbridge kind shows, the exclusion of users from production turns them into passive and literal consumers—just as the institutionalisation of teaching inhibits real learning. And as experience of the Hesketh Street kind shows, the continued existence of homes and neighbourhoods depends as much or even more on reponsible users and carers as on specialised builders. The production and use of inter-continental transportation systems, on the other hand, is a very different matter: the last thing aeroplane passengers wish to do is to share responsibility for piloting the airplane—only hijackers are willing to risk participation.

The intrinsically small scale of homes and neighbourhoods, and the intimate knowledge people have of their own priorities and space, are what make their necessarily infinite variety possible. If people's homes and neighbourhoods fail to provide a tolerable match with their personal priorities then they will either leave or minimise their efforts—with one important partial exception: 'Deficiencies and imperfections in your housing are infinitely more tolerable if they are your responsibility than if they are someone else's.' It is clear that 'housing' is a highly complex system, as soon as it is understood that 'The important thing about housing is not what it is, but what it does in people's lives [so that] dweller satisfaction is not necessarily related to the imposition of material building standards.'[10] What housing does for people depends on the matching of its location, built form, tenure and affordability with the residents' identity, security and future opportunities. Even within these generalised terms the functional complexity of housing (as an activity) is obvious.[11] The true nature of housing as it is experienced by the user is largely invisible. But when housing is seen and treated bureaucratically or commercially, as a welfare service or a consumer product, profound and counter-productive errors are made by those who believe that homes can be mass-produced like motor cars. The failure to understand the difference between complex machines with simple functions and mechanically simple systems (such as houses) with complex functions, continues to haunt professional and corporate thinking, reinforcing institutional barriers to the changes essential for resource economy and sustainable development.[12]

Complex systems involving ever-changing relationships between people, places and activities cannot be maintained economically by central management. Large organisations must standardise their procedures and products in order to keep overhead costs within competitive or practical limits. When building and managing large numbers of homes and neighbourhoods, centralised managements find the costs rise inexorably if they are to maintain social stability as well as keeping the buildings and surroundings in good repair. All three main political parties in Britain have now come to accept, in one way or another, the necessity of 'privatising' publicly owned and managed housing stock. They have learned, through negative experience, to respect the Law of Requisite Variety: 'If stability [of a complex system] is to be attained, the variety of the controlling system must be at least as great as the variety of the system to be controlled.'[13] The corollary, which has led a rapidly increasing number of industries to decentralise, is that 'any organisation seeking management control over a complex system inevitably reduces its diversity to below that of the organisation itself.'[14]

People themselves have unique knowledge of their own situations: their needs, expectations and priorities. Therefore, it is obvious and essential that they should have personalised and localised control over their own personal and local space. The economic use of resources and stable social relations depend on each other. But neither can be achieved or maintained by residents and neighbours if they are unable or unwilling to make responsible use of their own knowledge and social skills. It should now be obvious to professionals and officials, looking at local situations from the outside in, that their point of view and, therefore, their access to knowledge, is different from that of the insiders looking out. From their professional or administrative (and often cultural) distance, those who make the rules and the plans and manage finance can see the overall situation and the connections between one place and another—but they cannot possibly take into account the ever-changing variety of individual user's priorities. On the other hand, the residents and users know their own situations and are uniquely placed to decide how to use resources in their own space—but they may not be able to see the wider connections and their implications. In other words, the insiders and outsiders need each other's knowledge and resources; they and the economy therefore need a complementary, rather than a confrontational relationship. As Tony Gibson puts it:

LOCAL KNOWLEDGE AND COMMITMENT
PLUS
PROFESSIONAL BACK-UP
EQUALS
TOWNS AND NEIGHBOURHOODS THAT WORK

The Law of Requisite Variety can be followed only through the practice of subsidiarity—making decisions at the lowest practical level. Europeans were suddenly confronted with this hitherto esoteric word while this paper was being written—popularised by political debate over the unification of Europe. Hopefully it will accelerate learning how governments can devolve control over local development decisions that must be made locally if they are to make economic use of resources— and if 'economic development' is to be stabilised as a vehicle for social and cultural development.

Writing in 1916, the renowned American anthropologist Edward Sapir described the consequences of denying people access to the traditional means for 'sharing in the production of non-utilitarian values' as he puts it—and the confirmation, or rediscovery of meaning in life:

> 'So long as the individual retains a sense of control over the major goods of life, he is able to take his place in the cultural patrimony of his people. Now that the major goods of life have shifted so largely from the realm of immediate to that of remote ends, it becomes a cultural necessity for all who would not be looked upon as disinherited to share in the pursuit of these remoter ends. No harmony and depth of life, no culture, is possible when activity is well-nigh circumscribed by the sphere of immediate ends and when functioning within that sphere is so fragmentary as to have no inherent intelligibility or interest. Here lies the grimmest joke of our present American civilization. The vast majority of us, deprived of any but an insignificant and culturally abortive share in the satisfaction of the immediate wants of mankind, are further deprived of both opportunity and stimulation to share in the production of non-utilitarian values. Part of the time we are dray horses; the rest of the time we are listless consumers of goods which have received no least impress of our personality. In other words, our spiritual selves go hungry, for the most part, pretty much all of the time.'[15]

Three generations later we find ourselves not only living with the social and spiritual, but also the material consequences of this attitude. We are knee-deep and sinking fast in the quicksand of our unsustainable 'waste culture', generated by the loss of personal and local control over production of the 'major goods of life', not least our homes and immediate surroundings. Along with most everyday things that used to be home- or locally-made, our own homes have turned into commercial or welfare products for passive consumers. This aspect of pollution is one which, in 1916 (when Sapir wrote his paper), very few would have connected with vernacular knowledge, still less with the threat to nature and our own future existence.

Tuggelite—Sweden's Oldest 'Ecological Village'

SUE AUSTIN

NESTLING IN THE SKERE HILLS a few kilometres north of Karlstad lies Tuggelite—the name means 'a little bite'. Karlstad is a major provincial town on the edge of the great Lake Vänner in the centre of Sweden, and most of the residents of Tuggelite work there as professionals: doctors, dentists, teachers, librarians, etc. Fully operational since 1984, Tuggelite ranks as Sweden's oldest 'ecological village'. Nearly all the inhabitants have been together for much longer than eight years though, since the inception of the project in the 1970s. Their beautiful and largely unspoilt countryside is dear to the heart of most Swedes, and as various threats to its survival were recognised, environmental groups sprang up round the country. Initially many of these were protest groups, especially anti-nuclear, which was quite respectable under a strongly socialist regime. Gradually the focus changed towards more 'green' issues and people began looking into ways of conserving natural resources and living more economically in terms of energy consumption and waste creation.

This was contrary to the accepted Swedish thinking on house design: in Sweden there are very generous specifications for building, with the result that the average living space there is one of the largest in Europe. Insulation requirements are also high and devices such as heat exchangers widely used, so that the energy loss is already minimised. The fact that research had already been done in these areas may help to account for the reluctance of major building firms to take on the Tuggelite project. It is also a fact of life in Sweden that building regulations are immensely complex and over-bureaucratic, making it extremely difficult for private schemes to get accepted. There are several projects for 'ecological villages' in the country at present which are foundering on the rocks of red tape and excessive professional meddling. The conventional building and planning sectors are compartmentalised and unused to ecological thinking; and despite a considerable amount of research on the subject the findings have not percolated through to the building firms. The result

A family outside one of the houses at Tuggelite.

is that the layman has to be prepared both to seek out expert help from various quarters and to fight for his ideas. Once a plan has finally been accepted, its implementation has to be carefully monitored; otherwise, as in the case of several of the seven operational ecological villages in Sweden to date, costs may escalate way beyond the original estimates.

This was not the experience of Tuggelite, but that was because of very detailed planning in the first place. The financial and judicial aspects had to take precedence over idealistic considerations, although the group never lost sight of their main objectives: an energy-saving, environmentally friendly community where people could live together in a mutually supportive way. Thus the physical site had to fulfil certain criteria, and there was no compromise on these. Credit for seeing the project through this fraught period must go in part to a civil engineer in the group who was familiar with the rules and regulations. But the planning stage was not a one-man show: Tuggelite's residents claim that they all shared the responsibility and that decisions were taken democratically. Many could help in lobbying for example, and all could help with manual labour when the foundations were being laid. In the end the cost of building Tuggelite, in spite of the extra-thick concrete walls (36 cm) and additional features such as greenhouses and porches, compared favourably with conventional buildings of a similar size. The subsequent running costs of Tuggelite are considerably lower of course; up to a third less than buildings of a conventional design.

Tuggelite consists of a cluster of 16 houses joined together in small groups around a community centre which houses the boiler, the laundry room, an activity room complete with weaving loom and photographic lab, a kitchen, and a large main room used as a day nursery during the week and by Tuggelite's residents in the evenings and at week-ends. The long south-facing walls of the houses have greenhouses built on to them; the solar heat which builds up in these is channelled into the living area by means of a ventilation system through the walls. Small porches are built on to these walls too; these help to keep out draughts. The north-facing walls in contrast have small windows, which like those facing south are triple-glazed. The principle is to conserve and make use of all the solar heat available and also to minimise heat loss. In the cooler seasons the heating is boosted by a boiler in the community centre fuelled by wood pellets produced from a fusion of bark, peat and wood. There are two large solar panels in the roof of this building too.

The individual houses grouped around the community centre are joined together, under cantilevered roofs to protect them from excessive sun, rain or snow, while maximising heat storage. The extra insulation in the roofs and outer walls of the houses, composed of a 36 cm thick wad of mineral wool behind the wooden facade, ensures that very little heat is lost. The inner shell, flooring and joists are made of concrete, which has a very high capacity for heat absorption. Thus most of the solar heat taken in during the day is stored in the concrete, without raising the inner temperature significantly. At night the concrete gives off heat, keeping the temperature from falling too much. In this way the external insulation prevents heat from leaking out while the internal concrete structure stabilises the temperature. The greenhouses are effective in warming up the houses during the day even in winter: on a sunny winter's day the outside temperature can be down to -20°C while in the greenhouses it is +25°C. Cold air coming into the houses when people go in or out is reduced because of the porches on the cooler north-facing side. At night thick shutters keep the heat in. Overall the heat-saving is remarkable—around 50 per cent.

But the heating system in Tuggelite has not been all plain sailing. The first wood-pellet boiler proved too expensive to run and the development of a more cost-effective version was delayed by a drop in oil prices world-wide. In 1989 they acquired a new model which seems to be more efficient, though still needing daily maintenance. About this time too they installed the two 120 m solar panels as an additional source of alternative heat; however, in the event of a complete breakdown it is possible to switch over to an oil-feed for the boiler. Several of the houses have fireplaces installed in their living rooms to boost the heating as required.

The Tuggelite community decided from the start to use composting toilets. These would reduce considerably the daily use of water and in addition provide compost. Initially organic food waste was first disposed of down the toilets too, but their capacity was found to be too small; a separate composting system is now in operation for this. Each household is responsible for dealing with its toilet waste, which has to be emptied two or three times a year into containers, where it remains for a minimum of two years before it is used as manure around the trees and bushes outside. Waste water from kitchens and bathrooms which is free from bacteria and toxic products can be used on the flowers and vegetables in the greenhouses and allotments. The water is filtered through two-chamber wells and then pumped up into the greenhouses as required, using manual pumps.

The area surrounding the houses, which is jointly owned by Tuggelite's residents, has been carefully laid out. There are four earth cellars for storing root vegetables and a workshop next to the community centre where lawnmowers, snow shovels etc. are kept. Then there is a kitchen garden divided up into individual plots, one for each household, and a communal plot which ten families look after. And there is a children's playground right in the middle of the site, an important informal meeting place. One of the original aims of the Tuggelite community was that its members should have plenty of opportunity to meet each other in their daily lives, to avoid any feelings of isolation or anonymity. The money each household put down to purchase a share of Tuggelite included a contribution towards the cost of the communal facilities, the major expenditure being on the community centre of course. This is an integral part of everyday life there now. Apart from the shared amenities such as the laundry room and sauna, the building is used regularly in the evenings for courses and clubs or for individual activities. At weekends all Tuggelite's inhabitants, 61 at the last count, can get together there for meals or social gatherings. Its running costs are partly financed by the rent from the day nursery.

Another important concept behind the formation of Tuggelite was that it should be sparing on personnel too. No-one was to be employed to clean, garden, cook or indeed administrate. The tasks are shared out among the members of the community, many being carried out by 'teams', well-established units within the group. Working together is an effective way of looking after the social fabric. This is currently in good repair, to judge from the composition of the community: of the original sixteen households fourteen are still in residence more than ten years after they first got involved. Not a bad record for an experimental community.

Jörgen and Marianne were members of the original group out of which the idea of Tuggelite grew. Marianne is an attractive woman, mother of four and a primary teacher who is clearly very capable; convinced of her principles she is determined to put them into practice and in a quiet persuasive manner can carry others with her. She and Jörgen show a great deal of sympathy and understanding in the way they interact with and talk about other inhabitants of Tuggelite. Let Marianne tell the story of how it all began:

'We wanted to do something towards finding a way to live more in harmony with nature and our fellow man. That was back in the seventies when there was an active debate going on in Karlstad, as elsewhere, about how to right the wrongs done to the environment in our times. We joined a study group based on the findings of a research unit in Gothenburg. These and other materials formed a starting point for looking into energy production and consumption, the economics of energy-saving, more efficient use of resources and so on. Out of this group several like-minded people joined a newly formed association in the area which was planning to set up a self-supporting community. There was a lot of interest in the project, including many ideas from the Centre for Multi-disciplinary Studies in Gothenburg which was working on designs for a model ecological community. The original plan was for a self-supporting 'village' of 100 houses built on environmentally friendly principles of building design, organic cultivation, waste disposal and heating systems. But after many hours of discussion it became clear that it would be impossible to reconcile all the different interests. A number of people left the group but we stayed on, and new blood appeared as a result of contacts and advertisements. This time we were just a group of private individuals with no researchers or academics involved. We set our sights lower: a collection of private houses around a communal building which would be as environmentally friendly and would conserve as many resources as possible; and also, we hoped, provide an opportunity for people to share experiences and activities and to help and support each other. We investigated several sites but planning permission seemed hard to get. There was some opposition from conservative elements on the Council and many local people were suspicious of the proposed 'experimental' community.

'We kept on looking for a good site while trying to build up contacts and good relations with the authorities. We all began saving, and when in 1981 we reached our initial target we felt able to go ahead and offer the scheme to architects. It took quite a time to draw up all the plans of course; what was very significant was that we were all involved in the process of planning, and later in supervising minutely the building operations. We accepted the cheapest bid from a construction firm rather than looking for environmental commitment, we then had to watch carefully that the plans were being carried out exactly as stated. It was crucial that they didn't skimp on any of the specifications such as the thickness of the insulation in the walls which we had calculated was necessary to retain the maximum heat. The insulating material combined with the concrete makes the walls around 50 cm thick—we have nice wide window sills for our pot plants.

'We also had to decide what kind of ownership we were going to have. We felt we must own the property rather than rent it. So we chose a form of housing co-operative; together we own the site and each household pays a small rent to the group for its own dwelling. To all intents and purposes we own our houses. They are not identical; within the basic one- or two-storey design there is scope for individuality. We each chose our own kitchen fittings for example; ours was the only house with a dishwasher in the beginning but several other families with small children have bought them since. We do of course use environmentally friendly products in all our machines.

'We had decided on two sizes of house: a two-storey house of 120 sq. m and a smaller one-storey version of 96 sq. m. The idea of building greenhouses on to the south-facing walls (the positioning of the houses was carefully planned so that they would both collect warmth from the sun and protect each other from wind and cold) came from the book we had been studying. We also incorporated small porches at each front door to reduce heat lost when people went in or out. And then of course there were the earth closet toilets and the wells for collecting water from the kitchens for use on the gardens.

'Although we had originally planned a much bigger community I now think that 20-25 households is the best number. With that many members you can achieve a positive social effect—I mean shared child-minding for example, and safety. We don't have to lock up all the time here; we have our own in-built neighbourhood watch scheme. It's easier to take decisions within a small group too. We had very few real arguments at the beginning over the design of the houses, only minor disagreements over the colour of the outside walls, for example. The colour we settled on is a traditional dark red. I suppose that community life at Tuggelite hasn't developed to the extent that we thought it would. Some of the families already had small children when we moved in; more have been born in Tuggelite. The demands of a young family don't leave much time for socialising. But the parents who are taking maternity or paternity leave do eat together, with their children, twice a week and another group of adults eat an evening meal regularly together, without children. Personally we haven't got so involved in meal-sharing, partly because we still have many friends outside Tuggelite with whom we've kept in touch—we lived in an ordinary family house in Karlstad before.

'It's up to each household how much they share social activities, with no pressure being brought on anyone to join in. Then again, as our children grow into teenagers we enter a different phase and it's quite possible that we'll have more opportunity for socialising in the next few years.

'The effect on the older children of living in Tuggelite has been very positive. They appreciate the security the community gives them, and they are now beginning to make their own contribution. They readily help to organise the programme on a "workcamp day", adding their own suggestions. A few years ago they asked for a gymnastics group. The adults set it up for them and it bowled along nicely until the original group felt they'd outgrown it. But then the younger children wanted to join in, so the older ones took over as leaders. There is a strong bond between the children here who have all grown up together. We notice that there are few fights and often a very caring attitude. When the little ones start school, for instance, they find it quite easy to settle in, partly because they've been used to a wide age-range of children around them, but also because the older children from Tuggelite already at the school take special care of them.

'It's important that we all share in the maintenance and development of community life here. We started the practice of monthly "house meetings" right from the beginning. We ask for suggestions and ideas beforehand, and sometimes an individual or a group may introduce a topic, but generally the proceedings are very democratic. House meetings give us the chance to discuss various matters: different standards of cleanliness in the laundry room, for example, and work that may need to be done.

'Now that the community seems to be running fairly smoothly we've decided to hold house meetings less frequently, once every two months, as there's less to talk about.

'Another very important factor in the social organisation of Tuggelite is the work team. The adult residents are divided into five teams who are responsible, in rotation, for the communal tasks. Since we have taken on collective responsibility for cleaning the community centre, which includes the laundry room, the kitchen, sauna and the boiler room (the boiler has to be cleaned out every day) besides the main rooms which we use in the evenings and at week-ends, there is quite a lot of work involved. Then there is the outside area which we all own and look after jointly. Any practical jobs which need doing inside or outside are the responsibility of the work team. If there's a "work day" during the work team's duty period it's up to them to organise the programme for the day and to provide communal meals to sustain everybody. "Work days" are like mini-workcamps when we all get together to do the jobs that need to be done, like clearing up the communal areas outside, gardening or shovelling snow in winter. We arrange them as often as the need is felt, mainly in autumn and spring. They provide opportunities for social "cementing"; every one tries to be there, though of course it's not always possible. It's a chance to catch up with people you may not have talked to much over the last few weeks.

'Our own traditions are growing up here in Tuggelite. We always celebrate "Luciadag" (a traditional Swedish festival) together, on the Sunday nearest to the actual date, since we are all involved in other celebrations at school, etc. Then we have a party on Boxing Day and another in the summer when the schools break up. Although these are occasions for festivities all over the country Tuggelite is developing its own identity through its festivals.

'Over the summer holiday I'm afraid Tuggelite is rather empty as the families with small children tend to spend time away, often with grandparents. The people left here can feel a bit lonely. But I think this situation is inevitable at this stage of family life, given the traditional pattern of summer holiday behaviour in Sweden.

'November marks an important date on Tuggelite's calendar, the annual evaluation meeting. Besides offering a chance to assess developments over the year this is also an ideological forum when we look at the aims of the community and how far on we are towards meeting them. It gives an opportunity for anyone to challenge the direction we are taking and we sometimes have some quite frank discussions.

'Within Tuggelite we have particular roles for liaison with the society outside. At the moment I'm responsible for dealings with the day nursery staff. The nursery management is quite separate from us; it's a regular state day nursery—though possibly the only one in Sweden with composting toilets! But of course we have to liaise on matters like cleaning, which they do during the week and we do at week-ends.

'Integration into the wider society has come more slowly. We are now on better terms with our neighbours than at the outset. We organised a joint protest against a proposal to put an electricity transformer in the forest near here. We were successful in stopping it, which gave a boost to our morale, and a good opportunity to work together with our neighbours. Those who really objected to our being here have moved away, while others have begun to show an interest in what we're trying to do here at Tuggelite.

'Then Jörgen is active in local politics, working for the Green Party. He and I are acting as contact people for enquiries about Tuggelite from outside. Someone else is responsible for arranging study visits, and we all share the job of showing visitors around and explaining things to them. We get a tremendous number of enquiries, sometimes overwhelmingly so. Some people here think we should limit the number of visitors, and it's true that they can interrupt our lives quite a bit. But Jörgen and I both feel it's important that anyone interested in our style of community should be able to come and see what it's really like. It's vital to try to encourage other people to set up their own experiments; we can offer advice based on our experience, and sometimes practical experience too: one family has been living here with us for a year while they try to set up another ecological village in the district.

'And the future of Tuggelite? It lies with the children. Their reaction to being brought up in Tuggelite varies but I can tell you what my daughter said to me the other day: "I want to live in Tuggelite when I grow up because I feel safe here." '

Siv is a quiet, sincere person with an open friendly face. Although her smile is wonderfully warm her expression is a little care-worn, which you understand when you learn that her husband died in a cycle accident only eight months ago. She is staying on in the house in Tuggelite which he helped to design and was so enthusiastic about.

'I work in the administration at the technical college in Karlstad and my children have both attended a playschool in town rather than the one here in the community centre, simply because they, and we, were happy with that school; but this is definitely our home. My husband and I were involved in the planning, designing and building of Tuggelite from the beginning. That experience of working together in the preparation stages, which took a long time, longer than any of us had anticipated, was very valuable. It was probably necessary in order to build up strong working relationships between us and also to establish a democratic way of taking decisions. If one person had master-minded the whole operation I don't think it would have stood much chance. This way we all felt fully committed. There have been problems of course: I can't pretend everything has gone smoothly from the start. The boiler gave us some trouble at first and there have been various difficulties with the composting toilets. We try to share responsibility for the technical side of things; even if Lars is the expert on the boiler, for example, he's taught us all a fair bit about it. I can't say I'm very technically minded, but we all try and when there's a problem we can't solve there's always someone we can ask.

'This is an excellent place to bring up children. My two feel so secure here knowing they are part of a group where they are known, valued and cared for. Starting school doesn't present any of the traumas other children sometimes suffer. My daughter instantly recognised friends in the older classes, children who would keep a special look-out for her. So the strangeness of the new surroundings didn't matter so much. And of course our children are used to being together with others of all ages. There's always a playmate here if you want one—but if you don't, and you want to be on your own or with your parents, that's possible too.

'This is a difference between Tuggelite families and most families outside: after children are picked up at the day nursery (up to age seven) by working parents, there is little time or energy left for any wider socialising. My daughter, who's nine now, is happily off playing with the others a lot of the time, but my five-year-old boy prefers to spend his time with me. That's not surprising after losing his father so recently. What's good about Tuggelite is that we can cater for them both.

'But it's not just the children who benefit from the atmosphere of security and warmth we've managed to create here. I'm sure I have found my husband's death easier to bear because of the comfort and support I have had from my friends here, friends who I really trust and can go to any time I feel upset or down—there's always someone there. What's more these are people who were good friends of my husband too so they miss him as well, and we can share memories together. I've had lots of practical help too. Of course one major advantage of living here is that I can carry on with much the same lifestyle as before despite having changed my status to a one-parent family. So I don't have to deal so much with the loneliness that situation often brings. I don't feel trapped by my children as there's always someone to mind them at any time of the day. I appreciate Tuggelite even more now. I suppose in the beginning it was more of my husband's dream, but now I feel I need the comfort and acceptance I have here.

'We're not all that different from everyone else you know. Personally I think it's important not to be too radical too quickly. For one thing children can't cope easily with being too different from everyone else.

'Our children go to ordinary local schools and they have to stand up for Tuggelite as it is: already the composting toilets have created a stigma.

'I don't want my children to be labelled as "odd" all their school lives. Quite apart from that though I think it's a mistake to try to go too far too fast. We've taken a few steps here towards harmony with the environment with our building design, our conservation of energy, our recycling of waste and our sharing of resources. Several small steps are often more effective than one big one.

'We don't see ourselves as different to other people; most of us go off to work in Karlstad every day, unless we're taking maternity leave to be with our small children. Although the social dimension is a bit like a traditional village where everyone is known and thus people help and care for each other, we're not really like a village at all as our age range is so small; apart from two older single women, the adults are all within a ten-year age span. Then we're all financially independent, a precondition for buying into Tuggelite in the first place. If we hadn't put down the capital ourselves we couldn't have set up Tuggelite the way we wanted it.

'Besides the essential preliminary stage when we were doing the groundwork for Tuggelite together, I think an important reason for the success of this community is that nearly all of the original families stayed with us for the first few years. Since we moved in in 1984 only two families have left, and in both cases it was for personal reasons rather than dissatisfaction with the way Tuggelite was developing. I think a period of consolidation of, say, five years is crucial for establishing a community like this. You need to build up work patterns and social organisation. You have to learn how to deal with crises, such as a sudden shortage of wood-pellets for the boiler because the factory producing them was on strike, or the non-functioning of the toilets. During this settling-in period no new members should be admitted to the group; after that time you can start introducing new people but only a few at a time. The social balance is delicate and can easily be upset. In our case the long years of planning and working together have paid off: we have created an efficient and sustainable community which can be seen to be working.

'I feel needed and valued here, but I also feel that we are acting responsibly towards the environment.'

Hasse is a tall, slim, intense man with a sense of purpose about him. He normally works as a teacher in Karlstad but is currently taking paternity leave (quite common in Sweden) to look after his one-year-old child.

'I'm very involved with my children at the moment. They range in age from one to thirteen so I have an opportunity to observe the effect of living in Tuggelite at different stages in their lives. Three of my children were born here and have never known any other life. It's undoubtedly a positive and enriching experience for them when they're young, but who knows what their reaction will be as teenagers. I myself grew up in a house my family shared with another and so I was used to sharing living space. That was in Stockholm; I studied sociology at university and later worked as a play leader. I've always been interested in the way society functions and been looking for ways to make sure that everyone benefits. I moved to a job in Karlstad at the technical college and joined the study group along with Marianne, Siv and the others. That early period together before we moved into Tuggelite was vital to the long-term success of the community. It provided the solid base which meant that subsequent disagreements and difficulties could be contained and overcome. In a community like this everyone has to be very tolerant.

'We have learned to listen to each other and to be patient, which isn't easy when, as I do, you believe strongly in something. Of course we have differences of opinion: I for one would like to see fewer cars in Tuggelite but other people feel that private cars are still necessary. We shouldn't really need one car per household though. We did hire a minibus for a trial period but at the end of it nobody wanted to commit themselves by paying out to buy the bus. I was overruled on that occasion, but I still feel a community vehicle could replace several private cars here, or else perhaps one car could be shared between families. I enjoy the communal aspects of life here: I and my youngest child share a meal with the other parents and children at home twice a week, taking turns to prepare it. Then my wife and I join several others once a week to eat supper without the children. We're making progress towards group purchase of food: a number of families have a joint arrangement with a local farmer who leaves us fresh unpasteurised milk at the gate and also provides us with a whole lamb in the slaughtering season. I think this side of things could be developed a lot further. However I'm aware of the danger of being too idealistic and pushing my neighbours further than they feel ready to go. The evaluation meeting in November is a good chance to air any grievances and put forward new ideas. Recently two families brought up the suggestion of buying cable TV. The general opinion at the meeting was that the expense was unjustified and I think that the people concerned accepted the decision. We have since decided to pay for an extra Swedish channel, but of course if this is not enough the issue can always be raised again next year. On the other hand when the teenagers requested a stereo cassette for their gym dance sessions it was agreed to. Another group decision which provoked lengthy discussion was a fair price to ask for a house in Tuggelite when one family was moving out. We've been lucky that this has happened only twice in the history of Tuggelite: stability in the first few years is extremely important.

'It's true that we're a homogenous group of middle-class professionals—doctors, dentists, teachers and engineers—rather than a true cross-section of society. But if we had not been so in tune with one another and felt able to have open and rational discussions I doubt whether Tuggelite would have survived as it has. It would certainly have been difficult to get it off the ground, for we needed all the technical expertise and knowledge of official regulations, beside the contacts in the right places in order to get planning permission at all. Since then we have managed to get an award from a newspaper, which we have used to buy a new composting system for food waste. At first there was something of a problem with flies, which has not been entirely solved, but we're working on it.

'One growth point in Tuggelite just now is the cultivation of a kitchen garden. Outside the houses we have marked out an area for vegetables, a communal plot which is looked after by ten families, and additional individual plots. This is in addition to the fruit and vegetables we grow in our greenhouses. Produce from these gardens is stored in the underground earth cellars we built, which have proved very effective in keeping vegetables cool and fresh. Unfortunately we haven't had wonderful results with our home-grown vegetables as the soil here is so poor; just about good enough for potatoes and onions. What we can't grow we try to buy as a co-operative. We also buy all our cleaning products this way, and I think the system could be extended to more items on the family shopping list.

'What effect is all this environmental consciousness having on our children? I would say it depends very much on the child. I try not to indoctrinate my children: merely by living here they are making a statement to the world. They absorb the values of the community without trying, and that sets them a little apart from their schoolmates. My children have certainly been teased at school because they come from that strange place with the earth closet toilets. They seem to be able to cope with the taunts, but I'm not sure that I would want them to have to deal with being radically different. My thirteen-year-old daughter is highly motivated to try to save the planet, and frequently comes up with her own ideas: at the moment she's organising a collection of cans. My ten-year-old son is quite the opposite and much more of a conformist. For him it's much harder living in a place like Tuggelite since he resents the different way we do things here.

'We have to accept their differences in attitude and try not to be too critical. They must decide for themselves how they want to live as adults. The future of Tuggelite rests to a large extent with them and what's exciting is that we are now entering a new phase when the children are starting to tell us what to do to protect the environment. It will be fascinating to see what happens next.'

Sacredness is an attribute of the mind, not an attribute of the cosmos. Only when we approach the universe with a reverential attitude and behold it with a mind that is sacred, do we find the universe sacred.

Henryk Skolimowski, from *Living Philosophy*

Introduction to the Afterword

VITHAL RAJAN

'Is the Universe a Friendly Place?'

ALBERT EINSTEIN SAID it is important for us to ask whether the universe is a friendly place. The answer to this all important question is not out there, but within ourselves. Religious belief has accepted the poor as naturally forming the community of God, for it is only to Him that they can turn: 'Blessed are the poor in spirit for theirs is the Kingdom of Heaven.' For the ancient Buddhist, an important refuge was the *sanga*, a community held together by the Spirit, much like the early church, where two or three were met in His Name. It is a tragedy of civilisation that institutionalism and fundamentalism have swept the idea of the Spirit away from religion. In these uneasy, untidy times the Spirit rests, as it perhaps always has, in the coming together of ordinary people, who in rebuilding their communities show us a glimmer of the basic unity of nature, humanity and the cosmos. In my own country of India, the long forgotten idea of the *sanga* now finds new form in the *sangams*, or associations, of the poor, by which people with no resource except their labour come together for mutual support. By helping each other, they rediscover their own community, its strengths, its knowledge, and its culture. The oppressed find a name for themselves, a voice among the mighty, and show an example of true development, of a barefoot revolution, enriching the life of their community. And it is the poor women, as among the *sangams* of the Deccan Development Society in Andhra Pradesh, with which I had the honour to serve for ten years, who by looking after each others' simple needs show to the world what community spirit can do for people. Their small savings, their happiness in seeing that their children do not go to bed hungry, that there is a vegetable to eat along with the rice, that maybe they can put a tile roof on their hut, that herbs grow which can cure them, sound deep in the ears of the many like a grand orchestra. From simple frugality has come self-confidence and an unassuming dignity, and this in turn has brought them social and political recognition. Women working together and caring for each other and their families has not brought them the lust for power —though such temptation is not wholly absent. What they have achieved too is the beginning of a spiritual life together, though they have yet to give it a name.

But what they may discover is that building a community is an act of compassion, an act of love, 'which covers a multitude of sins', and which blesses the giver. It is the way by which we as a people can get in touch with the continually evolving cosmos, and find a comforting, affirmative answer to Einstein's question in our own hearts. **Sir George Trevelyan**, one of the best-loved thinkers and seers of our time ends this book on a note which, for all its poetry, is also simple commonsense.

Afterword:

The Resurgence of the
Community Spirit in Europe
or
The Rising Tide of Love

SIR GEORGE TREVELYAN

INDEED, THIS SEEMS to be happening in our time. Although there is still so much violence, negative emotion, fear and greed, it is palpably obvious to anyone open to it that there is also what I would call a 'rising tide of love'. Perhaps this will prove to be a major phenomenon in our time. It does not enforce itself. It simply flows and where it meets resistance and adverse emotion it seeps around. When a human being has overcome negative emotion, greed and criticism and is able to offer the chalice of self ready to receive it, then this tide of love will fill it. To those who are alert and awake, it is very clear that people are drawn into groupings of love and companionship.

The geographers and scientists can tell us of global warming, melting of the ice-caps, and the rising of the seas. In such a time of dismay and foreboding, the rising tide of love can bring joy. It draws people to try and work together in group endeavour. Some groups are small—and indeed it is right to begin small and develop organically. The most important example of a successful community in this country is Findhorn. This also started from the smallest unit, but from the first was a demonstration of working not for self but for the Whole, to the Glory of God and under divine guidance. It is a precarious way of living, but may be a clue for many in the coming period of change, when the economic structure of our society seems to be breaking down. This implies that the energies that vitalised the old structure, based on self-interest, are being withdrawn and in their place are being released living energies that are inherently powerful for the harmonising of all life. If we can take this concept, it can throw light on the present symptoms of breakdown, which could fill us with dismay unless we can accept that dying is always a necessary prelude to renewal, making way for the flooding in of transforming forces which could bring to birth a new society.

It may serve a really important function if groups working to build community make links with each other, and come together every now and then to look at what they are doing in the light of the greater picture. For the spirit has no meaning if it is working *in vacuo* and detached from life. We have to transform society, each one of us starting from precisely the point we are now at. Increasingly we see that the guidance and the wisdom we need are within us; less and less do we need to search outside. Having free will, we must learn to use it not for ego and self but for the whole. This is the coming to maturity of mankind. There never was such a generation to be alive.

Appendix

Examples of grassroots conservation initiatives in Europe

MICHEL PIMBERT

Belgium

A range of Belgian associations promoting biological farming and gardening, such as CRABE and VELT, are actively collecting, conserving, multiplying and distributing seeds of traditional varieties. Some commercial enterprises, like Biogarden, are also multiplying and selling organic seed, while a broad-based worker solidarity movement, Fraternité Ouvrière, is encouraging small-scale urban gardening and conservation techniques involving over 1,200 plant varieties, to promote family nutrition among low-income households.

France

Grassroots genetic conservation activities in France are well established and very popular. Farmers' and gardeners' organisations promoting biological production methods (FNAB, Nature et Progrés, Terre Vivante...) provide exchange platforms for traditional landraces. They also provide training and documentation and carry out research activities. Organic seed companies, such as the highly popular Biau Germe, specialising in old varieties not listed in the National Seed Catalogue, maintain, multiply and sell seeds by correspondence. Various local associations like Club Mémoire Verte or the Association for the Inventory and Conservation of Cultivated Plants are collecting and propagating rare vegetables. At last count, more than fifteen organisations are conserving and popularising local fruits, such as the nationwide network Croqueurs de Pommes. National Regional Parks and private individuals are maintaining traditional plants and animals for specific ecological zones or local industries. Since 1984, southeast France has engaged in a regional genetic heritage programme, PAGE PACA, involving inventorisation, conservation, documentation, training, and diversification of local agriculture. The programme is a cooperative effort between NGOs, national and regional parks, chambers of agriculture, INRA, schools, botanical gardens and other bodies. It puts emphasis not only on conservation and use of locally adapted species, but raising awareness, creating employment and capturing export markets for processed goods based on the region's genetic heritage.

Germany

A large part of the conservation activities carried out by the informal sector in Germany are organised through independent research centres, membership networks and biodynamic seed companies. Some independent plant-breeding associations, such as Pflanzenzuchtverein Werstein in Manleus, maintain collections composed of local landraces representing several hundred varieties of species. Together with farmers and horticulturalists they are pursuing crop improvement programmes and farming systems research for sustainable agriculture. Members of genetic resources exchange networks like Verein VEN, the SSE or Arche Noah, also maintain active collections, while the German biodynamic seed sector is one of Europe's largest. In the former GDR, some independent plant breeding research organisations and small gardeners' associations also maintain(ed) important collections of traditional plant genetic resources.

Greece

At the non-governmental level, individual farmers and rural communities are maintaining —sometimes rehabilitating—traditional varieties, especially cereals, often in marginalised territories. However, to date, there seems to be no organised programme or co-operative work going on.

Italy

Grassroots conservation work in Italy is highly fragmented. Biodynamic farmers' networks linked to the Demeter Association are conserving and utilising traditional landraces, and several large private amateur collections of fruits have been established. Mixed regional programmes promoting on-farm conservation and improvement of rustic fruits, cereals and vegetables are also under way (Tuscany, Marche). A range of farmers' co-operatives are collecting and reusing old local varieties of maize, emmer and durum wheat, vegetables and other crops. The larger environmental organisations, like Terranova, WWF and Lega per l'Ambiente, are also starting to set up orchards, experimental farms and germplasm reserves in order to conserve and breed crops for organic farmers.

Netherlands

There are several large-scale private and semi-private germplasm conservation programmes being carried out in the Netherlands. One of the largest, Het Hof van Eden, runs a genebank and an *in situ* collection of 30,000 species from all over the world. The collection, focussing on so-called 'minor crops', has been built up over the past 12 years and includes important materials from the Andes, Tibet and Ethiopia. Every year, 12-18,000 species are rejuvenated on a total of 1.2 hectares scattered among small farmers' fields to avoid cross-pollination. All data are computerised; a small non-profit seed company has been established to cover basic conservation costs. Other non-profit foundations are dedicated to rare tulip collections and conservation of horticultural species, in collaboration with national botanical gardens and public universities.

Portugal

Non-profit environmental groups are active in agroforestry projects to maintain and propagate locally adapted trees as a more sustainable alternative to high-yielding eucalyptus.

Spain

Farmers' organisations, private individuals and university-linked associations are engaged in a variety of initiatives to document, conserve, exchange and improve local landraces adapted to the different climates and production systems of Spanish agriculture. Whether affiliated with the ecological, biodynamic or conventional farming sectors, genetic resources exchange networks are gaining momentum and documentation is improving. The Catalan-based CAE and the Valencian CEIDER are playing lead roles in coordinating and stimulating this work.

UK

Grassroots conservation work in the UK is well established and attracting public interest. Some large collections are held by independent non-profit research associations devoted to sustainable agriculture, like the HDRA. HDRA's Heritage Seed Programme currently houses 200 varieties of vegetables, many of which have been taken off the commercial seed market. Training courses in saving viable seeds and raising awareness are part of their programme. Private individuals also collect, conserve, exchange and utilise traditional varieties not available on the British market.

NON-EC EUROPE:
Austria, Switzerland and Turkey

Grassroots conservation activities in **Austria** are organised through several groups, one of the largest being the Arche Noah network, formed as such in 1990 through the fusion of two long-standing groups. Current membership exceeds 200 people in the German-speaking countries (Austria, Germany and Switzerland). Particular collecting efforts are devoted to cultivars being dropped from National Lists, as a form of 'early warning system' for genetic erosion. Arche Noah carries out inventories of regional genetic diversity research in various conservation methods and facilitates germplasm exchange and awareness-raising through fairs, local markets, school programmes, the media and various publications. Voluntary conservation work in **Switzerland** is very well organised and receives government support. Major collections of plant and animal genetic resources are preserved on 600 farms through the membership programme of Pro Specie Rara, while Fructus is carrying out the largest fruit species conservation programme among Swiss NGOs. These and other groups make inventories, carry out research and public awareness campaigns, and liaise effectively with the Swiss genebank at Changins. As for **Turkey**, just a few projects on genetic resources conservation are being carried out at the community level.

Nordic Countries

NGO plant genetic resources conservation networks are particularly well structured in **Denmark** and **Sweden**. The Danish Seed Savers Exchange network currently has 50 members who are collecting, conserving, multiplying and exchanging heirloom seeds. For example, they recently saved a 100-year-old *Pisum* landrace being grown by an amateur and threatened with extinction. Germplasm maintenance, informal research and experimental breeding for alternative crop production systems is also being carried out by the Ethnobotanical Garden, run by a private individual. In Sweden, SESAM, a voluntary organisation with over 200 members is collecting, maintaining and distributing among its membership vegetables and cereals that are typical of Scandinavia. Rejuvenation work is given to experienced members while samples of all varieties are backed up through long-term cold seed storage. SESAM also carries out research on meristem tissue culture to clean up its virus-infected indigenous potato collection (100 varieties), and develops innovative regeneration techniques adapted to the various climates of Sweden. SESAM is developing contacts with grassroots conservation NGOs in **Finland** and, together with **Denmark** and **Norway**, the various groups are discussing the potential for full Nordic NGO cooperation.

Eastern Europe

Local conservation activities in Eastern European countries has remained limited to private initiatives, small gardeners' clubs and a few ecological plant-breeding societies. For example, the Gesellschaft für Ökologische Pflanzenzucht in the former GDR has been conserving a broad range of cereal genetic resources and developing breeding methods of low-input farming, and enjoyed collaboration with the Gatersleben genebank. Groups in **Hungary** and **Czechoslovakia** are also promoting the conservation and use of traditional fruit species for local markets and industry. Under current circumstances, however, major emergency NGO operations have had to be launched over the past year to identify and protect the genetic diversity still available at the farmer and market level in several East European countries.

Source: Hardon, J., Perret, P. and Vellvé, R. 1992. Common framework for an integrated EC programme on the conservation of plant genetic resources. Published by GRAIN, Jonqueres 16, 6D, E-08003, Barcelona, Spain.

References

Introduction: The Return to the Community
1. UBS International Finance, 12, Summer 1992.
2. Peter Kornbluh, Nicaragua - The Price of Intervention. Reagan's wars against the Sandinistas, Institute for Policy Studies, Washington D.C., 1987.
3. Ernest Gellner, Postmodernism, Reason and Religion, Routledge, 1992.
4. Sandra Harding, The Science Question in Feminism, Open University Press, 1986.
5. Gill Kirkup and Laurie Smith Keller (eds.), Inventing Women: Science, Technology and Gender, Polity Press, 1992.
6. Luther Standing Bear, Land of the Spotted Eagle, University of Nebraska Press, 1978.
7. Fritjof Capra, The Turning Point, Simon & Schuster, 1982.
8. Henryk Skolimowski, Living Philosophy, Arkana, 1992.
9. Edward Said, Orientalism, Penguin, 1985.
10. Pauline Marie Rosenau, Post-Modernism and the Social Sciences, Princeton University Press, 1992.
11. Richard Ashley and R.B.J.Walker, 'Speaking the Language of Exile: Dissident Thought in International Studies'. International Studies Quarterly, 34.3, 1990.
12. Michel Foucault, Power/Knowledge, Pantheon Books, 1980.
13. Vincent Descombes, Modern French Philosophy, Cambridge University Press, 1980.
14. His Excellency Ricardo Alarcon de Quesada, The Minister for Foreign Affairs, Cuba, at the United Nation's Economic and Social Council (ECOSOC): 'The Solution is called justice and true human solidarity', Granma International, July 19, 1992.
15. The Guardian, 17 July, 1992.
16. Susan George, A Fate Worse than Debt, Penguin, 1988.
17. The Guardian, 2 September, 1992.
18. Ronald Wright, Stolen Continents, John Murray, 1992.
19. D.G.Tendulkar, Mahatma. Vols I-VIII, Publications Division, Government of India.
20. Gunnar Myrdal, Asian Drama, Vols I-III, Penguin.
21. Vandana Shiva, Staying Alive, Nataraja, 1990.
22. Amartya Sen, Poverty and Famines, Clarendon Press, 1982.
23. David Seckler, 'Production, Poverty & Employment in Indian Agriculture', mimeo, USAID, 1985.
24. Bertrand Schneider, The Barefoot Revolution, A Report to the Club of Rome, Intermediate Technology Publications, 1988.
25. Swami Satprakashnanda, Methods and Knowledge, Advaita Ashram, India, 1974.
26. Richard Harland, Superstructuralism: The Philosophy of Structuralism and Post-Structuralism, Methuen, 1987.
27. Chogyam Trungpa, Journey without a Goal, Shambhala, 1985.
28. Paula M. Cooey et al., After Patriarchy, Orbis Books, 1991.
29. John S. Pobee, Who are the Poor?, WCC Geneva, 1988.
30. M.Scott Peck, The Different Drum, Arrow Books, 1987.
31. Nicholas Till, Mozart and the Enlightenment, Faber and Faber, 1992.
32. E.F.Schumacher, Small is Beautiful, Harper, 1975.
33. Marija Gimbutas, The Civilization of the Goddess, Harper, 1992.

Part One: Global Issues: Introduction
1. The Guardian, 12 August 1992.
2. Robert Chambers, Putting the Last First, Longman, 1982.

Waiting for UNCED: Waiting for Godot: Johan Galtung
Notes

The figures in connection with the nuclear reactors around the world are from the doctoral thesis by Johan Swahn at the Section for Applied Peace Research at Chalmerska Technological Institute in Gothenburg.

For the theory of biogas converter appropriation, see Johan Galtung, Development, Environment and Technology, New York, UNCTAD, 1979.

For the point about diet, a look at world smoking habits, or at least the European ones, is already instructive. The US is here ahead of others in prohibiting smoking in public spaces. In Europe, France is seen as most prohibitionist, Spain among the least (El Pais, 27 February 1992). I am grateful to Dr Terry Shintani, Honolulu, for estimates of the effect of the diet factor on human mortality.

A good example of simple alternative technology is the 'witch's stove', an insulated box where a pot that has been brought to boiling point can be enclosed so that the cooking continues without more energy consumption. A simple device indeed, saving 40-50% of energy usage (Korean Herald, 10 April 1992).

Economics & Sustainable Resource Use: Fulai Sheng
1. David W. Pearce & R. Kerry Turner, Economics of Natural Resources and the Environment, p.311, Johns Hopkins University Press, Baltimore, 1990.
2. Sally Jeanrenaud, The Conservation-Development Interface (Draft), WWF-UK, March 1992.
3. Worldwatch Institute, State of the World, p.150, W.W. Norton & Company, New York and London, 1992.
4. Anthony Luke, 'Spain: Too Poor to be Green', New Scientist, 25 July 1992.
5. World Resources Institute: World Resources 1992-93, p.9, Oxford University Press, 1992.
6. Worldwatch Institute, State of the World, p.3, W.W. Norton & Company, New York and London, 1992.
7. IUCN, UNEP, WWF, Caring for the Earth, Gland, Switzerland, 1991.
8. World Resources Institute, op. cit., p.136.
9. IUCN, UNEP, WWF, World Conservation Strategy, Gland, Switzerland, 1980.
10. IUCN, UNEP, WWF, Caring for the Earth, p.1.
11. Ibid.
12. UNCED, Agenda 21, Chapter 8, p.2 (advance copy), June 1992.
13. IUCN, UNEP, WWF, Caring for the Earth, p.1.
14. In WWF-Canada and WWF-US, the original name 'World Wildlife Fund' is retained.
15. WWF, Annual Review, Gland, Switzerland, 1992.
16. WWF, Focus on WWF in Europe, p.12, Banson, London, September 1991.
17. WWF-Spain, Environmental Effects of the Castilla-La Mancha Regional Development Plan (Summary), 1991.
18. CEPA (Coordinatora Extremena de Proteccion Ambiental), Dealing with Disparity: European Structural Funds in South West Spain, The Econologist, Vol 22, No 3, May/June 1992.
19. LPN (Liga Para a Protecçao da Natureza) and ADPM (Association for the Defence of Mértola's Heritage), CADISPA/Mértola, Portugal, 1992-1993.
20. H.E. Williams, 'Scope for the Development of the Environmental Sector in the Regional Context', Environment and Economic Development in the Regions of the European Community, ed. Frank E. Joyce and Gunter Schneider, Avebury, England, 1988.

21. Michael Wells, Katrina Brandon, and Lee Hannah, People and Parks – Linking Protected Area Management with Local Communities (draft), WWF-US, Washington, DC, 1990.

22. Sally Jeanrenaud, op. cit., p.24.

23. Ibid.

24. Ibid.

25. Ibid.

26. LPN and ADPM, op. cit.

27. The World Bank and European Investment Bank, The Environmental Program for the Mediterranean, p.10, World Bank, Washington, DC, 1990.

28. EC, 'Towards Sustainability—A European Community Programme of Policy and Action in relation to the Environment and Sustainable Development', 1992.

29. Ibid.

30. C.A. Vendrik, 'Recreation Planning for the North Holland Coast', Environment and Economic Development in the Regions of the European Community, ed. Frank E. Joyce and Gunter Schneider, Avebury, England, 1989.

31. Ibid.

32. EC, op. cit.

33. Ibid.

34. World Bank and European Investment Bank, op. cit., p.10.

35. Michael Wells, Katrina Brandon, and Lee Hannah, op. cit.

36. Sally Jeanrenaud, op. cit.

37. World Resources Institute.

38. Sally Jeanrenaud, op. cit.

39. Ibid.

40. Ibid.

41. Worldwatch Institute, State of the World 1992-1993.

42. This part draws on Sally Jeanrenaud, op. cit.

43. J.M. Ernecq, 'Some Aspects of Environmental Policy in a Traditional Industrial Region: The Case of the Nord-Pas-de-Calais Region in France', Environment and Economic Development in the Regions of the European Community, ed. Frank E. Joyce and Gunter Schneider, Avebury, England, USA, 1988.

44. IUCN, UNEP, WWF, Caring for the Earth, 1991.

45. World Bank, World Development Report 1992, Washington, DC, 1992.

46. WWF and World Bank, People and Parks (advance copy), 1992.

47. World Resources Institute, World Resources 1992-93.

48. Ibid.

49. Solon Barraclough, Land Tenure and the Social Dynamics of Deforestation, p.9, United Nations Research Institute for Social Development, 1992.

50. Ibid.

51. Ibid.

52. The World Commission on Environment and Development, Our Common Future, Oxford University Press, Oxford, New York, 1987.

53. Sally Jeanrenaud, op. cit.

54. Ibid.

55. Ibid.

56. Ibid.

57. Ibid.

58. Ibid.

59. EC, op. cit.

The Community-Nature Relationship: Michel Pimbert

1. A. Gomez-Pompa and A. Kaus, Taming the wilderness myth, Bioscience Vol. 42 (4): 271-279, 1992.

2. F. Couplan, Le régal végétal, Plantes sauvages comestibles, Encyclopédie des plantes comestibles de l'Europe Vol. 1, Debard, Paris, 1983.

3. P. Marchenay, A la recherche des variétés locales des plantes cultivées. PAGE PACA, La Thomassine, 1987.

4. PAGE PACA, Pour que vive la diversité, Page Paca, Manosque, France, 1990.

5. R. Vellvé, Saving the Seed: Genetic diversity and European agriculture, Earthscan Publications, 1992.

6. K. Dahl and G.P. Nabham, From the grassroots up: the conservation of plant genetic resources by grassroot organisations, Diversity Vol. 8 (2): 28-31, 1992.

7. P. Mooney, The law of the seed. Development dialogue 1983: 1-2, 1983.

8. PAGE PACA, op. cit.

9. M.P. Pimbert, Une pepinière d'actions locales, La lettre de Solagral, 66: 11-20, 1988.

10. B. Mollison, Permaculture: A Designer's Manual, Tagari Publications, 1988.

11. T.M. Groh and S.H. McFadden, Farms of tomorrow: community supported farms & farm supported communities, Biodynamic Farming and Gardening Association, Kimberton, 1990.

12. J.N. Pretty, Farmers extension practice and technology adaptation: Agricultural revolution in 17-19th century Britain, Agriculture and human values—Winter-Spring 1991: 132-148.

13. M. Thick, Market gardening in England and Wales. Quoted in J.N. Pretty, Agriculture and human values 1991: pp.132-148, 1985.

14. R. Chambers, A. Pacey and L.A. Thrupp, Farmer First, Intermediate Technology Publications, London, 1989.

15. J.N. Pretty, op. cit.

16. R. Rhoades, The coming revolution in methods for rural development research. User's perspective network (UPWARD), International Potato Centre, Box 933, Manila, Philippines, 1990.

17. P. Richards, Farmers also experiment: a neglected intellectual resource in African Science. Discovery and Innovation. 1(1): 19-25, 1989.

18. M. Worede, Ethiopia: a genebank working with farmers. In Growing Diversity, D. Cooper, R. Vellve and H. Hobbelink (Eds), Intermediate Technology Publications pp.78-96, 1992.

19. A. Hangerud and M.P. Collinson, Plants, genes and people: improving the relevance of plant breeding in Africa, Experimental Agriculture 26: 341-362, 1990.

20. J. Ashby, C. Quiros, and Y. Riviera, Farmer Participation in On-farm Varietal Trials. Discussion Paper, Agricultural Administration Network No. 22. UK: Overseas Development Institute, 1987.

21. D.M. Maurya, A. Bottrall, and J. Farrington, Improved livelihoods, genetic diversity and farmer participation: a strategy for rice breeding in rainfed areas of India, Experimental Agriculture 24, 311-320, 1988.

22. M.P. Pimbert, Participatory Research with Women Farmers, 30 min. VHS-PAL Video, ICRISAT Information Services, Distributed by TVE, Postbox 7, 3700 AA Zeist, The Netherlands, 1991.

23. R. Chambers, Participatory rural appraisals: past, present and future. Forest, trees and people Newsletter No. 15/16: 4-9, 1992.

24. RRA Notes, Nos. 1-16, Participatory Rural Appraisal—Proceeding of the February 1991 Bangalore PRA trainers workshop, Myrada and IIED. See especially No. 13.

25. H. Rose and S. Rose, The political economy of science: Ideology of/in the natural sciences, Macmillan Press, 1976.

26. E. Yoxen, The gene business: who should control biotechnology? Free Association Books, 1983.
27. R. Vellvé, op. cit.
28. R.J. Mac Rae, S.B. Hill, J. Henning, and G.R. Mehuys, Agricultural science and sustainable agriculture: a review of existing scientific barriers to sustainable food production and potential solutions, Biological Agriculture and Horticulture, 6: 173–219, 1989.
29. J.M. Lévy-Leblond, Ideology of/in contemporary physics. In: H. Rose, and S. Rose, The Radicalisation of science. Macmillan Press pp. 136–175, 1976.
30. R. Vellvé, and H. Hobbelink, Intellectual property rights on life forms: opportunities and concerns, ATAS Bulletin 8 (in press), 1992.
31. D. Baldock, Agriculture and habitat loss in Europe, WWF International CAP discussion paper number 3, 1990.
32. H. Lorenzen, Agriculture et ecologie, un marriage fertile, Green papers, 10, Published by the Green group in the European Parliament, 1992.
33. Lorenzen, op. cit.
34. SAFE, Draft document on CAP reform, unpublished. Available from SAFE, 21, Tower Street, London, WC2H 9NS, UK, 1991.

Part Two: Living in Harmony: Some Concepts: Introduction

1. Richard H. Grove, 'Origins of Western Environmentalism', Scientific American, July 1992.
2. Arturo Gomez-Pompa and Andrea Kaus, "Taming the Wilderness Myth". BioScience, Vol. 42, No. 4, April 1992.

Part Two: Living in Harmony: Practical Social Experiments: Introduction
For more information on the Cadispa projects, you can contact:

Marco Pagliani
WWF-Spain
ADENA
Santa Engracia 6
28010 Madrid, Spain
Tel: 01-308-23-09
or 01-308-23-10
Fax: 01-308-32-93

Magnus Sylven
WWF-International
Rue Mont Blanc
CH-1196 Gland,Switzerland
Tel: 022-364-9225
Fax: 022-364-3239

Peter Martin
WWF-UK
Panda House
Weyside Park
Godalming, Surrey GU7 1XR, UK
Tel: 0483-426-444
Fax: 0483-426-409

Spain: The Pyrenees: Introduction

1 & 2 Coordinatora Extremena de Proteccion Ambiental (CEPA): 'Dealing with Disparity', The Ecologist, Vol. 22, No.3, May/June 1992.

Part Three: Habitat and Communitas: Introduction

1. The Guardian, 14 October, 1991.
2. Revd Alan McDonald, 'Edinburgh, The Story of Pilton Community Ministry', in Wendy Godfrey(ed), Down to Earth, The British Council of Churches, 1985.
3. The Guardian, 8 July, 1992.

Community within the City: John Turner

1. Defined as 'meeting the needs of the present without compromising the ability of future generations to meet their own needs.' World Commission on Environment and Development, Our Common Future (the 'Bruntland Report'), Oxford, 1987.

2. The potential of community-building through self-managed local initiatives is illustrated by twenty cases in Africa, Asia and Latin America, in Building Community, a Third World Case Book, edited by Bertha Turner, Habitat International Coalition, 1988. Available from HIC (Europe), Habitat et Participation, Place du Levant 1, Louvain-la-Neuve, Belgium 1348.

3. Information on the Trowbridge estate was complemented and updated by Patrick Hamill, RIBA. The principal source for information on the Hesketh Street project is from Power to the People: co-op housing in Liverpool, The Architect's Journal, 18 July 1984. Sophy Krajewska, a co-author of the above, also provided updated information.

4. At one time, for example, minibuses were bringing young Australians from the Earls Court area of West London to squat in the vacant flats.

5. Planning for Real is a widely used methodology for participatory planning and design promoted by the Neighbourhood Initiatives Foundation, Telford, UK.

6. From his article in Power to the People: co-op housing in Liverpool, op. cit.

7. John F.C. Turner and Rober Fichter, editors, Freedom to Build: dweller control of the housing process, Macmillan, New York, 1972; trans, Italian, Spanish.

8. Hernando de Soto, in El Otro Sendero, la revolución informal (La Oveja Negra, Bogotá, Colombia 1987) describes how commerce and public transport in Lima, Peru, depend on the dominant 'informal economy' – and how legal regulations inflate costs to unaffordable levels. The late Graeme Shankland's Wonted Work, a Guide to the Informal Economy (Bootstrap Press, New York, 1988) provides a complementary view in the so-called 'developed' world.

9. Estimates vary too widely to validate particular references, most of which fail to specify what is included or refer to single factors. If the use of materials and energy for home and neigbourhood uses and furnishing as well as for building, improvement and maintenance are added, the total approaches half of all that is used, and more in low-income countries.

10. Colin Ward on John Turner's second and third 'Laws of Housing' in his Introduction to Housing By People, Marion Boyars, London, 1976 and Pantheon Books, New York, 1977; trans, Dutch, French, German, Italian, Spanish.

11. In Human Scale Development, Apex Press, New York and London, Manfred Max-Neef presents a much more detailed breakdown of factors which has been used to demonstrate the same issue.

12 . Le Corbusier is commonly blamed for this misinterpretation by calling a house a machine for living in—view shared by many professionals, politicians and industrialists with interests in mass-production (as distinct from 'production by the masses') since the 1920s.

13. W.R. Ashby, 'Self-regulation and Requisite Variety' in Introduction to Cybernetics, Wiley, London, 1956, reprinted in Systems Thinking, edited by F.E. Emery, Penguin Modern Management Readings, London, 1969.

14. Michael A. Franks in an unpublished working paper, 'Realising People's Productivity', co-authored with John F.C.Turner, 1991.

15. Eduard Sapir, 'Culture Genuine and Spurious', in The American Journal of Sociology, Vol. 29, January 1924.

Notes on the Contributors

Sue Austin, a social researcher, has lived and worked in several countries of Europe including Northern Ireland and Africa. She is at present working as a language teacher and living with her family in Sweden.

Ricardo Azon is the president of ADEPA and in charge of the Aragonese component of CADISPA-Spain. He is a veterinarian who sudied in Madrid and decided to go back to his hometown in Sabinanigo to promote conservation and development in Aragon.

Giorgos Catsadorakis, a biologist, is one of the most important experts on Greek fauna. He works in Prespa on several conservation projects.

Christa Dettwiler is a freelance journalist living in Zurich. She has worked for Greenpeace.

Paulo Faria is a biologist and biology teacher in a secondary school in Lisbon. He is the former Head of Education at LPN (Liga Proteaççao Natureza), and is an active volunteer for several Portuguese environmental NGOs.

Johan Galtung, one of the most renowned peace researchers of our times, has held over a dozen major positions and over 30 Visiting Professorships in five continents, and has consulted for all the major UN agencies. He has published more than 50 books and over 1,000 monographs. In 1987 he received the Right Livelihood Award, "the Alternative Nobel Prize", for his systematic and multi-disciplinary study of the conditions which can lead to peace. At present, he is Professor of Peace Studies, University of Hawaii, as well as Honorary Professor at the Freie Universitat, Berlin, Sichuan University, and the Universidad de Alicante.

Satish Kumar is the Director of Schumacher College at Dartington, south Devon, and Editor of Resurgence magazine. He travels widely, giving talks on ecological and spiritual issues.

Donald MacDonald, from the Island of Lewis in North Western Scotland, is the author of several text books on environmental and geographical themes. Since 1986 he has been the Head of Geography at Jordanhill Campus of the University of Strathclyde, Glasgow.

Myrsini Malakou, biologist, is the Managing Director of the Society for the Protection of Prespa, where she lives and works with all the main environmental NGOs in Greece. She is the Coordinator for CADISPA-Greece.

Peter Martin, Head of Education Policy, WWF-UK, has been a teacher, adventure training instructor, warden of a nature reserve and education officer of the Royal Society for the Protection of Birds. He initiated the development of the CADISPA concept which has now taken root in several European countries.

Giorgio Neri has been in charge of the communication aspects of CADISPA-Italy, on a voluntary basis, since the start of the project. He is a freelance journalist and writes for a number of local newspapers and magazines.

Hillka Pietila was head of the UN Association of Finland, and has worked and written for several years on issues related to world peace, human rights, the rights and status of women, third world development and the environment.

Michel Pimbert, Head of the Biodiversity Programme of WWF International, is an agroecologist, who initiated exemplary participatory research with poor Indian women farmers when he worked as Principal Entomologist with the International Crop Research Institute for the Semi-Arid Tropics (ICRISAT).

David Pitt is a member of the IUCN Commission on Environmental Strategy and Planning; a consultant on the UN Negotiating Committee on Climate Change; and Secretary, Alp Action Scientific Advisory Committee, Bellerive Foundation. He has published widely on environmental and development issues.

Miquel Rafa, a biologist, is the founder and current director of DEPANA, Catalonia's main environmental NGO. He has a long experience of "green" NGOs and studied the NGO movement in the USA. He is responsible for CADISPA-Catalonia, one of the two Spanish CADISPAs.

Vithal Rajan has worked in the areas of peace research, human rights, third world development and environment issues. He was the founder Chairman of the Deccan Development Society; Executive Director of The Right Livelihood Foundation, and Director, Ethics and Education, WWF International.

Jorge Revez, biologist, is the director of ADP, the NGO in charge of CADISPA-Portugal, he has been active for many years in the region of Mértola, where he has helped establish two cooperatives (woolweavers and beekeepers).

Enrique Segovia, biologist, began with WWF-Spain as a volunteer, becoming the education officer in 1990. His special concerns are the topics of consumption and sustainable development. He is the co-ordinator of CADISPA-Spain.

Fulai Sheng is an economist who has served with the Ministry of Finance of the People's Republic of China and with the World Bank in Washington. At present he works in the Sustainable Resource Use programme of WWF International.

Sir George Trevelyan, Bt., called 'a spiritual leader of the New Age movement', has written many books including: *A Vision of the Aquarian Age, Operation Redemption*, and *Summons to a High Crusade*. He founded the Wrekin Trust to inspire people towards a holistic world view, and was given the Right Livelihood Award in 1982, "for educating the adult spirit to a new non-materialistic vision of human-nature".

John F.C. Turner has developed the theory and practice of self-managed home and neighbourhood building in Peru, the United States and the United Kingdom. His several books on housing policy have been published in many European languages. As coordinator of Habitat International Coalition's NGO project, he carried out a global survey of local initiatives for neighbourhood improvement, and was given the Right Livelihood Award in 1988, "for championing the rights of people to build, manage and sustain their own shelter and communities".

Index